W9-BAX-453

Why Jazz Happened

Why Jazz Happened

MARC MYERS

University of California Press

BERKELEY   LOS ANGELES   LONDON

University of California Press, one of the most distinguished
university presses in the United States, enriches lives around the world
by advancing scholarship in the humanities, social sciences, and natural
sciences. Its activities are supported by the UC Press Foundation and
by philanthropic contributions from individuals and institutions. For
more information, visit www.ucpress.edu.

University of California Press
Berkeley and Los Angeles, California

University of California Press, Ltd.
London, England

Library of Congress Cataloging-in-Publication Data

Myers, Marc, 1956–
    Why jazz happened / Marc Myers.
        p.   cm.
    Includes bibliographical references and index.
    ISBN 978-0-520-26878-4 (cloth : alk. paper)
    1. Jazz–History and criticism.   I. Title.
    ML3508.M94 2013
    781.65′5–dc23

                                                        2012022218

Manufactured in the United States of America

22   21   20   19   18   17   16   15   14   13
10   9   8   7   6   5   4   3   2   1

In keeping with a commitment to support environmentally responsible
and sustainable printing practices, UC Press has printed this book on
Rolland Enviro100, a 100% post-consumer fiber paper that is FSC
certified, deinked, processed chlorine-free, and manufactured with
renewable biogas energy. It is acid-free and EcoLogo certified.

For Olivia,
the daughter I love madly.
And for Alyse.
My world, my love. Forever Alyse.

Contents

Acknowledgments

This book began after the eminent jazz writer and critic Nat Hentoff answered his phone. As a teen, I was in awe of Nat's jazz books and album liner notes—his authority, the quality of his storytelling, and the ease of his language. So in recent years it has been both thrilling and gratifying to receive calls from him regularly about my jazz articles for the *Wall Street Journal* and my posts at JazzWax.com.

In 2009, when I began to develop the idea for this book—approaching jazz history from the outside in—I called Nat to run it by him. Nat was excited and insisted immediately that I pitch my concept to Mary Francis, his editor at the University of California Press. Thanks, Nat, for your inspiring calls, unrestrained passion, and enormous generosity.

Thanks to my editor Mary Francis, whose fine ear, sage guidance, and cheerleading throughout this process—from proposal to cover—were invaluable. Mary truly is a jazz saint and arts hero, and this book would not have been possible without her input and support. And thanks to the University of California Press's Jacqueline Volin, Stephanie Fay, and Kim Hogeland.

A big thanks to . . .

The legendary photographer Herb Snitzer, whose daily support and generosity prove that artists from the '50s are indeed motivated by humanity and joy. Many thanks for everything.

The photographer and author Hank O'Neal, whose support, friendship, sharp eye, relentless optimism, and subversive wit always remind me why jazz matters.

The brilliant writer-critic and dear friend Terry Teachout, who first insisted that I write about jazz in 2007 and has been there ever since. The *Wall Street Journal's* Leisure & Arts editor Eric Gibson, who continues to encourage me to write about the musicians and events that excite me most. The jazz musician and writer-editor Bill Kirchner, who kept an eye on me. And producer Fred Seibert, who invented fun and always reminds me that thinking differently about everything is ultimately what's interesting. I thank them all.

Dan Morgenstern, Ira Gitler, and George Avakian—jazz's wise men—were there for me throughout the reporting and writing process. I am grateful for their insistence on scholarship, passion, and a great story.

Thanks to all the many musicians and eyewitnesses who were interviewed for this book: Burt Bacharach, Hal Blaine, Randy Brecker, Dave Brubeck, Gary Burton, Ron Carter, Teddy Charles, Buddy Collette, Chick Corea, Buddy DeFranco, Russ Garcia, Herb Geller, Ira Gitler, Benny Golson, Chico Hamilton, Bill Hanley, Nat Hentoff, Bill Holman, Marjorie Hyams, Dick Hyman, Joseph Jarman, Larry Kart, Dick Katz, Orrin Keepnews, Dick LaPalm, Yusef Lateef, John Levy, John Litweiler, Hal McKusick, John McLaughlin, Howard Mandel, Johnny Mandel, Edward "Chip" Monck, Dan Morgenstern, Lennie Niehaus, Dave Pell, Benny Powell, Phil Ramone, Sonny Rollins, Howard Rumsey, Ray Santos, Gunther Schuller, Grace Slick, Carol Sloane, Al Stewart, Billy Taylor, Creed Taylor, Jack Tracy, George Wein, Randy Weston, and Joe Wilder.

Thanks to my mother, Bernice Myers, a children's-book author and illustrator, who got me hooked on the printed word and images before I could walk. My late father, Lou Myers, an artist-writer, who taught me about deadlines, hard work, and the value of simplicity. And my brother, Danny, who, unlike me, actually became a professional musician.

My loving wife, Alyse, a beautiful writer, author, and muse, who provided unconditional emotional support and on-point editorial advice.

And my daughter Olivia, whose wide smile, deep love, and electrifying excitement always inspire me to go the extra distance and do my best.

Introduction

The history of recorded jazz can be traced back to February 26, 1917. On that Monday, members of the Original Dixieland "Jass" Band rode the freight elevator up to the twelfth floor of 46 West 38th Street in New York, where weeks earlier the Victor Talking Machine Company had opened its new recording studio. After assembling their instruments, the all-white quintet from New Orleans played "Dixieland Jass Band One-Step" and "Livery Stable Blues" into the long metal horn that served as a microphone back then. When the songs were released weeks later on either side of a single 78-rpm record, the band's highly syncopated and somewhat frantic "Dixieland" fox-trot became an overnight sensation. Appearing in music stores just days after the United States entered World War I, the record was promoted in newspapers as "a brass band gone crazy,"[1] and sales soon rivaled releases by the opera sensation Enrico Caruso and the march king John Philip Sousa.[2]

But the Original Dixieland Jass Band was less original than its name implied. Black musicians in New Orleans had already developed the up-tempo music style in 1906 as an instrumental offshoot of ragtime. Although the Original Dixieland Jass Band's white musicians were from New Orleans, and some had begun their careers playing in the city's integrated parade bands, the ensemble's formation in early 1916 was the brainstorm of Harry James, an enterprising café owner in Chicago who heard the musicians while he was in the Crescent City to see a prize fight.

By 1916 Chicago was already a music center. Tom Brown's Band from Dixieland was having some success at Chicago restaurants, and there seemed to be plenty of room in town for another Southern dance attraction. When James's recruited musicians began their Chicago engagement at Schiller's Café in March 1916, they called themselves Stein's Dixie Jass

Band, after their drummer, Johnny Stein. But after several name changes and personnel swaps, the group settled on the Original Dixieland Jass Band, to distinguish itself from all competitors. The new name—with its built-in point of difference—was somewhat boastful and helped the band stand out in a town noisy with entertainment. Toward the end of 1916, the group came to the attention of the singer Al Jolson, who enthusiastically wired Max Hart, his New York agent. Hart booked the musicians into the Paradise Ballroom at the Reisenweber Building near Columbus Circle in Manhattan.

The Original Dixieland Jass Band began its New York run in January 1917, and its new style of spirited dance music seemed to capture the times perfectly. Backed by a firm one-two beat, the musicians played with wild abandon, their notes coming and going in organized chaos—much like the herds of automobiles swerving madly around one another on the city's streets. The hectic music at once mirrored dancers' prewar anxiety and gave them welcome relief from the daily gloom of newspaper headlines.

Within weeks, the fuss created by the Original Dixieland Jass Band's appearance in New York caught the attention of the British-owned Columbia Graphophone Company. Executives, intrigued, invited the band to record at Columbia's Woolworth Building studio. But when the musicians arrived on January 31, their loud, unrestrained playing style overwhelmed the abilities of the studio's equipment. Taken aback by the music, Columbia executives aborted the session and paid the band members for their time. Undeterred, members of the band immediately approached Victor, Columbia's recording rival. There, they found a far different reception. Executives were determined to succeed where their main competitor had failed. On February 26 the Original Dixieland Jass Band recorded two of its most popular songs for the label.

The band's session at Victor would probably have ended the same way as their Columbia encounter if not for the technical savvy of Victor's engineers. At the dawn of recorded music, the pandemonium of a clarinet, trombone, cornet, piano, and drums all playing in a confined space presented many acoustic problems, because those instruments have distinctly different sonic personalities. Opera singers, symphonic orchestras, and marching bands were quite manageable for recording engineers, given their unified tonal consistency. But the sudden and exuberant surges of a Dixieland quintet were a different matter. So Victor's head sound engineer placed the musicians in different locations around the pickup horn in the studio, which the company called the Laboratory. The band's cornetist stood twenty feet from the horn, with the drummer five feet behind him.

The trombonist was roughly fifteen feet from the horn, the clarinetist five feet, and the piano closest of all, since it was the least likely to be heard.[3]

Nick LaRocca, the band's cornetist, recalled the recording session years later: "First we made a test record, and then they played it back for us. This is when they started moving us around in different positions. After the first test record, four men were rushed in with ladders and started stringing wires near the ceiling. I asked them what all these wires were for, and one of the men told me it was to sop up the overtone that was coming back into the [pickup] horn. The recording engineer at Victor had the patience of a saint. He played back our music until it sounded right."[4]

In retrospect, the songs the band chose—a blues and a dance number—were apt selections to inaugurate the history of jazz recording, and prescient, considering jazz's future direction. Over the next twenty-seven years, jazz would rely exclusively on the blues and dance tempos to win over listeners and build a mass-market audience. By adhering closely to the blues, syncopation, and eventually the music of Tin Pan Alley, jazz was able to remain in vogue without dropping the musical characteristics that made it special and exciting to listeners and dancers.

But jazz's first commercial recording in 1917 didn't take place merely because the music sounded new and interesting. After all, the form had been kicking around New Orleans for years, and other black and white ensembles were already playing it when the Original Dixieland Jass Band stepped off that elevator in New York. Instead, events removed from the music converged to create an opportunity for jazz to be recorded. There were the band's own ambitions, the brainstorm of the band members to approach Victor after failing at Columbia, Victor's driving desire to outdo Columbia, the technological smarts of Victor's sound engineers, the public's expanding interest in phonographs and the availability of these machines, and the public's prewar jitters and need for an emotional release. Throughout jazz history, similar events unrelated to the music or the artists have influenced the emergence and direction of major jazz styles.

Of course, jazz would never have evolved without the creative genius of musicians and their desire to stand out and leave a mark. But their efforts certainly would have been slowed and in some cases suffocated without timely developments in business, technology, the economy, demographics, and race relations. In the years between the two world wars, several major jazz styles emerged in response to such forces. New Orleans–style jazz was joined by Chicago's hot jazz and New York's sophisticated orchestral jazz of the 1920s, followed by Kansas City's swing of the late 1920s and 1930s. In each case, musicians initiated a new style in response to the demands of employers and popular tastes during Prohibition and the Depression. But the history of jazz in the twenty-seven years following the first jazz recording would be incomplete without factoring in the proliferation and development of radio, records, the phonograph, the jukebox, and sound films, or "talkies"—technological revolutions that made music more accessible, more convenient, and a lot more pleasing to the ear.

After World War II—from 1945 to 1972—these influential nonjazz events became more abundant and potent. During this postwar period—when jazz was thoroughly transformed from dance music performed by entertainers to a sociopolitical movement led by performance artists—ten major jazz styles surfaced, with a new one emerging roughly every five years. These major postwar styles were bebop, jazz-classical, cool, West Coast jazz, hard bop, jazz-gospel, spiritual jazz, jazz-pop, avant-garde jazz, and jazz-rock fusion. In each case, a significant event external to jazz itself greatly enabled the music's development and popularity—from the bebop of Charlie Parker and Dizzy Gillespie in the mid-1940s to the jazz-rock fusion of Tony Williams, Miles Davis, John McLaughlin, Chick Corea, and Herbie Hancock in the late 1960s and early 1970s.

Before World War II, the chief benefactor of jazz's widening appeal was the recording industry, which was dominated by Victor, Columbia, and Decca. By the late 1930s each of these record companies had an extensive roster of white and black swing, jazz, and pop artists under contract. In the 1930s the big three record companies were all offspring of large entertainment conglomerates, which held enormous sway over music's direction and development. The Victor and Columbia record labels were owned by the Radio Corporation of America (RCA) and the Columbia Broadcasting System (CBS), respectively. Starting in the 1920s, these companies managed burgeoning national radio networks that influenced the tastes of the millions of American households that tuned in nightly. Although Decca in the United States did not own a radio network, the company had considerable financial backing from Britain's Decca label until 1939, and it specialized in pop and jazz.

All three companies' records were pressed and shipped to small local stores around the country for sale to customers, and elaborate and tightly controlled national marketing efforts were used to whet the public's appetite for recordings. During the 1930s, when the musicians' union was powerful enough to limit the playing of records on the air to preserve the jobs of live radio musicians, record companies used a one-two punch to stimulate sales: First, musicians toured regularly, performing in ballrooms and appearing live on the radio—a practice that exposed audiences to their music, sparked word of mouth, and boosted name recognition. Second, jukeboxes in public spaces gave consumers—and everyone else in the room—a chance to hear favorite recordings and new releases. Both strategies resulted in the emergence of national musical stars, an increased appetite for dance music, and skyrocketing sales of radios, phonographs, and records.

Records and the machines that played them not only made jazz styles popular nationwide but also generated enormous revenue for record companies. But as these companies grew wealthier and extended their reach, they tended to repeat the same successful music formulas over and over again and suppress excessive creative risk. To be sure, plenty of important recordings of improvised jazz were made during the music's first twenty-seven years—Louis Armstrong's "West End Blues," Bix Beiderbecke's and Frankie Trumbauer's "Singin' the Blues," Duke Ellington's "Mood Indigo," Fats Waller's "Honeysuckle Rose," the Benny Goodman Sextet's "Rose Room," and Coleman Hawkins's "Body and Soul," to name just a handful. But such documented expressive adventures by individuals were hardly the norm.

By contrast, during the twenty-seven years that followed World War II, jazz was reshaped frequently by external events. After the war, the vise-like grip of the three major record companies on the industry weakened in the wake of labor actions, increased competition from new labels, changes in the radio industry, and the promotion of concerts. As a larger field of record labels emerged and competed, jazz musicians gained greater creative independence. From 1945 to 1972, the ten major jazz styles that emerged certainly reflected their times. But instead of conforming to proven blues and dance models, jazz began to be filtered through the viewpoints of individual artists rather than solely through the commercial interests of a few large record companies. For the first time, jazz played an assertive role, reflecting and shaping America's values and culture rather than merely mirroring them. As all the arts began to reflect the personal vision and freedom of the artist, jazz's natural reliance on self-expression allowed the music to pivot neatly from syncopated dance music to individualistic statements.

The first nonmusic event to dramatically alter the evolution of jazz in the crucial postwar years was the 1942–44 recording ban by the American Federation of Musicians (AFM), which prohibited its members from making records. The AFM's move was an effort to force record companies to pay a royalty on the sale of records to a union trust fund that would subsidize live music by hiring musicians left unemployed by the rise of records, the phonograph, radio, and the jukebox. Once the ban began, in August 1942, the only new material by union instrumentalists that the major record companies released was the music it had stockpiled prior to the job action—a supply of recordings that thinned out as the ban continued. The first phase of the union standoff lasted until September 1943, when Decca, running short of cash and warehoused recorded music, signed a four-year contract with the AFM, agreeing to pay royalties into the AFM's fund. Meanwhile, Capitol, which had been formed on the West Coast in 1942, also signed with the AFM, followed by many new and existing small labels.

Columbia and RCA Victor, however, held out for another year, hoping that the federal government would intercede on their behalf. But when Washington refused to step in, the two companies capitulated in November 1944—after President Roosevelt was reelected—and signed the same deal that Decca and other labels had accepted. In the interim, the record industry had undergone a major transformation. In the fourteen months that Columbia and RCA Victor had been idle, hundreds of small labels rushed to form and sign with the AFM, hoping to carve out a niche while Columbia and RCA Victor's studios remained dark. One result of this proliferation of new labels was the recording of a new jazz style in 1944 that would become known as bebop.

But merely recording bebop did not guarantee its popularity or success. In fact, bebop was not fully accepted and appreciated on a national scale until four years later, in 1948. Its success owed much to the contract terms the record companies had signed with the AFM—the second event to transform jazz. Once the companies agreed to pay royalties on record sales to the AFM, the union no longer stood in the way of radio stations playing records on the air. Airplay meant increased record sales, and increased sales meant fatter royalties for the AFM's fund. As more radio stations played records to fill airtime during the day and at night, a new generation of jazz boosters emerged to champion bebop. These advocates included jazz disc jockeys, jazz concert promoters, and jazz magazine writers and critics—all working in support of bebop and bebop musicians and burnishing their own reputations in the process. Thanks to their efforts, bebop by 1948 became more than an exotic New York jazz style. It had overtaken swing, going so far as to influence fashion, language, and jazz itself.

The third event to alter jazz's direction was the G.I. Bill. Passed in 1944, it allowed millions of returning veterans to attend college for free, giving musicians who had served the opportunity to enroll in accredited schools and colleges with intensive music programs. By the late 1940s jazz musicians who qualified for such programs began to graduate, having studied formal and modern classical theory and composition. As they reentered the music industry full-time, they had a profound influence on the quality and direction of arranging, composing, and performing. The jazz-classical styles that surfaced included cool jazz, concert jazz, and chamber jazz, along with Gunther Schuller's Third Stream in the late '50s.

The advent of the extended jazz solo would have been impossible without the introduction of the $33\frac{1}{3}$-rpm long-playing record in 1948 and the widespread use of magnetic tape in recording studios by the early 1950s. Both technological advances represent the fourth transformative event, resulting in the emergence of single-record jazz albums—first in a 10-inch size and then 12-inch. The album's proliferation, in turn, led to the widespread use of graphic art and photography on LP covers, creating new appetites for the music inside. Liner notes on the backs of LP jackets explained the music, provided biographical information about the musicians, enabled writers to express their views and enthusiasm, and gave consumers an opportunity to read about the music prior to purchase.

On the West Coast, the suburbanization of Southern California in the late 1940s and early 1950s was the fifth event to change the music by ushering in a new harmony-rich jazz style that was neither as dense nor as rhythmic as the jazz that surfaced in urban markets. The region around Los Angeles developed aggressively from the late 1940s onward, and builders hired to develop massive tracts of land needed cookie-cutter solutions to complete large-scale, inexpensive housing tracts quickly. For mostly white jazz musicians looking to buy a home, the area surrounding Los Angeles was idyllic. The weather was pleasant year-round, and work opportunities in the rapidly expanding record, movie, and TV studios were plentiful. As more white musicians relocated to the West Coast, the comfortable, harmonious, and conformist lifestyle began to be reflected in jazz that emphasized airy counterpoint played by reeds and horns and deemphasized the more urban churning sound of the piano, bass, and drums.

The sixth group of events to change jazz was the introduction of the 45-rpm format by RCA Victor in February 1949, the subsequent battle with Columbia's $33\frac{1}{3}$-rpm records, and the rise of Broadcast Music Incorporated (BMI) as the leading music-licensing company for jazz and rhythm and blues (R&B) composers. As the Federal Communications Commission issued a growing number of licenses to new radio stations after World War II, the number of smaller stations independent of the major networks increased in urban and rural markets throughout the country. The expansion of radio boosted the demand for singles and created an opportunity for the new 45-rpm record. When RCA Victor had first unveiled the smaller disc with the large center hole, the company marketed it as a compact rival to Columbia's 33⅓-rpm LP. But as the larger format caught on with record companies, the 45-rpm needed to be repurposed. By default, the disc began to replace bulky 78-rpm singles on the radio and in jukeboxes, making it ideal for R&B, which was becoming increasingly popular with teens in regional markets where independent radio was thriving. R&B's success in the early 1950s wasn't lost on jazz record companies or artists who developed a new style—hard bop. This jazz style shared some of the characteristics of both West Coast jazz and R&B—notably the former's emphasis on reeds and horns and the latter's big driving beat. In the LP era, when more music was needed to fill albums, more hard bop composers found they were able to license their compositions through BMI, leading to a greater percentage of original works on jazz albums starting in the early 1950s.

The seventh influential event was the acceleration of the civil rights movement following the Supreme Court's *Brown v. Board of Education* decision in 1954. When many states refused to halt their segregationist policies following the decision or protect those attempting to integrate public facilities, civil rights protests grew more intensive, particularly in the South. Public confrontations led to mounting violence, which was covered extensively by newspapers, radio, and television. The graphic results helped inspire more spiritual and freer forms of jazz that had deep roots in the black church, gospel music, and back-to-Africa movements of the 1920s and 1930s.

In 1964 the commercial value and status of jazz began to slip, particularly among younger record buyers. When the Beatles' success proved more than just a fad, a surge of British and American copycat acts followed in 1965. Motown also had enormous success with its black R&B artists, whose smooth-sounding records routinely crossed over to the pop charts and white audiences. This dramatic shift in music tastes among black and white teens in the mid-1960s—the eighth event—altered the commercial landscape and priorities of virtually all record companies, which subsequently devoted more of their resources to rock, folk, and R&B artists than to jazz. Among the effects of the shift was the embrace of pop music by notable jazz artists, in the form of instrumental interpretations of pop-rock radio hits.

But not all markets, jazz artists, or record labels turned to pop. Jazz artists in Chicago in the mid-1960s, alienated from the mainstream music scene, chose to take control of their art by creating a self-supporting organization that freed them from the pressures of commercial conformity and the demands of radio and jukeboxes. The formation of the nonprofit Association for the Advancement of Creative Musicians (AACM) in Chicago led to the rise of a freer, more abstract style known as avant-garde jazz. Many of the musicians who belonged to the AACM were inspired by Ornette Coleman, Cecil Taylor, and other free-jazz artists as well as local community-organizing efforts and civil rights actions in Chicago in 1965—the ninth external event.

The final series of events that influenced the evolution of jazz from 1942 to 1972 was the rise of electronic instruments and powerful concert speaker and lighting systems in the late 1960s. As more folk-rock and hard-rock bands featured electronic instruments, and sound systems grew larger and louder, outdoor rock festivals began to attract huge crowds—particularly the Monterey Pop Festival (1967), the Atlantic City Pop Festival (1969), the Woodstock Music and Art Fair (1969), and the Altamont Free Concert (1969). Young jazz artists, responding to rock's mass appeal, began to embrace electronic instruments in hopes of reaching younger, larger audiences. Artists also incorporated rock's longer and more expressionist song formats, creating jazz-rock fusion.

Jazz would continue to evolve after 1972, albeit more slowly and less definitively. Smooth jazz, adult contemporary, the acoustic-jazz revival, acid jazz, and other styles would all be shaped by artistic visions, audience tastes, and events external to jazz. But the years from 1942 to 1972 remain the most prolific, dynamic, and significant for the evolution of jazz. During this critical period, jazz styles changed more rapidly than in the preceding decades—and more profoundly than they did in the years that followed. Jazz also established itself as high art with national appeal—without losing its integrity or purpose.

1   Record Giants Blink

On February 16, 1944, a dozen jazz musicians met at a New York studio to record three songs for Apollo Records. The band's leader was the tenor saxophonist Coleman Hawkins, who at age thirty-nine was the oldest jazz musician present and easily the most famous. Almost five years earlier, Hawkins had recorded "Body and Soul," on which he seemed to improvise seamlessly for about three minutes without once playing the famed song's original melody—except for the opening four bars. Hawkins's brash reworking of the Tin Pan Alley standard had become a jukebox hit for RCA Victor and made Hawkins a saxophone sensation. But jazz reputations in the 1940s required reinvention and fresh achievement. To remain ahead of the creative curve, Hawkins frequently invited younger jazz musicians to challenge him in clubs—a risky move because it exposed him to a possible besting by up-and-comers. But the open invitation also allowed Hawkins to stay sharp and remain in control. The musicians who assembled that day for the Apollo Records session were both his admirers and his stylistic rivals.[1]

The February 16 gathering at Apollo was the label's very first recording session. Apollo had been founded just weeks earlier by Teddy Gottlieb, the white owner of the Rainbow Music Shop on 125th Street, one of Harlem's most popular record stores.[2] With the Apollo label, Gottlieb hoped to create a pipeline for his record store by having musicians re-create on disc the excitement of Harlem's after-hours clubs. He also fully expected the label's records to sell well in the store's neighborhood, particularly among younger buyers, who weren't old enough to gain entry to the clubs. In Gottlieb's favor was the Rainbow Music Shop's regular sponsorship of the *After Hours Swing Session*, an overnight radio show on WHOM hosted by "Symphony Sid" Torin.[3] The animated disc jockey had been on the air in New York since 1937, spinning jazz records by black musicians, and the show was revered by Harlemites.[4]

What Gottlieb did not know—and could not have known on February 16, 1944—was that Apollo Records was about to make history. On that day Hawkins and the other musicians—the trumpeters Dizzy Gillespie, Vic Coulsen, and Eddie Vanderveer; the saxophonists Leo Parker, Leonard Lowry, Don Byas, Ray Abrams, and Budd Johnson; the pianist Clyde Hart; the bassist Oscar Pettiford; and the drummer Max Roach—would take part in what is now considered the first commercial bebop recording.[5] The music they recorded that February wasn't known officially then as "bebop"—it was too new, and the word *bebop* wouldn't be used in print to describe the new style of jazz until later in the year, when magazine writers needed a snappy word to summarize the animated style. But the musical language of bebop—with its strange-sounding notes and breakneck tempos—had been developing aggressively over the preceding years, at jam sessions and in black big bands.

To the average ear, bebop sounded significantly different from the more predictable "swing"—the most popular jazz style in 1944. Swing was primarily dance music; black big bands had first developed it in Kansas City in the late 1920s and early 1930s before it was leveraged by white bands in the mid-1930s. Swing's crossover to national prominence began in 1935 when Benny Goodman's band appeared at the Palomar Ballroom in Los Angeles, met there by frenzied local teens who had heard the band play on NBC's *Let's Dance* radio broadcasts.[6] For the most part, swing featured a less frantic tempo than earlier jazz styles, often with an emphasis on the second and fourth beats.

Bebop, initially, was everything swing was not. Its explosive excitement centered on individual musicians, who took turns playing improvised solos. Often bebop was performed at a pace far too fast for dancing. And while swing relied predominantly on parts written for a large group of musicians—with an occasional space for a brief solo or two—bebop was intended to be played by small groups that joined together only briefly at the beginning and end. Bebop was so intricate that most musicians—even experienced jazz musicians—could not imitate it with ease.

The sound of bebop resembled that of no other form of jazz previously played or recorded. There was a happy urgency and sly hipness to it, a bouncy, slippery informality and liberated feel that left listeners excited and energized. The secret of the new music rested in soloing musicians' interpretations of the song's chords—they added notes in some cases and left out notes in others.[7] Speed, improvisational risk taking, and on-the-fly harmonies also played big roles in the music's high-wire act. This was music for showing off the talents and dexterity of the individual, not the whole ensemble.[8]

"Bebop wasn't a secret language," said the pianist Billy Taylor, one of bebop's early practitioners. "It was an expansion of many aspects of the complex musical language that already was being played at the time by Art Tatum and others. In 1944, Dizzy demonstrated bebop to me on the piano of the Onyx Club on New York's 52nd Street. He said, 'Look, if you play this chord and add this note, this will happen. Then if you leave this note out, it will take you in a different direction.' Dizzy had spent years working this out."[9]

The musicians who recorded for Apollo Records in February 1944 weren't strangers. They knew one another and had performed with each other since late 1943 at New York's Onyx Club and Kelly's Stable.[10] In addition, several of the musicians were already established jazz stars. Some weeks earlier, for example, two of twelve musicians—Coleman Hawkins and Oscar Pettiford—had been named top artists on their respective instruments by *Esquire* magazine's jazz critics' poll. But of all the musicians present that day, Gillespie was far and away the one who had done the most to develop and codify the new style of jazz they were recording. His nickname, Dizzy, was perfect—describing how the spiraling music made listeners feel while also fooling rivals into underestimating his extraordinary skills. The nickname had been given to him in the late 1930s, while he was in Teddy Hill's band. "Dizzy stayed up there [in the trumpet section] with his overcoat on—in fact he did everything in an unorthodox fashion," said Hill in an April 1947 interview in *Metronome* magazine. "Embarking on a new arrangement, he was as likely as not to start reading an interlude or the last chorus instead of taking it from the top. I said to him, 'Boy, you're really Dizzy.' 'Yes,' said Gillespie cheerfully. 'That's right.' I said, 'I think I'm going to call you Dizzy.' And that's the way it has been ever since."[11]

Gillespie had also been the most articulate explainer of how the new jazz should sound, often teaching fellow musicians to play it. "Dizzy tried to hum everything to everybody to get them to see what he was still talkin' about," tenor saxophonist Budd Johnson told Ira Gitler. "Diz would sing, and actually that's how I think the music got its name, bebop. Because he would be humming this music, and he'd say, 'Ooop bop ta oop a la doo bop doo bad.' So people said, 'Play some more of that bebop'. . . and actually I think that's how it got its name, because that's the way he would have to sing it to make you get the feeling that he wanted you to play with."[12]

But if Gillespie and other bebop pioneers—including the alto saxo-phonist Charlie Parker, the drummer Kenny Clarke, and the pianist Bud Powell—had been developing the jazz form since 1941 and 1942, why did it take until February 1944 to record the music? And how did a frantic form of improvised music played mostly by black musicians in dimly lit nightclubs for audiences seated in chairs rather than moving about on dance floors manage to become a national sensation four years later, not to mention jazz's predominant style?

SWING AIN'T THE THING

The recording of bebop in February 1944 occurred largely because Decca and smaller record companies had settled with the American Federation of Musicians in late 1943, ending a recording ban by musicians that had started in the summer of 1942. All the labels that signed with the union in the months that followed hoped to take advantage of a marketplace without new releases from RCA Victor's and Columbia's star bandlead-ers. Those two major labels refused to settle with the musicians' union and would hold out until late 1944. With Victor and Columbia idle, small independent labels were able to rent studio time and record on a shoestring budget. Many of these smaller labels in New York turned to musicians who could assemble groups and record exciting music at a high level. Apollo was among these microlabels, but the number of new record ventures multiplied quickly as Victor and Columbia held out.

When Dizzy Gillespie and Charlie Parker began to record bebop, other musicians bought their records and transcribed their notes to figure out what exactly they were doing. "How did I learn bebop? There was no school to learn," said the clarinetist Buddy DeFranco. "You had to figure out what was going on musically. In 1944, I was in Charlie Barnet's band. Dodo Marmarosa, the piano player, and I collaborated quite a bit during our down time. One day we ran into trumpeter Charlie Shavers. He said, 'There's a guy up in Harlem who plays alto saxophone. His name is Charlie Parker. You have to go hear him.' . . . So on a night off, we went up there. We were dumbstruck by what he was doing on his instrument. We spent as much time as possible there but we only picked up so much. It wasn't long after that night that Parker started making records with Dizzy Gillespie, introducing the idea of bebop. We played their records over and over again when we began to figure out what they were doing. Dodo said to me, 'Why don't you try to play the clarinet like Parker?' I said, 'That's exactly what I was thinking.' So I did."[13]

Bebop's roots can be traced back to the early 1940s, when black big-band musicians began experimenting with new ways of playing improvised solos. From the start, their goals were to gain the admiration of their audiences with these solos and to achieve a level of fame and respect from their peers. A black musician who became a renowned soloist could start his own band or land a coveted record deal with a major label. By 1940, several black jazz musicians, including Louis Armstrong, Art Tatum, Fats Waller, Lionel Hampton, Teddy Wilson, and Coleman Hawkins, had already reached star status by having commercial crossover success as soloists. For young black musicians in bands in the 1940s, the only way out was up, and the only way up was to stand out by being exceptional.

But from the perspective of bandleaders, the success of individuals in their bands was bad for business. Running a swing orchestra was a daily challenge requiring entrepreneurial skill. Bandleaders had to resort to managerial and psychological tricks to retain top young talent. The stakes were highest for the major swing bandleaders who had lucrative contracts with record companies and appeared on the labels' radio networks. Similar contracts did not exist between the bandleaders and the musicians they hired and had to retain. Without formal contracts with bandleaders, musicians in swing orchestras typically remained with a band until they received a better offer from another one or were fired—a frequent occurrence, since bands were constantly being overhauled and fine-tuned by bandleaders. Musicians who wanted to break free of this hired-fired cycle and improve their job security had to develop a distinct sound on their instrument. In other words, their performances had to wow audiences without eclipsing the talent and egos of bandleader bosses.

For an individual musician, quitting a band without having lined up another offer was risky. Leave a band to do what? Without star power and sizable capital from a backer, forming one's own band was a challenge for the novice. Record companies were few during the 1930s, with Columbia, RCA Victor, and Decca making up 85 to 90 percent of the market by 1940.[14] From the record company's standpoint, recording, to be cost-efficient, required perfection. The odds were slim that one of these record companies would take a chance on an unknown musician or a band whose errors could result in cost overruns and subpar music. Though a handful of smaller jazz labels existed before World War II, they recorded primarily older styles, and their products were marketed to record clubs and collectors and other enthusiasts of traditional jazz.

If you were a jazz musician in the late 1930s and early 1940s, you had little choice but to cling to the swing bands that recorded and toured. In turn, bandleaders constantly had to develop ways to feed the egos of their talented sidemen—without overinflating them. As many bandleaders discovered, a fine line existed between recognizing talent and heaping on too much praise. Keeping star musicians happy compelled swing bandleaders to order up arrangements that provided solos for them. Bandleaders also formed small groups within their bands to give their best musicians a chance to shine.

For a time, these spotlight opportunities satisfied the ambitions of many leading band musicians. But by 1941 the novelty of playing in a big band's small breakout group began to wear thin for younger and more talented sidemen, particularly in black bands. With 78-rpm records able to hold only about three minutes of music on each side, solo time was minimal. Increasingly, this spare solo space failed to satisfy the creative spirit and abilities of top talent. These musicians came to realize that they had only one shot: to stand out with hopes of developing a following and being discovered by record companies. It was a risk, but a risk many felt they had to take. As a result, more ambitious artists began to experiment with new ways of playing solos, to make them memorable.

Chief among these musicians was Gillespie. Born in Cheraw, South Carolina, Gillespie had attended a nearby music school on scholarship and studied piano and trumpet.[15] In 1937 he traveled to New York and joined Teddy Hill's band, emulating the famed trumpeter Roy Eldridge's fiery style. In 1939 Gillespie joined Cab Calloway's orchestra, one of the most successful black bands in the country. But the bandleader didn't particularly appreciate Gillespie's approach to soloing, calling the unorthodox notes "Chinese music."[16] In March 1941, Calloway hired the more traditional trumpeter Jonah Jones to handle the solo parts. In addition, Gillespie was increasingly excluded from the band's small group, the Cab Jivers. Gillespie's frustration grew, and in response he boldly exhibited his penchant for sophomoric pranks.[17] In September 1941, the two men came to blows. Calloway, after a performance during which he thought Gillespie had thrown a spitball, took the trumpeter to task. Words were exchanged, and when Calloway reached out to strike Gillespie, the trumpeter reportedly pulled a knife. The bassist Milt Hinton interceded, but Calloway grabbed Gillespie's wrist, and the two men scuffled until other band musicians pulled them apart. But by then, the knife had cut Calloway, and Gillespie was fired.[18]

After Gillespie left Calloway's band, he began to freelance in New York, playing at clubs in Harlem. Jam sessions at Minton's Playhouse, Clark Monroe's Uptown House, and other establishments typically featured small clusters of musicians, mostly horn players, backed by an aggressive rhythm section. At these clubs, musicians played extended improvised solos based on blues and Tin Pan Alley standards, competing for peer and audience approval. The musicians in the house rhythm sections prodded and provoked soloists with unexpected piano chords, bass lines, and drum patterns, hoping to egg them on to even more exciting results—or failure and humiliation. Gillespie, during the months after he left Calloway's band, sharpened his ideas at these clubs and in the sextet of the alto saxophonist Benny Carter. In early 1942 Gillespie subbed in Woody Herman's band and sold several of his arrangements to Herman and Jimmy Dorsey. In May 1942 Gillespie joined Les Hite's band in New York and recorded a brief solo on "Jersey Bounce" using his new style. The record was a hit, and Gillespie was only too happy to share his new musical discoveries with other musicians.[19]

The trumpeter Joe Wilder, who sat next to Gillespie in Hite's band, recalls that Gillespie's bebop style was already in place in 1942: "We didn't call it bebop then, of course. It was just a new way of playing, and Dizzy had already recorded some of those new things months earlier in Cab Calloway's band. Instead of playing the chords that were written, Dizzy was into flatted fifths and ninths, and harmonic playing. What was fascinating was that Dizzy could be both precise and loose. Between songs, Dizzy would start telling me jokes and cracking me up. Then Les would give a downbeat and I couldn't stop laughing. Les would say, 'Hey Junior—that was my nickname—you had better play and stop fooling around back there.' Dizzy, of course, would have an innocent expression on his face, as if he had no clue why I was laughing. He wasn't trying to throw me. Dizzy wasn't competitive like that. He was happy to show me things all the time on the trumpet and he also had solos on songs, just like I did. Dizzy's humor kept him relaxed, and his style of playing in Les' band was very different."[20] By July 1942, Gillespie recorded with Lucky Millinder's band, and his solo on *Little John Special* demonstrated that his new jazz ideas were developing rapidly.[21]

Halfway across the country, the saxophonist Charlie Parker also was experimenting with a new solo approach for many of the same reasons as Gillespie. Born in Kansas City, Kansas, Parker began by playing baritone horn in a school marching band and eventually picked up the alto saxophone. In 1936 the fifteen-year-old Parker was urged to sit in with seasoned members of Count Basie's band, including the tenor saxophonist Lester Young and the drummer Jo Jones. But Parker played "Body and Soul" in the wrong key and was so lost in thought that the didactic Jones tossed one of his cymbals at Parker's feet to get his attention. The brass disc fell with a deafening crash and Parker, humiliated, packed up his instrument and departed.[22]

Discouraged but undeterred, Parker spent the next year practicing intensively—mastering scales and blues runs in every key.[23] Because jazz in Kansas City in the mid-1930s relied more on improvisation than on elaborate arrangements, Parker was forced to develop fingering for speed and an ear for inventing blues riffs.[24] In 1937, when he returned to the jazz scene in Kansas City after his self-imposed exile, he was a more mature and confident player. During the next three years, he moved from Kansas City to Chicago and then to New York in search of playing opportunities—at one point washing dishes at a Harlem club just to hear the pianist Art Tatum.[25]

But by 1939 Parker had become bored with the static music he had been playing in bands: "I kept thinking, there's bound to be something else. I could hear it sometimes but I couldn't play it. Well that night I was working over 'Cherokee,' and as I did I found that by using the higher intervals of a chord as a melody line and backing them with appropriately related [chord] changes, I could play the thing I'd been hearing. I came alive."[26]

Parker returned home to Kansas City in 1940 for his father's funeral and soon took a job in Harlan Leonard's band. But Parker's chronic lateness forced Leonard to fire him. Parker joined Jay McShann's swing band and toured the Southwest with the blues orchestra for the next year and a half. When McShann arrived in New York in January 1942, the band appeared at Harlem's Savoy Ballroom opposite Lucky Millinder's orchestra, which at the time featured Dizzy Gillespie in the trumpet section.[27] Like Gillespie, Parker also played jam sessions at after-hours clubs. During one of these appearances, in 1942 at Clark Monroe's Uptown House, Parker's improvised performance of "Cherokee" was captured on an acetate disc recorded by Jerry Newman, a Columbia University student. As evidenced by the recording, Parker's solo was breathtakingly fast and fluid, demonstrating an unrivaled feel for the new modern sound that Gillespie and his disciples were crafting separately in Harlem clubs.[28] By the summer of 1942, Gillespie was experimenting with new chord voicings and harmony while Parker was exploring how to phrase solos differently and infuse the blues into virtually every one he played.

Both Parker and Gillespie had just about perfected their new approaches to jazz when their ambitions to record were halted. In August 1942 the American Federation of Musicians launched a job action against record companies that prohibited all union musicians from recording. The ban was the culmination of a fifteen-year battle the AFM had been waging over new sound-recording technologies that had displaced thousands of musicians. Bebop in 1942 would have to wait a little longer to be recorded.

DIALS, NICKELS, AND PINK SLIPS

In the years preceding World War II, music had become the country's most affordable form of entertainment. Movies were popular, too, of course, but they had two big drawbacks: They could not be viewed at home, and you had to pay each time you wanted to see them. By contrast, music could be heard free—again and again—after the initial purchase of a radio or a phonograph and records. As radio networks expanded their reach nationwide, music became an even more popular Depression-era pastime, with millions of Americans listening to the same programs at the exact same time, often in the comfort of their living rooms.

As the quality of recorded music improved, starting in the late 1920s with the introduction of the electronic microphone, the recording and radio industries prospered. Network radio featured live studio performances of musicians while records allowed consumers to hear favorite artists on their home phonographs and on jukeboxes in public. The two media—radio and records—worked hand in hand, and sales of both soared. From 1927 to 1930, the bandleader Duke Ellington appeared more than two hundred times on the radio,[29] establishing himself as a formidable recording artist and major crossover attraction. But radio and records spelled trouble for the vast majority of average musicians who earned a living performing in theaters, taverns, and other public places in America's small towns and big cities. Owners of bars or restaurants who added a radio, phonograph, or jukebox to their establishments no longer had to worry about musicians' salaries or the rules imposed by the musicians' union. They simply flipped a switch and turned up the volume.

In 1926, soon after radio sets began to be mass-produced, the American Federation of Musicians' president promised members that there was "absolutely nothing to fear from radio. Radio will have the same result as the phonograph . . . it will ultimately increase the employment of musicians."[30] In all fairness, recording and playback technology was in its infancy, and music performed onstage or live over the radio sounded far superior to the scratchy, coarse results coming through phonograph horns. But after the development of electric recording equipment in the mid-1920s, the sound of records began to improve dramatically, as did the at-home phonograph.

During this period, the simplicity and affordability of the radio made it a family necessity. In 1925 there were 571 radio stations in operation in the United State, and radios in more than four million households, or about 10 percent of the total, leaving enormous room for growth.[31] In November 1926 RCA launched its NBC radio network by broadcasting a dance-band program from New York that reached twenty-five stations as far away as Kansas City. Consumer demand for radio programming was so strong that by January 1927 the United Independent Broadcasters (UIB) radio network was formed in Chicago. That same month, RCA launched a second network, renaming its existing one the Red Network and the new one the Blue Network. In 1929 the struggling UIB was sold and renamed CBS by its new owner, which expanded the network by emphasizing dramatic programming for the at-home market.

In its infancy, radio was a mess. Signals weren't uniform, causing one station to override another on the dial as the number of operators increased. With the passage of the Radio Act of 1927, the government began to license stations, bringing order to the near-chaotic market and the signals beamed by stations. With efficiency came a well-ordered radio dial, leading to a surge in sales. In 1927 three hundred thousand employees worked in twelve hundred radio plants, most of them in seven major cities. By 1929 some plants were producing a thousand radios a day.[32]

The first significant threat to musicians from technology came in 1926. That year, Warner Brothers introduced its Vitaphone sound-picture system in short-subject films, laying the groundwork for the "talkie" movie. From the start, music for talkies was recorded at movie studios in California and then synchronized to the action in films. The new technology's impact took a little time but ultimately proved devastating for movie theater organists and orchestras. The number of musicians employed to accompany silent films in movie houses around the country began to drop precipitously. Within a few years of the Vitaphone's launch, an estimated twenty-two thousand musicians—half of the instrumentalists employed by movie theaters at the time—were out of a job.[33]

"Sound movies didn't start all at once across the country," said the saxophonist Lennie Niehaus. "Talkies were something of a novelty early on. Smaller movie theaters continued to play the older silent movies with live music behind them. The big theaters got the new movies with the sound. But as the years went on and talkies took hold, the live orchestras were cut down to smaller groups, and then to just a violin and piano and drums for local theaters. Finally, the work just dried up. As soon as talkies began to take hold, the Hollywood studios started to hire their own orchestras. My dad heard about opportunities in the studio orchestras out there, so he packed up our family and moved us to Los Angeles."[34]

The trend toward recorded music only accelerated with the repeal of Prohibition in 1933. As the number of bars proliferated, so did the number of jukeboxes installed. The modern commercial coin-operated machines had first emerged in 1927 after electronic microphones improved the fidelity of recordings and the electric amplifier made built-in speakers possible. The jukebox's popularity surged during the 1930s—not only in bars but also in restaurants, hotel lounges, and anywhere people ate and drank. By 1936 Wurlitzer alone was earning a net annual profit of about $500,000, and by the following year the company held a 50 percent market share. In the late 1930s, the company was rolling out up to seven new models a year.[35]

During the Depression, as the popularity of radio, records, talkies, and jukeboxes continued to grow, unemployment among musicians increased. For the American Federation of Musicians, fewer musicians collecting wages meant fewer members paying union dues, and a decline in membership meant the AFM would have less clout. The federal government tried to aid musicians with the Works Progress Administration's Federal Music Project (FMP), which from 1935 to 1939 employed nearly 12,500 musicians in symphonies, small orchestras, brass bands, and opera or choral groups.[36] But the effort led by Washington did little for musician employment overall. By 1942 an estimated 50–60 percent of the AFM's 138,000 members were unemployed.[37]

No other occupation in America had ever faced such a threat from technology. In most industries, technology helped workers make more products faster. For example, a car built on a newly outfitted Detroit assembly line required the labor of autoworkers to operate the machinery. With the radio, records, the phonograph, and the jukebox, however, a single master recording made by musicians could be used to press millions of copies of the same song with no further participation by the original workers—in this case the musicians—in their production.

In addition, consumers could play those recordings repeatedly at home with no need for a new copy, no further payments to make, and no new efforts on the part of the musicians who made the original recording. In other industries, workers could be retrained to operate new methods of automation. But the new recording and playback technologies produced no alternative jobs for musicians. Instead, jobs that had been available to musicians, in silent-movie theaters, on the radio, and in other public places, simply disappeared as recorded sound made those positions unnecessary. By the 1930s radio posed the largest threat to musicians' jobs, especially as records began to be played on the air.

The AFM had little choice but to either fight the trend or face the real threat of marginalization and diminished power. Many of the tactics that the AFM would implement had been used by the American Society of Composers and Publishers (ASCAP) in earlier battles against radio. ASCAP was formed in 1914 after the composer Victor Herbert heard the unlicensed performance of his music at a New York restaurant. After complaining to the restaurant's owner that the unauthorized performance was in violation of the copyright law, Herbert was told there was no copyright infringement because no admission had been charged at the door. In retaliation, Herbert and 170 composers and 22 music publishers formed ASCAP, which would be responsible for collecting fees from orchestras, theaters, and anyone else who wanted to perform members' compositions in public for profit.[38] In the 1920s the courts extended the composers' right to collect such fees to radio.

At first, ASCAP had given radio a pass on these fees, since the airplay of members' songs by live orchestras meant strong sales of sheet music and records, resulting in ASCAP royalties. But as the popularity and profits of radio climbed in the 1930s, ASCAP reversed itself, demanding not only a fixed royalty fee but also a percentage of a station's commercial income. Fearful of depending on songs written by ASCAP composers and having to pay royalties with no end in sight, the radio industry formed Broadcasters Music Incorporated (BMI) in 1939 to generate its own inventory of songs and to form a lower-cost alternative to ASCAP's near-monopoly over radio.

But in March 1940 ASCAP's newest fee hike became the final straw. Although ASCAP proposed a substantial reduction in the fee it was charging smaller stations, it announced a new 7.5 percent fee on the income of the major radio networks. The networks viewed this fee as a tax, and when the ASCAP royalty agreement with radio networks expired at the end of 1940, the networks refused to renew it under the new terms. For ten months—from January to October 1941—the country's three existing radio networks subsisted entirely on live and recorded music written by BMI composers or tunes in the public domain.[39]

Phonograph records and radio transcriptions—recordings of performances for replay on the air after their initial airing—had been used during the 1930s by radio stations. But court cases during the decade continually attempted to halt or restrict the on-air use of records. In 1941, with war looming in Europe and the Pacific, the government moved to resolve ASCAP's battle with the radio industry. By then nearly nine hundred radio stations were in existence, with five hundred of them representing more than 90 percent of the income of the broadcasting industry.[40] As the industry's regulator, the government believed that ASCAP was putting radio in a bind. When the government threatened to hold ASCAP in violation of antitrust laws, ASCAP dropped its 7.5 percent fee and agreed to allow the government to review its financial records.[41] Despite all the fuss, ASCAP's battle with radio had barely made a dent in the profits and expansion of the radio industry. From 1930 to 1935, radio industry jobs doubled, and by 1938 both RCA Victor and CBS owned movie studios as well.[42]

Throughout the 1930s the AFM had waged its own war with radio and the recording industry to try to slow the erosion of jobs. The AFM's battle in Chicago was particularly heated. Since the 1920s, the city had been an entertainment and recording center, and a hotbed of union activism. In 1935 the Chicago local even secured a deal with the radio industry ensuring that all recordings would be destroyed after a single broadcast. Additional airplays of records were allowed only after a station hired a "stand-by" orchestra whose number was equal to that of the musicians on the record.[43]

Inspired by the Chicago local's success, the national AFM in 1936 filed lawsuits in an attempt to limit the play of records to home phonographs only and prohibit their repeated on-air use by radio stations. When the courts failed to rule on the litigation, the more militant Chicago local, in February 1937, forbade its members from recording, stating that the prohibition was needed to halt the "menacing threat" of recorded music. Although a nationwide ban of records and radio was also considered, it was averted when the networks and their affiliates agreed, in August 1938, to increase their budgets significantly over the next two years to hire studio musicians.[44]

The AFM may have been winning small battles here and there, but the union had dramatically overstepped its bounds. In 1940 the Department of Justice declared that the collective agreement between the AFM and radio was illegal, an incursion on radio's freedom of speech. As a result, the AFM's favorable agreement with radio was not renewed.[45] After ASCAP lost its own battle with radio in 1941, the AFM also realized that any assault on radio in the future was unlikely to succeed in Washington, especially after America entered World War II in December and radio was increasingly viewed as essential to national communication and security.

But in other efforts, the AFM was undaunted. In 1940, with the naming of James Petrillo, the former Chicago union leader, as the new national president, the AFM embarked on a series of moves to consolidate its power. It annexed other musicians' unions around the country and successfully pressured the Boston Symphony Orchestra, which was the country's largest nonunion orchestra, to join. And while radio presented the greatest threat to AFM jobs and clout, the union needed to aim at a softer target. So in 1942, the AFM went after radio's most profitable source of content: the record industry. The AFM's position was that unless the recording industry was stopped, radio would continue to find ways to play records instead of airing live music, resulting in a steady drain of dues-paying musicians.

MUSICIANS PULL THE PLUG

In 1942, if you flipped on a radio to listen to music, chances were about fifty-fifty you would hear a record playing. Although today such an occurrence hardly seems worth noting, the trend back then was worrisome. In the 1930s recorded music had rarely aired on the radio during the day. Most radio stations had employed orchestras full-time to generate much of the music they broadcast. But as records became more popular, more radio stations began spinning them.

When the Federal Communications Commission conducted a survey of 796 of the 890 radio stations in operation in 1942, it found that while the average station devoted 76 percent of its broadcast time to programs containing music, more than 55 percent of those programs used recorded or transcribed music. What's more, 230 of the 298 stations that were unaffiliated with the networks relied on recorded music for over 80 percent of their musical programs.[46] Increasingly, the only jobs available to musicians who weren't employed by bands, radio stations, and movie recording studios were low-paid teaching jobs and local gigs.

From the union's standpoint, unless something was done to stanch the decline of dues-paying members, it would have diminished strength to enforce the rules governing pay, hours, and staffing—and record companies and other employers would surely flout them. More important, the smaller the union's membership, the less influence it would have lobbying in Washington. From the AFM's standpoint, the only way to halt the drain was to slow the growth of radio, records, and jukeboxes. The most effective way to accomplish this goal, the union believed, was to prohibit its elite members from recording.

The AFM had begun to explore the possibility of a nationwide ban on recording at its 1941 convention, winning a green light from members a year later at its 1942 summit. In June 1942 the president of the AFM, James Petrillo, fired the first salvo, sending a letter to all the record companies, stating that "your license from the American Federation of Musicians for the employment of its members in the making of musical recordings will expire on July 31, 1942, and will not be renewed. From and after August 1, 1942, the American Federation of Musicians will not play or contract for any other forms of mechanical reproductions of music."[47]

With America at war on two fronts, the Department of Justice tried to head off the AFM's planned job action by filing an antitrust suit against the union. But a federal district court and then the Supreme Court dismissed the suit. Once the ban started, on August 1, 1942, Congress tried to force the AFM's hand by claiming that World War II had created a national need for recorded music. But in truth, there was little Congress could do, especially when the influential American Federation of Labor, in October 1942, endorsed the boycott and the collective struggle of musicians at its annual convention.[48]

What made the AFM's recording ban particularly ingenious was the union's lack of stated terms for a resolution. Rather than issue a document outlining what it wanted, the AFM merely banned all recording by its members and remained mum on the conditions that needed to be met for recording to resume. Given the union's volatile history with radio, part of its initial strategy was to see whether a ban would force radio to increase its use of live musicians. By remaining silent, the union also hoped to dodge Congress's growing animus toward labor and unions in general.

The timing of the AFM's move was brilliant. Just after the start of World War II, America's unions collectively had promised Washington that there would be no strikes against wartime manufacturing. But because the AFM did not issue the terms of its job action, it technically was not on strike. Union members could still play in orchestras and bands, and their performances often were carried live on the radio. From the AFM's strategic standpoint, musicians simply had chosen not to work for the record industry, which didn't technically employ them full-time anyway. Record companies were perfectly free to issue records they had recorded before the ban began, so the AFM wasn't standing in the way of an industry's ability to produce or its ability to distribute the result. From the AFM's standpoint, the union was simply choosing not to perform as another industry's labor force—which is why it was known as a recording ban rather than a strike.

But perhaps the shrewdest move of all was the union's decision to target the record industry rather than radio. Regulated by the government since 1927, radio was untouchable during the war. The record industry did not share the "essential industry" status enjoyed by radio. Rather than take action against the companies whose labor practices it wanted to change, the AFM simply decided to stop making a product—records—that it felt was doing more harm than good to its membership.

In the fall of 1942 the Department of Justice tried a new tack against the AFM. It argued that the union, by banning recording, was attempting to prevent radio and jukeboxes from acquiring records, thereby eliminating competing forms of music production. Thus the ban, according to the Department of Justice, was in violation of the Sherman Antitrust Act. But that convoluted line of reasoning was a stretch. A district court in 1943 dismissed the complaint, but the Supreme Court took up the case on appeal. During the Supreme Court's review, the AFM grew uncharacteristically edgy. It had no idea how the court would decide, fearing the AFM could be viewed as taking an industry hostage because no terms for resolution had been put forward. Four days before the Supreme Court's decision was handed down, the AFM announced publicly its terms for ending the recording ban. The court wound up deciding in favor of the union.

For musicians to return to the recording studios, the AFM said, the record companies and radio transcription firms would have to sign a contract with the AFM agreeing to pay royalties to the union for each record and transcription made with AFM musicians.[49] The royalties, according to the AFM's terms, were to be used "for the purposes of reducing unemployment which has been created in the main by the use of mechanical devices and for fostering and maintaining musical talent and culture and music appreciation; and for furnishing free, live music to the public."[50]

All of the record companies refused to consider such terms, objecting publicly that contributions made to a fund "disbursed at the Union's uncontrolled discretion" would not be financially transparent and thus would be open to corruption. They also argued that being forced to make royalty contributions to a fund for musicians who never worked for them would set a bad precedent. Having previously failed to make its case using anti-trust laws, the record industry took its argument to the War Labor Board (WLB), which had been established under the War Labor Disputes Act of 1943 to step in when business disputes interfered with the war effort. Once again, the recording industry hoped to use the law as leverage to break the AFM ban.

Then something surprising happened. Just as the WLB began to consider the case, in the late summer of 1943, Decca Records threw in the
towel. Unlike RCA and Columbia, Decca did not have a massive stockpile
of recordings to release as the ban wore on, nor did it have coast-to-coast
radio networks to keep it flush or a warehouse of higher-priced recordings by classical artists to release. Decca reaped nearly all its profits from
popular music and in mid-1943 it was close to bankruptcy.[51] Hamstrung
by the halt in recording, it could make no new records. And yet it had just
purchased the World Broadcasting System for its recording studios and
lucrative radio transcription business.[52] Even though Decca itself held no
interests in radio networks, transcriptions were lucrative when leased to
radio stations for broadcast at their convenience.

So in September 1943 Decca accepted the AFM's terms and signed a
deal set to run until midnight on December 31, 1947. Within a month,
twenty-two smaller record and transcription firms signed the same deal
as Decca—including Capitol, which had been formed just before the ban
started in 1942. In the next few months, seventy-six newly formed record
companies accepted the Decca terms. For its part, the AFM agreed that it
would not seek wage increases during the term of the contract and that
it would keep royalty payments in a separate fund, to be used "only for
purposes of fostering and propagating musical culture and the employment
of live musicians, members of the Federation."[53]

None of these agreements swayed Victor or Columbia, which refused to
sign. They hoped that if they sat on the sidelines, the WLB would continue
its review and rule in their favor. And Victor and Columbia's gambit nearly
paid off. In March 1944 the WLB advisory panel reviewing the case issued
its report. While the panel had no problem with the AFM's control of its
royalty fund, it questioned the union's complaint, saying that the AFM
had failed to prove definitively that the employment of its members had
suffered as a direct result of the success of records and radio. The panel
also noted that while a third of AFM's members were able to find full-
time employment as musicians, the remaining two-thirds supplemented
part-time musical work with other forms of employment. So technically
AFM's members weren't unemployed. The advisory panel recommended
that the full WLB order the AFM to end its recording ban.[54]

But the full WLB did not follow its panel's recommendation. It accepted
the principle of the union's fund but urged an end to the recording ban so
that the issue of royalty payments could be resolved in arbitration. The
AFM, however, refused to comply, noting that Decca and other record
companies had already signed a union agreement. The WLB then referred

the matter to Washington's Economic Stabilization Director, who had the power to seize control of the union if he found cause. But in the fall of 1944, the director decided that the continued ban against Victor and Columbia would not impede or delay the war effort. President Roosevelt wired the AFM, informing Petrillo of the favorable decision, but he asked the union to comply voluntarily with the WLB's recommendation. Petrillo refused. Then, in November, with Decca busy recording Jascha Heifetz—who had just left Victor to join Decca and resume recording—and President Roosevelt reelected to a fourth term, Victor and Columbia grudgingly signed the AFM's royalty contract, ending the twenty-seven-month ban.

As for the AFM, the union had scored a major victory for its newly established fund: all companies were now on board to pay royalties on records sold.[55] Payments ranged from a quarter-cent on a thirty-five-cent record to 2.5 percent of the sale price of records selling for more than two dollars. On transcriptions, the royalty was 3 percent of the transcription company's gross revenue from the sale, lease, or license of recordings, except those used only once, which were royalty-free.[56]

The rapid rise of record sales in the years that followed the lifting of the ban meant increased royalty payments and a fatter AFM fund. In 1945 the industry sold 165 million records; in 1946, the number rose to 275 million; in 1947, it was 350 million. In addition, hundreds of small record companies had emerged during the months that Victor and Columbia refused to sign an agreement with the AFM.[57] These small companies were helped by the government's easing of restrictions on shellac—an ingredient essential to the manufacture of records. They also benefited from the relatively low cost of renting time at record and radio studios. As for the AFM's royalty fund, it would accumulate more than $4.5 million during the contract's three-year term.[58]

Although radio wasn't a direct target of the AFM ban, it was nonetheless affected by the job action. The massive profits earned in 1941 by NBC, CBS, and the Mutual Broadcasting System raised worries at the FCC, which decided that RCA's ownership of the Red and Blue Networks represented an unfair slice of the market. A court battle followed, and in July 1943 RCA agreed to sell its newer Blue Network to Edward Noble, chairman of the Life Savers Corporation.[59] The sale of RCA's Blue Network to Noble closed on October 12, 1943, a month after the AFM-Decca settlement. Clearly by 1944 RCA, with one radio network less, was under economic pressure to either take legal action to end the AFM recording ban or settle. The company needed to air newly recorded music and resume the sale of more lucrative classical albums.

During the period from September 1943, when Decca signed with the AFM, to November 1944, when Victor and Columbia finally gave up the fight, jazz thrived. In these fourteen months, many new smaller independent record labels gained a foothold in the marketplace, recorded new music, and won over music-hungry consumers. Because many of the big-name swing bandleaders were already signed to Victor, Columbia, and Decca, the smaller labels turned to jazz combos featuring musicians who weren't part of big bands whose leaders were under contract to the major record labels.

By the time Coleman Hawkins and the other 52nd Street musicians recorded "Woodyn' You," "Bu-dee-daht," and "Yesterdays" on February 16, 1944, and "Disorder at the Border," "Feeling Zero," and "Rainbow Mist" (a reworking of "Body and Soul") on February 22, the record industry had already begun to change. Competition was increasing for the first time—particularly in the jazz category. During this period of industry transition, Apollo Records was first to record Dizzy Gillespie's revolutionary new approach to jazz—soon to be called bebop. Going forward, jazz would emphasize the soloist and his or her spectacular skills and ability to improvise—not the orchestra as a whole or its singers. But bebop's story was far from over. Recording the music was an accomplishment, but turning bebop into a cultural phenomenon with national appeal was another matter. Bebop in 1944 was known only to a handful of musicians, club-goers, and critics in New York. Spreading the word and generating interest and demand would require passionate champions and a marketable mystique.

2   DJs, Promoters, and Bebop

As soon as the ink had dried on the agreements signed by Victor and Columbia, records became a cash cow for the AFM. The more records that played on the radio, the merrier for the AFM. Airplay led to consumer and jukebox sales and thus a fatter union fund devoted to hiring unemployed musicians to play concerts.

Once the union no longer presented obstacles to the airplay of records, radio began to make greater use of on-air personalities to play them, engage listeners, and lure them back. This on-air personality became more widely known as the disc jockey—a colorful character who soon became one of the most powerful forces in the music business. A disc jockey decided which records to play and what to say about them on the air. A larger-than-life figure whose talents rested on intimate knowledge of the music, the disc jockey also had unrivaled access to musicians and record industry executives who were eager to have specific records played. In the case of the jazz disc jockey, particularly in major urban markets, such access meant a familiarity with the jazz club scene, jazz gossip, and even jazz artists' lingo. Such information enabled the disc jockey to create a nocturnal mystique for jazz on the air—making listeners feel as though they were part of jazz's late-night inner circle.

In the years after the AFM ban ended, the jazz disc jockey, first in New York and then in other cities, helped to stimulate the public's interest in bebop. These disc jockeys championed the music and musicians by playing their records, promoting them, and broadcasting the music live from nightclubs. Not only did disc jockeys give a boost to bebop musicians with their on-air banter and airplay of records, but they also built their own reputations by becoming the music's spoken-voice ambassadors, reaching millions of listeners.

Conflicts of interest became the norm as many disc jockeys doubled as publicists, promoters, and producers—happily accepting gifts and favors in exchange for playing records on the air. The jazz disc jockey was soon joined by jazz editors and writers, jazz concert promoters, and a range of other powerful players orbiting the periphery of the music and finding that boosting bebop was in their own best interest.

BEBOP SPOKEN HERE

Dizzy Gillespie may have been among the first to record bebop in a small group, in February 1944, but he still had big-band ambitions. As far as Gillespie was concerned, leading a big band was prestigious and the most exciting commercial possibility for a jazz musician. Even in early 1944, a big band record was the most effective way to gain traction in the marketplace and impress those who controlled recording opportunities. In March 1944, a month after recording his bebop composition "Woodyn' You," with Coleman Hawkins, for Apollo Records, Gillespie approached the bandleader Boyd Raeburn about recording "A Night in Tunisia," which at the time was called "Interlude." As Gillespie noted in his autobiography, he had come up with the unusual melody at the piano, playing an A-13th chord resolving to D minor.

The saxophonist Hal McKusick, a member of Raeburn's band in 1944, remembers Gillespie's arrival with his "Interlude" arrangement. "We were at the Lincoln Hotel in New York in March 1944," McKusick said. "Dizzy didn't come off like a wild guy then. He and [the pianist-arranger] Tadd Dameron just walked into the ballroom where we were rehearsing. They were businesslike and carried attaché cases. Dizzy spoke briefly to Boyd, and he and Tadd took out the musical parts to "Interlude." Like any composer-arranger team, they hoped we would like the song and that Boyd would decide to formally record it. Dizzy knew Boyd was open to new things and had a lot of hip arrangers writing for the band.

"After we played down the chart, I remember thinking instantly how attractive it sounded and that it swung in an exotic way. We performed "Interlude" for an audience at the hotel soon afterward and recorded it at our next studio session. That was the first time I had heard a big-band approach to bebop, and it was much more interesting than the repetitive swing formula we had been playing."[1]

Gillespie's previous eights years of experience with big bands continued to present him with earning opportunities in 1944. After leading small groups at various clubs on 52nd Street, Gillespie joined the vocalist Billy Eckstine's big band in April 1944 and remained with the orchestra as its musical director through the end of the year. Though the band was fronted by Eckstine, its arrangements were decidedly bebop. Part of Gillespie's motive for joining Eckstine's band was his promise to Billy Shaw, his personal manager and booker at the William Morris Agency. Shaw told Gillespie that if he held Eckstine's fragile band together, Shaw would help make Gillespie a headline attraction. That's all Gillespie needed to hear. Soon after joining the band, he urged Eckstine to hire Charlie Parker, bebop's other major pioneer.[2]

In early January 1945 Gillespie and Parker recorded for the first time together in a small-group studio session led by the pianist Clyde Hart for the newly founded Continental Records. Days later Gillespie recorded with a bebop sextet for Manor, another new label. By February, a month after being named "new trumpet star" by *Esquire* magazine, Gillespie signed an exclusive contract with yet another new label, Guild Records. That month and again in May 1945, Gillespie and Parker recorded bebop for Guild. They also performed bebop at a series of concerts in New York.[3] With the popularity of Gillespie and Parker's new records, other small record labels began looking for musicians to record the same jazz style.

There was no shortage of bebop musicians in late 1945. The more Gillespie and Parker recorded, the better educated other musicians became. "When these guys started playing, no one could understand it," according to the jazz writer Nat Hentoff. "But once they made records, musicians could buy them and study what they were doing and figure it out."[4] By mid-1945, *Variety* listed 130 record companies nationwide[5]—many of them new and based in New York. Musicians who had been members of big bands left those orchestras as they found freelance work and were pursued by small labels for bebop recordings. The transformation was abrupt and would have been unimaginable only a few years earlier, when just three major labels dominated the market.[6]

What exactly was bebop? One of its most formidable arrangers, Walter "Gil" Fuller, wrote an essay in 1948 for a promotional brochure that was handed out at the Royal Roost, a New York jazz club that had opened that year on Broadway and 47th Street. The essay was meant both to bring the uninitiated up to speed and to serve as a modern artist's manifesto, outlining why the music was more than a novelty. "The conventional accents falling on the first and third beat of common time in the old two-beat era has now been superseded by accents falling on the second and fourth beats as well as the 'and' beats of a measure. A further development of the rhythmic structure appears by the super imposition of various meters upon the four-quarter or common time, known as polyrhythms. These accents usually stimulate the listener because they have two, three and four voice contrapuntal lines. . . . The harmonic structure of an ordinary pop tune when played by a 'bopper' has usually been altered. Much to the disappointment of many, all of the fifths, ninths and elevenths are not flatted, as some writers would have us believe. The dominant, tonic, and the other diatonic chords in most cases are altered by adding the sixth, ninth, eleventh and thirteenth. These notes may be chromatically raised or lowered depending upon the taste of the individual. Diminished and whole tone chords are almost extinct in Be-Bop and are rarely used."[7]

But in 1944, merely recording the new music for one of the new record labels didn't guarantee recognition or fame outside New York. Although recording was an important first step in documenting the new music, bebop needed to break out of the black neighborhoods where most of the records were sold and win over white jazz fans both in New York City and beyond.

GOING TO BAT FOR BOP

Although Dizzy Gillespie and Charlie Parker were magnificent musicians, their recordings of bebop for small independent record labels in New York in 1945 were hardly a breakthrough. The number of small record labels was growing rapidly, but none had much promotional muscle beyond the Harlem record stores.[8] RCA, Columbia, and Decca, plus Capitol on the West Coast, largely ignored bebop in 1945, viewing it as quirky and unsellable to postwar audiences that clung nostalgically to swing instrumentals and vocals. To raise bebop's profile and expose the new music to the larger white jazz audience, bebop needed champions who could take this music, known then only as "New York jazz," and make it a phenomenon.

No urban market in the country was more vital to ensuring the new jazz style's survival at the time than New York, where the music was performed and recorded. With the war in Europe winding down, the city was poised to emerge as an unrivaled port and entertainment and media center. Bebop was part of a broader avant-garde arts movement in New York that was shifting the world's cultural center away from Paris. The new modernism in painting, architecture, literature, and music would render postwar art forms from Europe virtually obsolete.

From Ayn Rand's *Fountainhead*, which reached no. 6 on the best-seller list in 1945, to the 1945 abstract works of the painter Jackson Pollock, artists in all fields were beginning to pursue a new radicalism, an "anarchist individualism" that combined unrestrained expression and a personalized vision.[9] In early 1945 New York's intellectual circles teemed with idealists, along with those who made a living evaluating, praising, and promoting them. In July 1945 *Down Beat* reported on a Manhattan art gallery that held a jazz jam session at the Village Vanguard, bringing musicians and artists together to discuss jazz and nonobjective painting.[10]

In the noisy traffic of creative movements, where the postwar artist spearheaded the new celebration of individuality and self-expression, promotion was essential to stand out. Fortunately for the music, New York was already the country's jazz, entertainment, and promotion capital. Major jazz writers were based in the city; New York hosted the country's largest concentration of nightclubs, theaters, and concert halls; all the major radio networks were based in Midtown Manhattan, and the radio dial offered the most diverse programming, twenty-four hours a day. Jazz, like other forms of music and theater in the city, had its share of street-smart agents, pushy publicists, tireless promoters, college-educated critics, and influential columnists. All these media power brokers jockeyed for power and competed to discover new jazz talent, hoping that their own profiles and influence would rise as the jazz artists they touted became stars. Most of bebop's early supporters were passionate about the music, but they were also intent on surviving and earning a living, and bebop was a way for them to build a formidable legitimate reputation.

Among bebop's earliest supporters and most ardent promoters were the personal manager and event booker Billy Shaw, the print media editors/writers Barry Ulanov and Leonard Feather, the concert promoter Monte Kay, and the radio disc jockeys "Symphony Sid" Torin and Fred Robbins. Each played a distinct role in raising bebop's profile and positioning the music and artists as highly exciting performers who needed to be taken seriously. Collectively, they would give bebop the promotional boost it needed to take on a life of its own. Individually, each found a way to profit from the music—by boosting the circulation of publications, increasing concert and club attendance, attracting wider radio audiences, and augmenting the number of records sold. Whatever their financial motivation, each individual was passionate about the new jazz style, and when they lent their names to the cause, they gave the music increased credibility. Little by little, they created a mystique for bebop that centered on hipness, black music and culture, and a nocturnal lifestyle that was both inviting and a little dangerous.

"These guys had enormous passion for the music and the artists, which made others take notice and helped raise bebop's overall profile—first in

New York and then in all the major cities around the country," said the jazz writer Ira Gitler. "Not everyone was a fan of bebop at first. Many resented the music, and older musicians who couldn't play it put it down. Barry Ulanov and Leonard Feather were journalists and were aware of bebop early on because they were always on the scene. Both promoted the music through recording sessions and helped raise the profile of *Metronome* magazine in the process. As for Monte Kay and Symphony Sid, they had been promoting the music for a long time—one through jam sessions and the other on small radio stations. But all four loved the music first and foremost."[11]

Barry Ulanov had been a fan and a reviewer of the new jazz as early as 1942. He had been born in New York to parents who had emigrated from Russia, and his father quickly became concertmaster of Arturo Toscanini's NBC Philharmonic Orchestra. Ulanov's father wanted him to become a violinist, but when an auto accident broke both of Ulanov's wrists, he had to give up an instrument he disliked. In 1939 Ulanov was named editor of *Metronome*, which began as a classical-music magazine that also covered swing bands. In short order, Ulanov and his co-editor, George Simon, transformed *Metronome* into a publication that focused on jazz, and Ulanov wrote many positive reviews of emerging bebop musicians and the new music.[12] As early as 1944, *Metronome* printed a feature on Gillespie and the new music.

Ulanov's love for modern music may have been influenced to some extent by his forward-thinking roommate at Columbia University, Ad Reinhardt, who would go on to become a leading modern abstract expressionist painter.[13] Miles Davis, in his autobiography, recalled Ulanov's early contribution: "There were a couple of white music critics, like Leonard Feather and Barry Ulanov, who were co-editors of *Metronome* music magazine and who understood what was going on with bebop, who liked it and wrote good things."[14]

Leonard Feather, a London-born jazz pianist, moved to New York in 1939 to seek playing opportunities. But he quickly became a well-regarded jazz composer, a record producer, and an influential deputy editor, columnist, and critic for *Metronome*. He was even a jazz press agent from 1941 to 1943.[15] "Leonard Feather isn't really given enough credit for promoting bebop," said Marjorie Hyams, a pianist and vibraphonist who worked on 52nd Street in the 1940s and was a member of the original George Shearing Quintet. "Leonard was a magazine writer, composer, piano player and ingenious A&R [artist and repertoire] man—and he was passionate about all of these roles and especially bebop. He always had great ideas and he was very generous with me. I lived in Greenwich Village at the time and he lived there with his wife. He was always looking at ways to promote bebop, creating new sounds using bebop as a base, and raising the music's visibility. I think he wanted to 'class' it up, to give it sophistication that would in turn catch on with many more people. Leonard knew it was great music but that it needed a hook to excite people who were put off or unfamiliar with it. From the mid-forties on, he wanted to turn bebop into a big deal—at least bigger than it was just on 52nd Street."[16]

In January 1946 an unsigned editorial in *Metronome* endorsed the new jazz style: "We feel that Dizzy, having become the focal point of this new scene in jazz history and being its most potent and fascinating personality, is a very important figure."[17] The magazine also named Gillespie's 1945 discs "Salted Peanuts" and "Be Bop" (for Manor) and "Salt Peanuts," "Hot House," and "Shaw 'Nuff" (for Guild) records of the year.[18]

Monte Kay produced weekend jam sessions in the early 1940s at the archipelago of clubs in New York that ran from Greenwich Village to 52nd Street. Kay began as a collector of Dixieland records, but his tastes shifted to small-group swing and the blues after he had heard Roy Eldridge and Ike Quebec. By 1944 Kay had been exposed to bebop, and in 1945 he and the Broadway press agent Mal Braveman formed the New Jazz Foundation to stage and promote small-group jazz concerts. "Kay was a soft-spoken, laid back kind of guy," Gitler recalled. "He was white but had an extremely dark complexion, and many people thought he was black."[19]

Kay's timing in the concert business was good. Jazz concerts held in symphony halls for listening rather than dancing dated back at least to Paul Whiteman's 1924 "Experiment in Modern Music" concert at New York's Aeolian Hall. In the 1930s bands appeared on theater stages as an added attraction to feature films. Benny Goodman's Carnegie Hall concert in 1938 was considered a success, as was Duke Ellington's 1943 concert in the same venue. But in each case the jazz concert fit a rigid format, featuring a large band onstage that tried to emulate the grandeur of the classical orchestras that ordinarily played there.

During World War II, material shortages of gasoline and rubber, as well as parts for bus and car repairs, made concert performances in urban centers more practical than touring. Promoters quickly realized that symphony auditoriums—vacant for many nights of the season—were ideal for popular music concerts of all kinds.[20] One of the first musicians to stage small-group concerts in large auditoriums was the guitarist Eddie Condon, who led a series of jam session concerts at New York's Town Hall in 1942. In the spring of 1945 Kay and Braveman's New Jazz Foundation staged the first in a series of bebop concerts at Town Hall featuring Dizzy Gillespie and Charlie Parker. The concerts introduced the new music both to audiences familiar with it from recordings and those who had only read about the two bebop stars."Monte Kay was quiet and unassuming," recalled the bassist and talent manager John Levy. "You'd never expect someone like him to be associated with the flamboyant groups and people he managed. He had a lot of money from his family and didn't have to do all this stuff with jazz. He liked the people he dealt with, but I don't know that he actually liked bebop. I think he just liked the people, the characters."[21]

By contrast, the concert promoter Norman Granz, who was based in Los Angeles during this period, had little use for bebop early on. In the summer of 1945, he traveled to New York to hear the new jazz for himself and size up the bebop talent pool for his Jazz at the Philharmonic tour, which was due to leave Los Angeles in November 1945 and arrive in New York in December. But Granz, who favored unrestrained jam sessions by established swing stars, found bebop almost nonsensical. "Jazz in New York stinks," he told *Down Beat*. "Even the drummers on 52nd St. sound like Dizzy Gillespie. . . . I can't tell you how disappointed I am in the quality of the music here."[22] But by the fall of 1948, Granz had had a change of heart, slating a JATP tour of twenty-eight concerts that included Charlie Parker and other bebop musicians. He gained his new outlook either because he needed to fill the recording pipeline for his Clef label, formed a year earlier, or because he had figured out how to leverage bebop effectively—by having artists record Tin Pan Alley standards.

But as the 1948 tour began, Granz's experience with Parker was anything but easy, given the alto saxophonist's drug problem and the dissatisfaction of the audiences with Parker's subpar performances.[23] While paying crowds may have been unhappy with Parker, they were moved by the other bebop musicians featured in Granz's gala shows, which exposed national audiences to bebop while establishing the value of individual artists who could deliver blistering, spectacular solos.

Although editors, jazz critics, and concert promoters gave bebop new respect and credibility, radio may have been the new jazz style's biggest and most important ally. In 1945 radio was a changed medium. After the settlement of the AFM's recording ban in 1944, the union had eased its hostility toward the playing of records by radio stations. The disc jockeys who rose to prominence thereafter had the biggest impact on the early acceptance and eventual popularity of the new jazz. The disc jockey chose which new records to play, introduced the music to the audience, and educated listeners, explaining to them in colorful language why a specific record or artist was exceptional. A good disc jockey also forged personal links to audiences with anecdotes, jazz news, banter, and a vernacular that captured the imagination of listeners. If a disc jockey was successful in creating an appetite for an artist's music, audiences would play the records on jukeboxes and buy the discs at record stores. Most important, the disc jockey was the ever-important hub for the record companies, concert promoters, jazz critics, and the listening public—serving as the music's seemingly independent screener and advocate.

The most animated and influential jazz disc jockey in New York in 1945 was "Symphony Sid" Torin. He had spent years on smaller New York stations, playing jazz records by black artists who received little airplay on mainstream music stations. He spoke in a hip, loose style that black audiences found familiar and white audiences found exciting. Born Sidney Tarnopol on New York's Lower East Side, Torin dropped out of college in the 1930s to become an errand boy at a Manhattan music store. In 1937, an executive from WBNX, a Bronx radio station, approached Torin and asked him to host a daily show. Torin agreed and was soon sponsored by a men's pants store and a hat company. One day, the station's program announcer opened Torin's show by saying, "Here comes the kid with the fancy pants and the fancy lid: Symphony Sid."[24] The name stuck, and his show became hugely popular across the river in Harlem.

Unlike most disc jockeys, Torin viewed himself as one of the musicians, not merely an announcer. His insider image was fueled by impromptu banter modeled after the urban jiving of musicians such as Cab Calloway, Louis Armstrong, and Fats Waller: "If you got eyes to be the sharpest, take a tip from old Daddy Sid and fall by Al's Pants Shop for the pants with the peg bottom and the wide knee," was typical of Torin's pitch for a sponsor's ad message.[25] But Torin was not merely a Runyonesque romantic. He had a knack for survival and instinctively knew how to make a buck. Pressured by advertisers early on to play pop records, not jazz, Torin ignored their advances and held fast to the jazz format. To protect himself, he began to conduct surveys among Harlem consumers to show the station's advertisers which of their products were most popular with his listening audience.[26]

In December 1940 Torin began broadcasting an all-night record program on New York's WHOM[27] and emceeing an occasional Sunday theater concert where he would play records.[28] He also hosted an afternoon radio show on WWRL. As his following grew, so did his reputation for introducing and promoting musicians favored in New York's black communities. By 1945 Torin was spinning on his shows many of the new bebop records released by small labels such as Guild, Manor, and Savoy—in part because of his close connection to Harlem's Rainbow Music Shop, one of his advertisers.

Torin first joined forces with the concert promoters Kay and Braveman in May 1945, when Kay staged the New Jazz Foundation concerts with Parker and Gillespie. Initially, ticket sales for the first event were so slow that Kay offered Torin 50 percent of the gate to promote it. Kay also provided the Guild records that Parker and Gillespie had recently made for Torin to play on his shows[29] In the weeks leading up to the May concert, Torin promoted the event on WHOM and WWRL. The strategy worked. By the day of the concert, thirteen hundred seats had sold, filling Town Hall to near capacity. "It was so good we did another concert a month after that," Kay told Ira Gitler.[30]

But the New Jazz Foundation was plagued by problems. Jazz artists didn't always show up for concerts when they were supposed to, and by November 1945 the foundation was seeking financial support through enlarged membership. Leonard Feather's comments in the July 1945 issue of *Metronome* were scathing: "Main fault of the concert was, as at the previous one, poor organization and production. Pretty soon the NJF will have to live down a reputation for broken promises. It cannot gain prestige until every musician advertised shows up, . . . the concert starts on time, the mike works, musicians stop coming on stage obviously high, and the whole thing, in short, lives up to the description 'concert.' I hope these things can be accomplished because the NJF's musical ideals are the best."[31]

In late 1945, Parker and Gillespie traveled to Los Angeles to perform. But they failed to win many fans for their new music. Unlike New York, Los Angeles was segregated, and black musicians were expected to be entertainers, not serious artist-musicians. Within weeks, Gillespie returned to New York, but Parker decided to stay on, appearing in concerts staged by Norman Granz, who had managed to turn a series of jam sessions he held at the Trouville Club in Los Angeles into a full-fledged concert series at the city's Philharmonic Auditorium. He expanded the concept to a tour in 1945 that he called Jazz at the Philharmonic. But in July 1946 Parker suffered a nervous breakdown and was institutionalized at California's Camarillo State Hospital, remaining there until early 1947.

A turning point for bebop came on February 1, 1946, when Billy Shaw, Dizzy Gillespie's personal manager, left the William Morris Agency to join the Gale Agency as a partner.[32] Shaw landed Gillespie a recording session with RCA Victor on February 22 for four bebop sides with a small group.

By matching Gillespie with one of the country's largest labels, one with the strongest record-distribution network, Shaw was able to place Gillespie's Victor 78-rpms in the hands of jazz disc jockeys nationwide. A month later, in March, Gillespie signed with the Gale Agency.[33] Gillespie began a lengthier period of recording for RCA in August 1947 that continued in December, this time with his big band. Shaw was now able to place Gillespie's records in all-important jukeboxes, reaching newly curious mainstream listeners. Shaw also helped organize a concert featuring Gillespie at Carnegie Hall in September 1947, under Leonard Feather's auspices. When Gillespie drew a standing ovation, Shaw began to plan a concert series around the country for the band as well as a tour of Europe in early 1948. Bebop proved a postwar sensation in Europe, an exciting exponent of American democracy and creative freedom. Behind the scenes, Shaw's publicity efforts on behalf of Gillespie were extensive—clipping articles and sending them off to editors, columnists, and disc jockeys. Gillespie's big band wasn't a threat to Stan Kenton's popular orchestra, but he was catching on fast, proving that a black band that played difficult music could attract a large enough audience to pay off.[34]

But Gillespie wasn't recording only for RCA Victor. In 1946 he also made recordings for Musicraft, which in November placed a trade ad for him and his band in *Metronome:* "The world's gone Dizzy Gillespie crazy. On tour, watch for them in your territory."[35] In the same November issue, Coleman Hawkins had no trouble picking out the modern musicians during a blindfold test conducted by *Metronome's* Leonard Feather. After hearing Gillespie's "That's Earl, Brother," he said, "That Milt Jackson could sound great—what he needs is a good set of vibes. That's Dizzy . . . the alto sounds like Charlie Parker, but it's not—I can tell the difference. It's Sonny Stitt. He's fine, too. Ray Brown's on bass. That's a good number, original conception and execution fine. It's modern; they're playing the right chords, they know the changes. It has a good beat, too; modern jazz has to swing, too. Three stars."

Meanwhile, records by dozens of other bebop musicians began emerging on both coasts. Disc jockeys such as Fred Robbins in New York and Al Jarvis in Los Angeles leveraged Torin's colorful tone, attracting a wide jazz-audience following.

SPINNERS PUT BOP OVER TOP

When Charlie Parker emerged from the Camarillo State Hospital in early 1947, he remained on the West Coast for several months, working with small groups of musicians and showing them how to play the new style of music that he and Gillespie had pioneered. In April, Parker returned to New York and formed a quintet with the trumpeter Miles Davis. California had been a bust for Parker, thanks to his court-imposed six-month stay at Camarillo and because Los Angeles, more racially segregated than New York, wasn't enthralled by bebop or its black hipster lingo and style.

Some record industry executives in Los Angeles even campaigned aggressively against bebop and its influence. In April 1946 radio station KMPC in Los Angeles announced a ban on bebop recordings: "The currently popular style of Bebop music is degenerate, a contributing factor to juvenile delinquency. It is suggestive and nothing short of dirty!"[36] By the spring of 1947, Dave Dexter—a jazz writer, record producer, and Capitol executive on the West Coast—had proclaimed that bebop was dead in Southern California. Dexter's negative remarks appeared in the *Capitol*, a newsletter published by Capitol Records, and were cited in a June article by Barry Ulanov in *Metronome*. Dexter wrote, "Note to bands and musicians planning to come to Hollywood: no be-boppers wanted! . . . Beboppers attract attention . . . by running six thousand notes a minute, bad notes, good notes, in between notes, just so they're notes, regardless of the chords."[37]

Nonetheless, back on the East Coast, bebop was performed at Carnegie Hall in September 1947, when Parker appeared there in concert with the Dizzy Gillespie Quintet. Even the major record labels were paying attention to bebop, though many of the early bebop artists they signed were white musicians who had figured out how to play the music. "I was signed up with RCA Victor, which wanted to get it because bop was catching on as the form of music," the tenor saxophonist Charlie Ventura told Ira Gitler in *Swing to Bop*. "But the average laymen, or the average listener, they thought bop was only associated with people that were on drugs, and goatees and this, and led a dirty life, and that they would gear their children to stay away form the beboppers, nothing but a bunch of hopheads. RCA Victor said, 'We want to use the word Bop.' Then I said, trying to get it to the producer, 'Amongst the people, don't let it sound like a dirty word.' So that's when I said 'Bop for the People.' That's how that came about."[38]

Other large record companies were quick to jump on the bebop bandwagon—provided that established white artists were involved. As the bebop vocalist Babs Gonzales told Ira Gitler, "Capitol didn't do much promotion. They promise you the moon. Their transition into bebop was really more or less pointedly [about] the big names. At that time, they acquired Benny Goodman and Woody Herman, and their sales and promotions went directly to these two biggest cats. . . . I had a dictionary [of jazz slang] out at that time. And Capitol didn't say nothing to me. They just took the dictionary and reprinted it with BG and Woody, like they were the big things. And way at the bottom, in small little print [was], 'By the courtesy of Babs Gonzales.' So I said I'd better not sue these people because I'm suing Victor at the moment. So I'd better cool it else I won't get heard nowhere."[39]

Bebop's sophistication also impressed musicians who favored modern classical music. The pianist Lennie Tristano, attempting to define bebop in the July 1947 issue of *Metronome*, noted that "bebop has made several contributions to the evolution of the single line. The arpeggio has ceased to be important; the line is primarily diatonic. The procedure is not up one chord and down another, nor is it up one scale and down another; the use of skips of more than a third precludes this seesaw motion. The skillful use of new scales fosters the evolution of many more ideas than does the use of arpeggios, since an arpeggio merely restates the chord."[40] Along the way, bebop became the music of youth, creating a sharp dividing line between old jazz traditionalists and young individualists. In November, Barry Ulanov extolled bebop's virtues in *Metronome* after interviewing Charlie Parker and Dizzy Gillespie, explaining that the music "weeded out poseurs, separating the moldy figs from the moderns."[41]

But bebop's recording momentum would soon be halted. In June 1947, the Taft-Hartley Labor Relations Act was passed to limit the expanding power of America's labor unions. The law prohibited all unions from collecting fees from companies and then managing the funds themselves, which Congress saw as likely to lead to financial abuse and extortion. The move was a swipe at the AFM's royalty fund, to which all the nation's record companies were contributors. Congress's goal was to ensure that the AFM's methods wouldn't become a model for labor—namely, calling a strike that wasn't officially a strike to settle grievances that were never officially defined and then forcing an industry to pay royalties to support union members who never worked for the companies that paid them. In the eyes of business and Congress, the stalemate that had occurred between the AFM and the record companies from 1942 to 1944 couldn't play out again between workers and any number of industries vital to the emerging cold war effort, including the manufacture of rubber, steel, aluminum, and airplane parts.

But the Taft-Hartley Act didn't scare the AFM. Concerned that the law would eventually set the union's clock back to the years before the ban, the AFM announced in October 1947 that when its royalty contract with the recording industry expired, on December 31st at midnight, recording by member musicians would again be banned. On January 1, 1948, the union made good on its promise, and the second recording ban began and lasted until December. Upon settlement, the AFM established the Music Performance Trust Fund, which took advantage of the Taft-Hartley Act's big loophole—that a third party could collect and manage royalty fees for a fund. The AFM would continue to collect royalties on records sold, but in compliance with the Taft-Hartley Act's stipulations.[42]

Though recording ceased for much of 1948, the year proved transitional for bebop. Clubs on 52nd Street began to close down—victims of a shift in postwar demographics and tastes. The gritty basement clubs in brownstones that stood shoulder to shoulder on 52nd Street and had appealed to audiences during World War II no longer retained their charm. Many of those who had been single during the war were now married and had moved into homes in leafy enclaves of New York. Others viewed 52nd Street as seedy, inconvenient, and located too many blocks east of Broadway—the city's entertainment center.

Despite the decline of 52nd Street, bebop was thriving. In January 1948 Gillespie appeared on the cover of *Metronome* after his orchestra had been named Band of the Year for 1947. Throughout the country, young bebop musicians were sporting berets, goatees, and eyeglass frames similar to Gillespie's. As the magazine noted, "Young boppers with their own little bands began to lead from the waist and the rump; some with perfectly good eyesight affected the heavy spectacles. Dizzy was a character; he had a personality to go with his music; he was well on his way to national importance."[43]

On the radio, jazz disc jockeys went to bat for bebop, becoming the music's most powerful and fanatical advocates. "The importance of the disc jockey grew completely out of proportion to the capabilities of the great majority of these men during the past year," *Metronome* reported in January 1948. "But as has often been pointed out in these pages, little or no music talent was uncovered by the networks, so that the recording companies, manned by much more public-wise personnel, were able to capture a huge audience merely by giving it something that sounded different.

"All the jockeys had to do was spin these new platters, catch audience reaction and then help launch the new stars and the new records, which the public seemed to like. Perhaps the most scorching success was scored by Fred Robbins, fast-talking, word-inventing twirler, who's not only a good performer, radio-wise, but who also knows and takes a keep interest in the records he plays. From a New York station WOV, his fame spread countrywide via his work as successor to Martin Block on Columbia's *Record Shop* show. The smooth, glib, sometimes too oily Block seemed better than ever in 1947, probably because of the obvious comparison drawn with his bandwagon-jumping rivals."[44]

The rise of the jazz disc jockey coincided with the decline of New York's 52nd St. In April 1948 Leonard Feather wrote a gloomy article for *Metronome* under the headline "The Street Is Dead: A Jazz Obituary."[45] In it Feather noted that whereas four years ago buildings on 52nd Street housed seven clubs—Kelly's Stable, the Hickory House, the Three Deuces, the Downbeat, the Onyx, the Spotlite, and Tondelayo—"Today, several are [occupied by] Chinese restaurants while others feature less jazz-related acts. In fact, the Onyx can't make money with live music and has decided to install the popular Symphony Sid, who now plays records for his audience and interviews visiting celebrities. Harlem is no substitute. The cause? High cost of living, lack of talent with drawing power, managers and agents who put a high price on talent, and rotten liquor."

In June, however, the disc jockey "Symphony Sid" Torin took a new job, switching from WHOM to WMCA, which had a much stronger broadcast signal, a wider reach, and a larger audience.[46] At WMCA, Torin played bebop records from midnight to 6 A.M. and eventually broadcast live on the weekends from a club called the Royal Roost, which in April had begun featuring bebop on Tuesdays in the heart of the theater district, on Broadway and 47th Street.[47] His show, by airing in the early hours of the morning, when hundreds of other stations were off the air, was able to reach into the Midwest and the South as well as all parts of New York.

The Royal Roost was originally a Broadway chicken restaurant, whose owner, Ralph Watkins, had converted it into a jazz club at the insistence of Monte Kay and Torin. "I knew there was an audience for jazz but [fans] were a little tired of standing up at the bar on 52nd Street and nursing a beer through a whole set," Kay told Ira Gitler.[48] Kay had first suggested back in February that Watkins feature jazz, and Watkins began his jazz nights on March 11, with the Jimmie Lunceford Orchestra.[49] When Watkins agreed to start a bebop night on Tuesdays beginning in April 1948, Kay, with Torin's assistance, began promoting the club. The first night that bebop was played, the police had to be called to handle the overflow.[50] The same size crowd turned up the following Tuesday, encouraging Watkins to add weekends to the lineup later that month.[51] In May the club expanded its schedule to feature bebop nightly,[52] and by August *Billboard* was hailing the Royal Roost on page 1 as a raging success: "Jazz on B'Way Brings Bux Back Alive: Watkins Experiment Boffo." The article touted capacity crowds and bebop's appeal: "Consensus now is that Watkins, his partner Bill Faden, and producer Monte Kay have shown them. Patronage has consistently grown from show to show with bebop aficionados more than willing to traverse the extra five blocks from the street downtown to the Roost to catch favorites like Thelonious Monk, Lucky Thompson's All Stars, Dizzy Gillespie and, now, the top-drawer Billy Eckstine–Charlie Ventura–Tadd Dameron offering."[53] Part of the Roost's charm was its centralized Broadway location and the roped-off section dubbed the Metropolitan Bopera House. Here, patrons paid a small admission and could sit and listen to the music without having to order drinks—a big change from the adults-only drinking clubs on 52nd Street.

The Roost—and bebop—also were greatly aided by Torin's live WMCA broadcasts from the club starting in the summer of 1948 and Birdland on WJZ starting in 1949. Torin promoted the music and musicians on the air and also, by describing the action at the Royal Roost, created for listeners a mental image of an environment that was exciting, intimate, and larger than life. By setting the scene, interviewing musicians, and allowing listeners to hear the sound of glasses clinking and patrons chatting and laughing, Torin turned jazz into a reality radio show.

"Down in Virginia, I had a small radio in my bed that I listened to very late at night," the record producer Creed Taylor recalled. "When everyone was asleep, that radio could pick up the frequency from New York stations coming over the mountains. I'd hear Symphony Sid's broadcasts from Birdland. He'd paint amazing pictures on the air. Between sets he'd observe what was going on. He'd say things like, 'Well look over there, it's Kai Winding talking to Diz at the bar. And Count Basie just walked in to catch a set.' Stuff like that. Everything that Sid talked about was so cool and clear in my head, not just about the music but also the social surroundings of the jazz players. All I could think of was, 'Wow, this music is something else.' I couldn't wait to get up to New York and start meeting the people Symphony Sid was talking about."[54]

The romantic, on-air scenes Torin described weren't lost on the vocalese singer Jon Hendricks. "Radio played such a big role back then. Whatever record Sid played on the air became hot. I thought Sid was an American cultural prophet. All those radio guys were the prophets of American culture. Sid was a cultured gentleman. He was eloquent, too, and could speak the vernacular, which connected with black listeners and intrigued white ones."[55]

When Gillespie opened at the Royal Roost with his big band in mid-1948, writers, critics, and disc jockeys were in attendance—including the editor and writer Barry Ulanov, the producer John Hammond, the critic Leonard Feather, and the disc jockeys Torin and Fred Robbins, who also was promoting concerts at Town Hall. In August, *Billboard* wrote: "Each attraction seems to outdo its predecessor. When Dizzy opened several weeks ago, it was hard to fathom anything creating more excitement."[56]

By the end of the year, disc jockeys had named Gillespie's band the no. 1 orchestra in the country and Gillespie the top trumpet soloist.[57] "Bebop's popularity took off with Symphony Sid," said clarinetist Buddy DeFranco. "He played a lot of records by hip jazz guys like Roy Eldridge and Ben Webster. He created this mystique that nighttime was when great things happened. He was the first one I can remember playing Parker's and Gillespie's stuff on the radio. But bebop's popularity was a combination of things. Bebop was a new kind of jazz, but bop's feeling was intriguing. It kind of made you feel good. It was happy and absolutely interesting. It was more polished and had more depth than standard jazz, especially on improvised solos. In fact, improvisation was expected.

"I decided to play bebop on clarinet after hearing Parker. I consider Parker the premier player. No one has done that much in such a short span of time. I think my playing is for the most part pretty good, but there's much to be desired. The big problem with playing jazz, especially bebop, is your brain must always be several beats ahead of your ability to play. You're constantly trying to catch up with what you want to do. Parker said the same thing to me."[58]

Torin continued to work hard on behalf of jazz musicians and the music. In July 1948 he even took a poll of his listeners and announced that Dizzy Gillespie was their no. 1 pick. In return, grateful jazz musicians wrote songs for Torin, hoping he'd use them as his theme. Among the best known Torin tributes were Lester Young's "Jumpin' With Symphony Sid" (1947) Arnett Cobb's "Walkin' With Sid" (1947), Illinois Jacquet's "Symphony in Sid" (1948), and Tadd Dameron's "Sid's Delight" (1948). When the jazz and bebop singer Sarah Vaughan appeared at the opening of New York's Clique Club on Broadway, between 52nd and 53rd Streets, in December 1948, the *Chicago Defender* reported that she attracted more than fifteen hundred people, including celebrities and notables such as Stan Kenton, Charlie Barnet, Benny Goodman, June Christy, Mickey Rooney, and more than a dozen disc jockeys, including Torin and Fred Robbins,[59] who by then was chairman of the National Association of Disc Jockeys.[60]

Perhaps Walter "Gil" Fuller summarized the scene best in his promotional essay, handed out at the Royal Roost: "The first promoters to successfully present 'bop' were Monte Kay, who produces the nightly concerts here at the Royal Roost, and Symphony Sid, the WMCA all-night disc jockey. In 1945 they sponsored the concert debut of Charlie Parker and Dizzy Gillespie at Town Hall and since then have been active in presentation and promotion of Be-Bop in New York. Several other disc jockeys have been instrumental in bringing the music to a wider audience: Fred Robbins and Bill Williams of WOV, Leonard Feather of WHN, Willie Bryant and Ray Carroll of WHOM, Jerry Roberts and Bill Cook of WAAT, Woody Woodard of WLIB, and Dan Burley and Fred Barr of WWRL. Robbins has also made a series of musical shorts for Columbia Pictures including one with Gene Krupa which introduced Be-Bop to the screen."[61]

By the end of 1948, when the second AFM recording ban had ended and musicians returned to the studios, bebop was the dominant jazz style, thanks to the perseverance of musicians, jazz writers, concert promoters, disc jockeys, and agents—all of whom gained visibility and profited from bebop's rise. Some five years after the first recording of bebop, in February 1944, the new music was being played on the radio in nearly every major urban market. In 1948 and 1949 even swing giants like Woody Herman, Benny Goodman, Buddy Rich, Harry James, Charlie Barnet, Tommy Dorsey, and Artie Shaw attempted bebop-flavored recordings, with varying degrees of success. Some of them, like Goodman and Dorsey, did so grudgingly, since they weren't skillful practitioners of the new style. But they were aware of the music's importance and their own need to remain relevant. Even the vocalist Bing Crosby, in April 1949, took a shot at the music with "Bebop Spoken Here."

As for Parker and Gillespie, both established themselves as unrivaled leaders of the new jazz style. In the October 11, 1948, issue of *Life*, the magazine devoted its regular feature *"Life* Goes to a Party" to images of Gillespie and an essay headlined, "Bebop: A New Jazz School Is Led by Trumpeter Who Is Hot, Cool and Gone. Bebop Is a New School of Discordant, Offbeat Jazz Which Has Mushroomed into as Big a Music Cult as Swing." The article addressed the trend, identifying Ava Gardner as "a bop fan" and showing her in a Hollywood club wearing a beret, glasses, and a mock goatee while listening to Gillespie perform.[62]

The *Life* spread included a series of photos illustrating how boppers salute each other upon meeting. "Bebop greeting begins as Dizzy Gillespie hails Benny Carter with 'Bells, man, Where you been?' The sign of 'the flatted fifth,' a note common in bop, is flashed by both men. The shout 'Eel-yah-dah!' which sounds like bebop triplet notes, is next. The grip [handshake] establishes friendship and ends the ritual. Beboppers can now converse."

Bebop, a national sensation by the end of 1948, was widely considered the new sound of mainstream jazz. As music, it was a liberating and exciting approach to jazz pioneered largely by black musicians. As a cultural phenomenon, it compelled the music establishment to take exceptional black musicians seriously. Ulanov and Feather, Kay and Granz, Torin and Robbins, and Shaw—all had done their jobs well. By 1949 bebop was the most influential force in jazz, with Gillespie earning $3,500 a week as the music's public face. The individualist had not only arrived in jazz, the individualist was now king, and through records, radio, and concerts, more musicians would gain access to the wider jazz audience as well.[63] As Torin told the New York writer Virginia Wicks in October 1949, "I run a modern jazz show and in spite of what the hit parade picks as top tunes, we play what we and our audience believe to be the music of today."[64]

But as bebop became increasingly popular among musicians and audiences, the style began to lose its electrifying, revolutionary qualities. Just as the blues had been drained of its stunning originality in the 1920s as soon as pop musicians figured out its seductive formula, the shock of bebop's new sound wore off as larger numbers of musicians deciphered its structure and recorded it. The qualities that had made the new jazz style special began to dissipate with familiarity. By 1949 bebop was no longer the exclusive domain of a handful of black practitioners. As it became more commonplace and predictable, a new, more complex form of jazz emerged. This new style would be pioneered not by blues musicians or big band exiles hoping to make a name for themselves but by black and white jazz musicians who had studied formally with teachers and in music schools.

3   G.I. Bill and Cool

Bill Holman had no clue what he wanted to do after his discharge from the navy in July 1946. When he was in high school before the war, he had played tenor saxophone and listened to big-band broadcasts on his family's radio in Santa Ana, California. In the navy he was trained as an engineer. Back home after the war, he tried to enroll in the music program at Los Angeles City College, but he was rejected; the school was already bulging with high school graduates and returning veterans. Badgered by his parents, Holman decided to finish his engineering studies at UCLA. "Within a year, it was clear that engineering was not for me, and since I had always had music in the back of my head as a career, I decided to move in that direction," Holman said. With tenor saxophone in hand, Holman made several trips to Central Avenue—Los Angeles's busy jazz strip in the heart of the city's black neighborhood.[1]

Jazz clubs had first appeared on Central Avenue as far back as 1908, when New Orleans musicians took the railroad to Los Angeles in search of work and settled there. In the 1920s, with the mass production of the automobile, a growing number of paved roads, and the proliferation of single-family homes, whites began moving to the city's outskirts and beyond. Los Angeles's thirty-nine thousand blacks, however, were less fortunate. Racism, segregationist policies, and real estate covenants restricted them to their neighborhood on the south side of the city. A self-contained economy emerged along the neighborhood's main thoroughfares, including a range of jazz clubs and hotel dance halls. During Prohibition, the demand for entertainment grew proportionately with the city's rapidly expanding film industry. Even during the Depression, when the city's black community experienced a 29 percent unemployment rate,[2] the Central Avenue club scene was vibrant, thanks in part to the arrival of talkies and a fresh surge of growth and hiring by Hollywood's movie studios.

By late 1947, during Holman's visits to Central Avenue, many of the clubs were hosting jam sessions that featured small pickup groups experimenting with bebop. Dizzy Gillespie and Charlie Parker had introduced the jazz style to West Coast musicians in December 1945, when they opened at Billy Berg's nightclub on Vine Street in Hollywood.[3] Interest in bebop among jazz musicians on the West Coast developed even further during Parker's extended stay in Los Angeles, from 1946 to early 1947.

During the day, black and white jazz musicians would congregate on Central Avenue in hopes of putting together small groups for club gigs that night. Holman had no trouble finding work, since saxophonists were in demand. But as more jazz musicians settled in Los Angeles after the war, the competition among them on Central Avenue intensified. Holman soon realized that learning how to arrange and improve his overall musicianship would greatly help his career. When Holman voiced his scholastic interest to trombonist Britt Woodman after a jam session, Woodman suggested that he enroll at the Westlake College of Music. Westlake was one of a growing number of music schools in Los Angeles that courted musicians seeking professional training under the G.I. Bill. With the federal government paying veterans' tuition directly to qualified teachers and institutions, new schools were formed to take advantage of the demand and the funding, while existing schools were quick to widen or start programs in commercial music.

"The guy who ran Westlake wanted to prepare students for opportunities in pop music," recalled Holman, who, in the mid-1950s, would become one of the West Coast's most significant and influential saxophonists, arrangers, and composers. "But when the jazz guys entered Westlake, they took the program their way, away from pop and toward jazz study. The G.I. Bill covered two years of my musical training as well as private lessons. When I finished, I could sight-read music, compose, and arrange. The experience changed who I was, what I could do musically, and where I was heading."[4]

The draft during World War II swept up many young musicians like Holman who had musical ambitions or had already landed jobs in big bands. Once on military bases, enlisted musicians with sufficient talent auditioned for an opportunity to enroll, after their basic training, in military music programs and bands. Thanks to the proliferation of radios, phonographs, records, and jukeboxes in the 1940s, music played as vital a role on military bases as it did in civilian life. Live music was needed on army and navy bases for medal ceremonies, parades, and other formal events. But it was also invaluable for entertainment and emotional comfort.

When the war ended in 1945, many of these enlisted musicians returned home in search of work. But the big-band business wasn't what it had been before the war, and jobs in bands were scarce. Factory production slowed with the end of the war, reducing both the number of jobs and the demand for live dance music, which made sense since the priorities of couples who had married during or just after the war were shifting to home buying and starting a family. Adding to the postwar strain on live music was a 20 percent federal amusement tax that had been enacted during the war. Because that tax applied to establishments featuring dancing,[5] many ballrooms scaled back or folded in the postwar economy. Instead, a greater number of smaller, more cost-efficient clubs emerged in their place, where audiences sat and drank while listening to live music. Even top musicians faced tough times when they were discharged. Many of them who had played in leading big bands found their seats filled by younger musicians. Work playing in small jazz groups was available, but the pay wasn't nearly as substantial or consistent as their former big-band salaries. In addition, many returning musicians were not yet familiar with the intricacies of bebop—the emerging small-group style.

Musicians weren't alone. The roughly 15.5 million veterans who returned home after the war needed jobs, but in many cases they weren't qualified or trained for the jobs that were created during the war.[6] The G.I. Bill was intended to stagger their return to the work force and provide training. Fearful that riots by unemployed servicemen like those that broke out after World War I might occur again, Congress had passed the bill in 1944, providing benefits for qualifying veterans that included enrollment at accredited colleges for free. The G.I. Bill was intended to help train veterans for America's future, but it also conveniently removed millions of discharged servicemen from the job market until the economy could once again catch its breath.

But in the case of musicians, most accredited colleges and music schools taught neither jazz nor swing just after the war. In fact, academic administrators—most of them at the time classically trained scholars with Eurocentric interests—disparaged jazz. The curriculum at most American music schools centered on formal theory and training, which meant traditional classical music—with some modern classical taught by professors who had escaped Fascist Europe. When jazz musicians who took advantage of the G.I. Bill graduated from colleges and music schools in the late 1940s, many emerged with classical skills they would never otherwise have acquired, given the relatively high cost of tuition and what their families could afford. Yet these newly graduated musicians didn't set out to find jobs in symphony orchestras. The competition for those positions was fierce, and open chairs typically went to musicians with strong classical backgrounds. Instead, most swing and jazz musicians who attended music school on the G.I. Bill retained their passion for jazz upon graduating and viewed a career in jazz and commercial music as more exciting and promising than one in a symphony orchestra.

But they didn't forget their training. Many of these classically educated musicians developed new jazz forms that were tempered by counterpoint and modern classical theory. Musicians like Dave Brubeck, John Lewis, Bill Holman, Dick Hyman, Shorty Rogers, Buddy Collette, John Carisi, Bill Triglia, Britt Woodman, and many others who studied under the G.I. Bill developed jazz styles with a sophisticated formal flare. Musicians who combined classical and jazz also influenced other skilled jazz musicians who no longer found bebop as radical or as challenging as it had once been.

The decision by jazz musicians to pursue formal studies under the G.I. Bill couldn't have been more timely. By the late 1940s, more recording, movie, and television studios—particularly on the West Coast—needed greater numbers of "schooled" musicians. As the consumer demand for records and movies surged, so did the need for trained instrumentalists. To contain costs, recording studios increasingly required polished artists who could not only sight-read music but also compose, arrange, double on a range of instruments, and perform perfectly the first time during recording sessions. As a result, graduating jazz musicians gravitated to New York and Los Angeles, where much of the studio work was concentrated, leading to the emergence of new jazz-classical forms on both coasts.

Such hybrids ranged from counterpoint and 12-tone forms to polytonal and chamber jazz. All these styles had roots in traditional classical music and modern classical theory, and all required highly skilled composers, arrangers, and players. Though not every jazz-classical musician had attended music school on the G.I. Bill, and not every music school graduate played a role in altering jazz's direction in the late 1940s, they nonetheless developed a general awareness of and admiration for the new classical forms.

JAZZ LEARNS TO SALUTE

The war had a profound effect on musicians and the draft took a toll on big bands and their individual sounds. All big bands had a "book" of arrangements, with a different part written for each musician. Played collectively, these arrangements gave each band a signature sound. Count Basie's band, for example, sounded different from the ones led by Duke Ellington, Benny Goodman, and Tommy Dorsey. Individual musicians helped shape their band's musical personality—how they phrased notes on their instruments, how strongly they played, and how distinct their tones were played a critical role in giving a band its distinctive sound. The loss of key players who had been drafted to serve in the war could alter an orchestra's impact and flavor.

As military inductions accelerated in the United States once the war began, bands lost players faster than they could replace them with musicians of near-equal talent and skills. In many cases, the new musicians were younger and less experienced than those they replaced. Just one new trumpeter, for example, could alter the sound of a band's horn section, especially if that trumpeter needed time to learn a part and get up to speed. Moreover, the bands that could find top talent to replace musicians lost to the draft always risked losing the new hires in the same way. The trombonist and bandleader Jack Teagarden, for example, lost seventeen musicians to the draft in just four months after America entered the war.[7] Increasingly, bandleaders had little choice but to pay less-qualified replacements more money to fill out the empty band seats. Forty-two of the musicians who played at one time or another in Tommy Dorsey's band—one of the biggest moneymaking orchestras of the period—wound up in the armed forces.[8] "I'm paying some kid trumpet player $500 a week," Dorsey complained, "and he can't even blow his nose."[9] The growing number of male musicians in the armed services also resulted in more than a hundred "all-girl" bands that toured and played for dances, entertained troops, and helped to sell war bonds.[10] Even name bands hired women: Woody Herman employed the trumpeter Billie Rogers and the vibraphonist Marjorie Hyams during the war. Bandleaders also were drafted. A total of thirty-nine of them served during World War II, and some, like Artie Shaw and Glenn Miller, enlisted. Those who were rejected—Tommy Dorsey, Benny Goodman, and Harry James, for example—were able to maintain their commercial prominence.[11]

Musicians were essential to the war effort. Live entertainment was both a morale booster and a diversion for soldiers, giving them a unifying interest and purpose, despite their different regional and cultural backgrounds. Records also could be found on military bases in barracks, thanks to portable phonographs, and in canteens, which had jukeboxes. Listening to music was essential on many levels, so an army or a navy inductee who could read music or be trained to do so was typically diverted early on to military bands or military music schools.

Off the bases, military officers routinely encouraged civilian musicians to enlist in the army or navy with the promise of a chair in one of the bands on nearby bases. The saxophonist Buddy Collette recalled a navy officer coming into the black musician's union Local 767, on Central Avenue, to recruit for an all-black navy reserve band to be stationed near San Francisco. Once Collette was drafted, he was sent to Great Lakes Naval Training Center on Lake Michigan north of Chicago. "There must have been hundreds of musicians from all over the country," he recalled. "A number of people from the West Coast were there: Marshal and Ernie Royal, Jerome Richardson, Wilbert Baranco, Andy Anderson, Quedellis Martyn and many others . . . Clark Terry kind of ran things. You'd have 20 saxophones, 16 trumpets and about 15 trombones, all in this big hall waiting to introduce themselves musically. And if you played well, you were sort of like a hero. People would like to know you based on how you sounded."[12]

As the draft continued to deplete home-front big bands, the average age of replacement musicians in those bands declined. By 1942 teens as young as sixteen were in chairs that had been occupied by seasoned musicians in their twenties or thirties. "My first professional date was at the local USO, where we entertained soldiers," said the trombonist Benny Powell, who played after the war in Count Basie's band. "For the longest time I thought I was a genius for being hired so young. But soon I realized I got the job because all the older guys were in World War II, and dance bands and halls needed anybody who could play."[13] The vibraphonist Teddy Charles also played his first professional job before he could legally buy a drink. "By the time I was fourteen years old I was playing gigs at Westover Field, the big air base near where I grew up in Massachusetts," Charles said. "We'd get the gigs because there were no older musicians around. They were all in the army. We were probably horrible, but it was fun."[14]

Soon, many musicians in their late teens who were lucky enough to find positions in bands received their own draft notices. "In 1943, when I auditioned for Les Brown, I replaced one of his players who had been drafted," recalled the alto saxophonist Hal McKusick. "I was with Les for about six months. That's when I received my draft notice. When I got to the draft office, they gave me a choice of going into the army immediately or waiting to be called later for the infantry. I decided to take my chances by deferring until the next round. Eventually I was able to do my service in a band entertaining troops in the U.S."[15]

A large number of musicians who entered the armed forces before 1944 were viewed by commanding officers as indispensable and often protected from being sent overseas. Base commanders in the United States took enormous pride in the bands they assembled from musician recruits and won respect from higher-ranking officers. The more polished the orchestra, the happier the troops being trained and the greater the respect for the base commander. As the war stretched into 1943, the navy became particularly attractive to musicians facing the draft. It was assumed by many to be less risky than the army's infantry, and the music school at the Anacostia Naval Station, near Washington, D.C., was highly regarded.

"I had been studying trumpet privately and enlisted in the navy in late 1944, when I was seventeen and a half years old," said Al Stewart, a trumpet player from Brooklyn, New York, who later played in the bands of Louis Prima, Benny Goodman, Dizzy Gillespie, and the Goodman/Louis Armstrong All Star Jazz Concert Tour in 1953. "I went into the service in February 1945. Once I finished boot camp at the Sampson Naval Training Center in Sampson, New York, they sent me to the U.S. Navy School of Music in Anacostia, Virginia, just outside of Washington, D.C. There, I studied with Leo Prager, a professional trumpeter who had been a teacher before he entered the navy."

Within two months, Stewart was transferred to the Naval Air Station in Norfolk, Virginia, to join Admiral Patrick N. L. Bellinger's Air Force Atlantic Fleet Band. "I learned a lot about playing in that big band from Bill Forest, the lead trumpeter," Stewart said. "He made me aware of phrasing, concept, supporting and playing in tune with good time. Basically, it was all about listening. Bill was a fine player and had been in Del Courtney's bands and other orchestras before his navy service."[16]

But musicians did not escape the boot-camp hardships faced by other troops. Frank Mathias, who wrote of his own stint in the service, reported that "each day began with a long hike. This was followed with rehearsal, ear training, individual practice, marching band drill, dance band rehearsal and finally retreat ceremonies. After this, the dance orchestra, combo and show band often left for jobs at variety shows, athletic events, service clubs of all stripes, USO clubs in town and civilian functions, like bond rallies and dedications."[17] The pianist Dick Hyman joined the navy. "I had enrolled at Columbia University as a freshman in the fall of 1944," he said. "The following year I enlisted in the navy because I knew that if I didn't, I likely would have been drafted into the army. I also was encouraged to sign up as a radio-electronics trainee at a higher grade—Seaman 2nd Class. In boot camp in Illinois, I played clarinet in the marching band, something I had done in high school. A couple of months later, the war was over, but my nautical career wasn't quite finished. The next phase—in the radio-electronics school—was decisively not for me. I flunked out and found myself in general personnel. My piano-playing ability was discovered by the music department of the Great Lakes Naval Training Center near Chicago, and I began to perform for various navy dance band affairs around the base and at affairs in Chicago.

"Around this time, someone in our barracks came into possession of the first Dizzy Gillespie–Charlie Parker records. That was the first time I had heard bebop. What a revelation that was. Then I began writing a musical show with a buddy, and we actually got into first rehearsals. But for reasons never explained to us, the whole project was canceled, and shortly after, I was on a troop train to California, where I found myself at Mare Island Navy Yard, north of San Francisco, repairing a destroyer escort back from the war in the Pacific. Finally, after only thirteen months of service, another troop train brought me back East where I was discharged, and I returned to college."[18]

After D-Day, in June 1944, many musicians lost their privileged status on U.S. bases. With the invasion of Europe, the demand for troops escalated, and music took a back seat to the ever-increasing need for soldiers to fight in France. In some cases, musicians continued to perform for troops in Europe and the Pacific between battles. Overseas they were "like birds twittering in the mouth of a cannon," wrote Mathias.[19] One of those "birds" was the pianist Dave Brubeck, who had enlisted in the army in 1942 to play in a military big band stationed at a base near Los Angeles. But after D-Day, the base band was broken up, and the musicians were sent to Europe as members of the infantry. Brubeck arrived in France in September 1944 and was immediately sent north by rail to Verdun.

"We were in a place called the Mud Hole," Brubeck recalled. "One day, these girls with the Red Cross pulled up in a truck and asked if anyone could play the piano. They were singers and had a piano in the back of their truck. No one raised their hand. So I did and played for them. The next day I was in a lineup at the Mud Hole preparing to go into battle. Three names were called. One of them was mine. The Colonel had heard me play piano the night before and said, 'I never want that soldier to go to the front.' He hid my records so nobody would know where I was, including my wife. One of my letters eventually got through to one of mother's best friends, so they knew I was alive." Brubeck soon found himself leading a big band just behind the front lines. "We didn't have sheet music, and we played instruments we obtained by trading cigarettes," he said.[20] Brubeck remained in the service until 1946.

When the wars in Europe and the Pacific ended in 1945, musicians who were discharged found that the home front had changed. Bands they had left when they were drafted no longer existed or had been drastically reduced in size. Sometimes the musicians who had replaced them were performing multiple roles, making it difficult for veterans to get their old jobs back. In one case, William McLemore, who had been the guitarist in Erskine Hawkins's band, was denied his old job because his replacement was playing and writing band arrangements. White musicians faced a similar fate. The singer John Huddleston, an original member of Tommy Dorsey's vocal group the Pied Pipers, sued the band in an attempt to win back his job.[21]

The sound of jazz had changed, too. Musicians who had entered the service as swing musicians and had played in military dance bands during the war returned to find bebop—a more difficult and demanding style—in vogue. "When I got back, improvisation not only was encouraged in jazz; it was expected," Brubeck said. Other returning musicians found the new music alien. "I felt lost, as if everything had changed while I was gone," said George Wein, who played jazz piano in the service and founded Storyville in Boston and the Newport Jazz Festival. "I didn't think of myself as a musician when I went into the army. I just knew I wanted to play. When I came out in 1945, I attended Boston University on the G.I. Bill to study premed. Playing piano at the time was always something I did; it wasn't something I was going to do for a living. Frankly, I don't know why I didn't pursue becoming a jazz musician. Later, of course, I realized that by studying, I could have played like many of the pianists I knew—not like the great ones but the good ones. I just didn't have enough confidence in myself as a player. The G.I. Bill changed my life completely. I managed to save about five thousand dollars in gifts for my education, so I had enough to pay for college. But because of the G.I. Bill, I didn't have to use my savings. Instead, I used those savings to open my Storyville nightclub in Boston."[22]

CLEFFERS HIT THE BOOKS

The G.I. Bill that changed George Wein's life was not overly popular in Congress when it was being crafted in 1944. Opening the nation's colleges to veterans by giving them a tuition subsidy had been President Roosevelt's idea. But many in Congress saw a college education as a privilege reserved for the elite who could afford it and for exceptional students who could win scholarships. In the House resistance grew over fear that the federal government was trying to mandate compliance by state colleges and therefore abridging states' rights. There was also growing concern in the House that free college for millions of veterans would produce an elitist, overeducated class that would result in millions of chiefs but far too few workers willing to do the heavy lifting.

But these concerns were code for far deeper fears over free education for G.I.s. More than a million blacks had served in the armed forces during the war—and many were from the South.[23] The thought of forcing colleges to integrate under the new legislation rankled House members from Southern states. They believed that black veterans with college degrees would wind up better educated than nonveteran whites and white veterans who chose not to attend college. From there, it was an easy leap for some congressmen to imagine integrated dating on college campuses and eventually Southern whites' having to answer to black bosses at work.

A deadlock ensued in a House subcommittee until John Gibson, an ailing congressman from Georgia who favored passage but had returned home to recuperate, was put on a plane to vote and break the tie.[24] Congress quickly approved the bill once it had cleared the committee, and President Roosevelt signed the Servicemen's Readjustment Act (G.I. Bill) on June 22, 1944. The new law offered veterans zero-down, low-interest home loans and a stipend of $20 a week for fifty-two weeks while they sought employment.[25] The most significant part of the new law was the educational benefit: Veterans were now entitled to up to $500 a year for college tuition and other educational costs—ample funding for college at the time. An unmarried veteran also received an allowance of $50 a month for each month spent in uniform, or $75 monthly if he or she had dependents. The length of time participants could attend institutions or study with qualified educators was based on the duration of their military service. The federal government would pay tuition directly to colleges.[26]

Eventually, 51 percent of those who had fought in World War II—or 7.8 million veterans—took advantage of the G.I Bill's education and training benefits. By 1947 veterans made up 49 percent of students enrolled at American colleges.[27] Years later, the bill was widely credited with leading to the most important educational and social transformation in American history, democratizing the colleges by allowing students of all economic and racial backgrounds to enroll. Black males made up 9.5 percent of the male population between eighteen and forty years old in the United States, but only 8.5 percent of the military, because of a higher disqualification rate among them.[28] Of the 15.5 million veterans returning after World War II, roughly 1.3 million were black.[29]

Government data on the G.I. Bill do not distinguish between musicians and nonmusicians, because it's impossible to know who entered the service as a professional musician, who became a musician during his time in the service, and who remained a professional musician upon discharge. But universities throughout the country did begin expanding music programs just after the war to win government-subsidized tuition, while new music schools surfaced to absorb the overflow of applicants at established institutions.[30] At the prestigious Manhattan School of Music in New York, for example, the conservatory—anticipating a surge in the number of veteran students—had applied for and received permission to offer a bachelor's degree in music in 1943 and a master's degree in music in 1947. The decision to become accredited in these areas of study enabled the school to meet the needs of discharged soldiers seeking to study on the G.I. Bill, and by 1951 they constituted half the school's 511 students.[31]

Music schools on both coasts featured a new breed of professor—émigrés who had escaped from Europe in the late 1930s, before the war. Professors such as Darius Milhaud, Mario Castelnuovo-Tedesco, and Stefan Wolpe were modern classical composers and theoreticians who favored polytonality, tone rows, modal scales, and other nontraditional approaches. American-born teachers like Wesley LaViolette also subscribed to these revolutionary approaches. The music schools in which those approaches were taught exposed musician-veterans to new music theory, ear training, composition, and arranging, as well as to instructors with avant-garde tastes. Other colleges, particularly on the West Coast and in the Southwest, began adding teachers who had both commercial and classical backgrounds to meet the needs of students interested in careers in the growing recording industry.

In February 1947 the Juilliard School of Music in New York placed a full-page ad on page 3 of *Metronome*. The ad's headline conveyed which particular students the school sought: "Training for Professional Musicians in All Branches of Music."[32] Today the ad seems commonplace, but in 1947 it was a dramatic departure for one of the country's most venerable music institutions to advertise in a jazz magazine and tout its curriculum as ideal for all types of musicians. Since 1926 Juilliard had specialized in classical training and producing the country's finest symphonic musicians at the undergraduate and graduate levels. Its founding mission was to be the U.S. equivalent of Europe's finest music schools. In 1945, Duke Ellington sponsored a Juilliard scholarship that was won by three students, among them Elayne Jones, a classical percussionist and timpanist.[33]

By 1947, New York was setting the world's cultural standards and agenda, and Juilliard was playing its part. The school's *Metronome* ad featured a list of instructors, among them a new professor, Vincent Abato, who offered instruction in "bass clarinet and saxophone." Abato had joined the Juilliard staff just that year, and the school was providing saxophone instruction for the first time. While Abato was giving classical instruction on the instrument, he was no stranger to jazz. Vincent "Jimmy" Abato had played with Paul Whiteman and Tommy Dorsey and had recorded extensively with Glenn Miller and Claude Thornhill. Abato was also a member of the prestigious Metropolitan Opera Orchestra. In the late 1940s, while he was teaching at Juilliard, he also was taking part in jazz and classical studio recordings. The Latin-jazz saxophonist Ray Santos, who attended Juilliard starting in 1948, remembered taking private lessons at Abato's 48th Street studio: "One time he had a bottle of cognac there. He told me Sarah Vaughan had just given it to him for his alto-sax solo at the beginning of her recording of 'Deep Purple.' And this was at Juilliard. Jimmy Abato not only was a legit player but he also had jazz chops." In Santos's other classes, students analyzed modern classical composers like Stravinsky and Bartók. "Many of the students there were on the G.I. Bill. Many had jazz experience because they had played in bands in the service. We analyzed everything in the repertory, from Beethoven to Bartók. We'd analyze scores both formally and harmonically. That's where I really got into twentieth-century classical music, especially Debussy, Ravel, and Stravinsky. A lot of their harmonic things really fit into jazz very well, especially the scales and modes they used."[34]

Teo Macero, who would later become a producer at Columbia Records, also attended Juilliard and studied with Vincent Abato from 1948 to 1949 and again in 1952 and 1953. He took summer school sessions in 1949 and 1950, receiving a bachelor of music in saxophone in 1952 and a master of music in saxophone in 1953. His Juilliard transcript is stamped "G.I."[35] In earlier years, jazz saxophonists who were admitted to music schools and conservatories like Juilliard could study only the clarinet—a woodwind instrument found in classical orchestras. The saxophone wasn't considered a legitimate instrument for study. There were no teachers to provide serious formal instruction and few, if any, mass-produced practice books for the instrument.

But by 1947 Juilliard and other top music schools in New York and around the country were expanding their programs to accommodate musicians who had served in World War II and were seeking formal training. At Juilliard, for example, the number of veterans who enrolled in the summer program alone jumped from 21 in 1945 to 650 in 1946, pushing the school's total enrollment up from 1,380 to 2,134, while the number of faculty climbed from 93 to 139 professors.[36] The jazz pianist Dick Katz studied music theory at the Manhattan School of Music from 1946 to 1950 under the G.I. Bill. When he auditioned for Janet Schenck, the head of the school, he played two classical compositions. "She could hear that I had little or no formal training," Katz said. "She said, 'I understand you play other kinds of music.' From the piano bench, I said, 'Yes, I do. I play jazz. But I didn't want to tell you that. I was afraid of not being admitted.' Schenck said, 'Why don't you play some of that.'" Katz did and was accepted into the program.[37]

The trend by jazz musicians to seek formal training wasn't new. Prior to World War II and the G.I. Bill, many jazz musicians received such training if their families could afford it. Musicians understood that it would make them finer sight readers and instrumentalists, boosting the odds of employment in both the jazz and classical worlds. But in the years immediately after the war, jazz musicians who attended music schools under the G.I. Bill had every intention of pursuing a career in jazz. They no longer viewed classical training as a fallback career move.

Instead, the classical compositions and modern classical forms they learned in schools and colleges became the basis for a new approach to jazz and enabled them to grasp and build on other musicians' more complex arrangements. Aspiring jazz musicians realized that the counterpoint of baroque music by composers like Bach, Handel, and Vivaldi could be adapted neatly to small-group jazz, while the polytonality of modern classical composers such as Darius Milhaud could be adapted for jazz orchestrations. "Musicians may have been studying classical music in school under the G.I. Bill, but what they really were studying was harmony and voicing," said George Wein. "They took what they were studying and found ways to work it into jazz. That's why they were there, and that's what they added to jazz when they came out."[38]

As more jazz musicians enrolled in music programs or studied privately, formal training became a rite of passage for many jazz artists and was viewed as a ticket to more lucrative composing and arranging jobs. By the late 1940s traces of superiority were creeping into the attitudes of musicians who saw value in classical forms, as the pianist Lennie Tristano suggested in his remarks in the June 1947 issue of *Metronome:* "Jazz has not yet found acceptance with the American public; and bebop, an advanced a complex outgrowth of that jazz, exists precariously above the uncomprehending ears of the average person. But it is the musicians themselves, the vendors of jazz, who in many cases made their own lives difficult. . . . The supercilious attitude and lack of originality of the young hipsters, constitute no less a menace to the existence of bebop. These young beboppers spend most of their time acquiring pseudo-hip affectations instead of studying and analyzing modern jazz with the aim of contributing something original to it."[39]

On the East Coast, Miles Davis had studied at Juilliard in 1944 and 1945 but wasn't entirely pleased by the experience. "When I say that Juilliard didn't help me, what I mean is it didn't help me as far as helping me understand what I really wanted to play," he wrote in his autobiography. "I figured there wasn't nothing left for me to do at that school . . . I was playing with the greatest jazz musicians in the world, so what did I have to feel bad about?"[40] Though he quit Juilliard to play with Charlie Parker, Dizzy Gillespie, and other bebop artists, one can assume that his experience there helped him understand and appreciate the classical forms that would be fundamental to his work with Gil Evans in what later became known as the *Birth of the Cool* sessions in the late 1940s and Evans's orchestral albums of the mid- and late 1950s.

When John Lewis, one of bebop's major pianists, enrolled at the Manhattan School of Music in 1946 under the G.I. Bill, however, more jazz musicians began to see the value of formal undergraduate and graduate studies. At the Manhattan School of Music, Lewis remained a student on the G.I. Bill through 1953. He was a music theory major in the composition and theory department, which at the time was headed by Vittorio Giannini, an émigré from Europe. As an undergraduate, Lewis started studying composition only in his third year. The first two years were devoted to studying harmony, formative analysis, and instrumentation— disciplines essential to his jazz compositions during this period.[41]

The pianist Dick Hyman majored in music at Columbia University in the late 1940s under the G.I. Bill. " I was a liberal arts student," he said. "In addition to the core studies, I could choose various electives, and of course I chose music classes in sixteenth-century polyphony, which has done me no good whatsoever in my career. I also studied music history and composition with Jack Beeson, who became a recognized composer. I also began serious piano studies with my uncle, Anton Rovinsky, who was a concert pianist and teacher. He opened my ears to Beethoven. I had

had lessons with other teachers, but those with my uncle were a lot more impressive.

"As a jazz musician, studying classical piano was just common sense. It was also a tradition in my family. There was more to be known about music than winging another chorus of 'I Got Rhythm.' Working with Uncle Anton helped me pin down some technical skills, and he gave me a heightened appreciation of music in general. I also was inspired by the idol of my generation—Art Tatum. There was no question that he had had a wonderful classical background and was using those techniques to accomplish things never heard before in jazz playing.

"A little later I was exposed to the requirements of being a studio musician, and I began to be on call for recording sessions, radio, and television shows. You had to be able to play any part put in front of you. For a lot of pop music, however, the piano parts were left incomplete, and you were expected to fill out or add embellishments in whatever style was called for. Of course, my ability as an improviser helped in this kind of situation."[42]

On the West Coast, musicians returning from World War II who sought a college education under the G.I. Bill influenced the way other musicians viewed classical music, theory, and composition. The saxophonist Buddy Collette enrolled in the Los Angeles Conservatory of Music. "I got four years of study for free, as well as books, metronomes, reeds and all of that covered. I attended the L.A. Conservatory of Music and Art, where I met Bill Green, and I had three private teachers. I started studying with Merle Johnston, who had a studio . . . Things were changing and there were more new musicians in town and many had the G.I. Bill for studying. That was the period, too, when I took up the flute."[43]

The trombonist Britt Woodman enrolled at the Westlake School of Music in Los Angeles under the G.I. Bill. In *Central Avenue Sounds*, he looked back on his formal training: "I was focusing more on solfeggio, ear training. I needed a much better ear for jazz. My brother, William—he's the one that had the ear. A person who plays music, especially jazz, you're supposed to have an ear. The chords are not important. Hearing them is what creates the melodies or a song or a tune. . . . I had two classes of solfeggio and arranging, and two classes of concert band—playing my baritone horn—and the jazz band. We had some great cats come out of Westlake College. Some of them were in Stan Kenton's band, did the arranging for his band. Bill Holman, he was one from Westlake College. I was there until Duke [Ellington] called me in '51.[44]

In Oakland, California, Dave Brubeck began his studies with Darius Milhaud at Mills College in 1946. "The G.I. Bill allowed me to become exposed to one of the great classical composers of our time," Brubeck said. "For most of the musicians I knew, the G.I. Bill gave us a chance to study. We were pulled away from worrying about how to make a living. I was in the service for four years, from 1942 to 1946, and was out of touch with the jazz world when I returned. Under the G.I. Bill, you were able to study with the best teachers right across the country. The sound of jazz changed as musicians became more educated."[45]

Brubeck had formed a relationship with Milhaud before his enlistment, and Milhaud had invited Brubeck to study with him when he returned from the war. "From Milhaud's compositions and his classes I became more aware of polytonality and polyrhythms and the usage of Bach-like counterpoint in both classical and jazz. Milhaud insisted that all of his students study Bach chorales and to recognize the importance of fugues," recalls Brubeck. "I was so enamored by Milhaud's approach that my original title for *The Duke* was *The Duke Meets Darius Milhaud.*

"When Milhaud visited New York to have some of his works performed, he was fascinated by the jazz scene. He liked to visit Harlem clubs. His association with Erik Satie and Igor Stravinsky, who also loved jazz, may have had something to do with his fascination. Milhaud believed that jazz influenced European art between the wars. Five of us in the Dave Brubeck Octet studied composition under Milhaud. It naturally influenced our playing and, in turn, I'm sure influenced others. In my first recording you can hear a Bach-like reference in the introduction to 'Back Home in Indiana.' On the octet recording, 'Fugue on Bop Themes,' by Dave van Kriedt, you can hear a prime example of what came out of Milhaud's classes.

"I don't know about Milhaud being the true father of West Coast Jazz and I don't know what influence our octet's sound had on Gil Evans and Miles Davis's *Birth of the Cool* band. I do know that Milhaud was the true father of my octet. His influence ranged widely, but at the same time there were other European refugees in Hollywood that were influencing and teaching young musicians. Pete Rugolo studied with Milhaud, as did my brother Howard, who wrote *Dialogues for Jazz Combo and Orchestra.* Also Bill Smith, a member of the octet, was associated with West Coast jazz and recorded and wrote for the Modern Jazz Quartet and other groups on the L.A. labels that were part of that movement."[46]

Nelson Riddle was an important postwar jazz-flavored arranger who used the G.I. Bill to study formally. In 1947, with time off from NBC, his employer at the time, Riddle studied first with Wesley LaViolette, who taught Shorty Rogers, André Previn, Stan Kenton, Bill Holman, and

Jimmy Giuffre. Riddle again used the G.I. Bill to pay for weekly lessons with Mario Castelnuovo-Tedesco,[47] a classical composer who, with the help of Jascha Heifitz, composed movie scores for MGM. Tedesco was a significant influence on many other major film composers, including Henry Mancini, Herman Stein, André Previn, Jerry Goldsmith, and John Williams. Among the West Coast musicians who, like Riddle, studied under the G.I. Bill was the saxophonist Bill Perkins, who attended the Westlake School of Music. Perkins, when he was interviewed in 1987 by Les Tomkins, recalled his days of study: "I went to the University of California at Santa Barbara and got a degree in music, but, especially in those days, it was not much of a preparation for being a jazz musician. And Westlake was an early effort at doing something—like Berklee School of Music, and like North Texas State did so well. But there were great players there, because it was just after World War II, and a large number of fine professionals had come on the scene and were studying at Westlake—such as Milt Bernhart. And Bill Holman was there—I have known him since 1948. So as a student it was a great experience for me. I did learn a great deal at that school."[48]

North Texas State College played a significant role in the lives of musicians studying there under the G.I. Bill. It gave them strong formal instruction and advanced training in jazz and arranging. The school even offered a bachelor of music with a major in dance band. Among its graduates in the late 1940s were the bassist Harry Babasin, the guitarist Herb Ellis, the arranger Gene Roland, and the saxophonist Jimmy Giuffre. As George Simon, the editor of *Metronome*, wrote in 1948: "The whole thing started in 1946, when Dr. Wilfred C. Bain set up a dance band program [at North Texas State]. The idea was to give a break to some of the enterprising musicians who weren't too keen about going through four years of college, prepared only for symphony work. Dean Walter H. Hodgson of North Texas State went along with the idea. But it took an instructor, Gene Hall, to put real teeth into the whole thing. This coming college year will tell just how sharp those teeth are."[49]

At Westlake, Bill Holman studied with the trumpeter Lloyd Reese. "My lessons with him were paid for on the G.I. Bill. What I should have had was a legit sax teacher to show me how to play the instrument. Lloyd was a trumpet player but taught everything. He had me learning chord changes on the sax so I could run arpeggios. I should have been learning how to make a good sound on the horn but those lessons turned out to serve me well. A short time later I auditioned for a band that saxophonist Lucky Thompson had been in previously. I was able to run all these changes with arpeggios, and I got the gig. Lloyd wasn't on staff at Westlake. In fact, you didn't get a degree from Westlake at the time. I think you got a pin [*laughs*]. But I definitely was a different musician coming out than when I went in. I learned how to write and arrange, thanks largely to my studies with Russ Garcia."[50]

Garcia wrote one of the earliest how-to books on jazz arranging, called *The Professional Arranger-Composer*. "When I got out of the army after World War II, I needed a job," said Garcia. "So I took one teaching at the Westlake College of Music in Los Angeles. Once they gave me the job, I asked myself what I would teach my students. So I wrote a four-page outline. Then I added musical examples to illustrate the points. That became the book. I taught all my classes at Westlake all the tricks I knew, including polytonality, tone row writing, rhythmic curves, Schillinger techniques, and contrapuntal techniques. In my classes were most of the musicians in Kenton's and Les Brown's bands as well as some of Woody Herman's alumni and lots of the greatest Hollywood studio musicians. Many were there on the GI Bill. Some took private lessons on harmony, counterpoint, orchestration, and composition."[51]

Ultimately, the musicians who served in World War II and studied under the G.I. Bill created informal networks, suggesting fellow musicians for performances and recording jobs.

CLASSICAL COOLS BOP'S HEAT

After World War II, many jazz musicians who took advantage of the G.I. Bill played gigs while they studied, to stay sharp and help make ends meet. As these musicians shuttled from campus to clubs, they brought with them a new modern-classical sensibility that made the sound of jazz more complex and sophisticated. Bebop had emerged in the mid-1940s and came to dominate the sound of jazz, but by 1949 its novelty had begun to wane as leading-edge jazz artists developed new styles.

Dizzy Gillespie and Charlie Parker—bebop's primary architects—were already experimenting in 1949 with new forms of orchestral music. Gillespie was leading a big band with Afro-Cuban influences, and Parker was recording with strings and a Latin big band. More important, many of the musicians who had been studying in two- and four-year programs under the G.I. Bill were graduating and eager to change the sound of jazz by leveraging what they had learned. They were more advanced players who understood the nuances of the new jazz-classical styles. Arrangers who did not serve in World War II but studied formally on their own also raised the stakes for all musicians. This group included Ralph Burns (New England Conservatory of Music), Lennie Tristano (American Conservatory of Music), George Russell (Wilberforce University), Pete Rugolo (College of the Pacific), and Gil Evans (College of the Pacific).

"The G.I. Bill changed jazz by adding a lot of highly educated people to the music," said George Wein. "Before the war, I studied piano with Sam Sachs. There was some education in jazz among musicians but no formal training in schools, at least not for large numbers of musicians. After the war, bebop emerged. Where it came from originally—who knows? A lot of different places and from many different musicians. By comparison, the jazz musicians who studied formally took classical music classes. But they were interested primarily in how to adapt the harmony and voicings they found in classical music for their individual jazz purposes."[52]

The new forms of jazz that surfaced were heavily influenced by classical composers and modern classical theorists. Many of the large orchestras of the late 1940s, including those led by Stan Kenton, Woody Herman, and Claude Thornhill, became concert bands. "The G.I. Bill of Rights was a tremendous force in this cross-fertilization," said the jazz-classical composer-musician Gunther Schuller, who played in Miles Davis's *Birth of the Cool* band. "The G.I. Bill enabled many of these people to go to music school or study privately for free. I knew many musicians who did this, but it became so common that you didn't even think of it that way. It was a natural progression. Where else would Lennie Tristano have heard atonality but during his studies? Where else would Gil Evans have heard impressionism? You see, when those older guys studied classical music or they had classical music teachers, that was kept kind of quiet. Classical and jazz were segregated then. One didn't mention that you had a classical teacher. For jazz, it was too square and all those kinds of implications, which of course are nonsense. One of my obvious rationales for combining jazz and classical was that both musics had a lot to learn from each other. Musicians may not have known that at first, but they discovered it soon enough. Especially the form. The forms of jazz back then were primitive, despite the enormous dexterity and skill of the musicians. In a very short period of time, jazz steadily became much more intricate and developed."[53]

In 1948 on the West Coast, Dave Brubeck brought what he had learned when he studied with Darius Milhaud to his experiments with unusual meters and modern contrapuntal voicings in his octet ("Prisoner's Song," "Rondo"). On the East Coast, Miles Davis, who had studied briefly at Juilliard, was spending more time with John Lewis and Gil Evans. Their collaborations resulted in Davis's forming a nonet. The nine-piece band included two instruments more often found in a symphonic orchestra—the tuba and French horn. Both Lewis and nonet member John Carisi had studied formally on the G.I. Bill, while Evans had studied at the College of the Pacific and the baritone saxophonist and arranger Gerry Mulligan had trained on the clarinet with a band arranger in Philadelphia.

Carisi reflected on his studies in an oral history in 1984: "I had come out of the Army and had worked for a couple of bands including Ray McKinley, where I met Eddie Sauter. That's how I got to Stefan Wolpe. I told Eddie that I was scrapin' the bottom of the barrel. I'm stealin' from myself and I keep writing the same things. [Eddie] was funny. He went through a whole string [of teachers]. 'I studied with Marion Bauer,' and he named all of these big East Coast teachers. I'm not saying that that's who he said, but names like that. 'But don't go to any of them. Go see a man by the name of Stefan Wolpe.' Stefan Wolpe had great classes [at his Contemporary Music School in New York in 1948 and 1949], because they were small, and there were mostly professional people that had already good backgrounds, like myself, commercial musicians. No nonsense. I took another class with one of his other students, James Timmens, in ear training, which was invaluable. I also took a marvelous class with Stefan himself in analysis. We analyzed Beethoven, Mozart, Bartók scores, whatever was up at the time. He had a marvelous approach. He didn't think that the study of any of the little details was of any importance. . . . To him musical devices and means were part of one's arsenal. He said, 'I give you these techniques to put in your arsenal, what you can use.'"[54]

Interestingly, almost all members of Miles Davis's nonet had received some formal musical training in school or in military bands during the war. In their first public appearance, billed at the Royal Roost in 1948 as "Impressions in Modern Music," the band attempted to reproduce in more compact form the dryer, cooler impressionism of Claude Thornhill's orchestra. The Lennie Tristano Sextet, another group that was exploring a new, avant-garde jazz-classical approach, also featured formally trained musicians.

Trained musicians on the East Coast produced a new form of jazz that eschewed vibrato, so the instruments and lines would feature a pure tone and each could be heard more distinctly. Most of this new music was played at a fast speed, paying tribute to the bebop style that was still in vogue. Although the new cool style's aesthetic was unpopular initially—viewed by many as atonal, elitist, and unmelodic—the incorporation of space, counterpoint, and modern classical harmony led to the development of jazz-classical forms, eventually becoming what Gunther Schuller in 1957 called the Third Stream—the formal fusion of jazz and classical music.

On the West Coast in the late 1940s, similar efforts to fuse jazz and classical were taking place. Shorty Rogers, who had moved to California in 1947 to study composition and arrangement at the Los Angeles Conservatory on the G.I. Bill, became one of the major forces in West Coast jazz. In a 1983 interview with Les Tompkins, Rogers said, "When I was in the Army, I was part of a group with a four–horn front–line and a rhythm section, and we were doing a lot of the material that Duke Ellington, Johnny Hodges or Barney Bigard would do on dates, where they would use a smaller group rather than the whole Ellington orchestra. We had a whole book of *Things Ain't What They Used to Be, Squatty Roo* and a bunch like that. So the few arrangements I got to write in the Army were my very first things."[55]

Buddy Collette, a West Coast jazz and studio musician, spent four years studying with different teachers from the Los Angeles Conservatory on the G.I. Bill just after the war. "I studied with classical teachers. One was Henry Woempner, who played flute on a lot of MGM pictures. He was a tough guy and helped get me in shape. I lucked out. Formal study changed me as a musician. I studied the Schillinger system on flute, clarinet, and saxophone. I also was composing and writing. I was disciplined, and four years was a long time to be in school.

"By 1948 many jazz musicians gradually began to realize that classical music was something also great and that there was nothing to be ashamed of. It was a great music that had been kept separate from jazz, and jazz had been separate from classical. These were two segregated worlds. But people like John Lewis, who because of his background—he had studied classical piano, and there were other isolated cases of jazz musicians studying with classical teachers—influenced many musicians to take jazz more seriously. Benny Goodman had studied with a player who was with the Chicago Symphony. Other jazz musicians were already aware of classical music, but it was a segregated field.

"That all began to change after the war. A guy like John, when he was in the Army during World War Two, he'd take leave in Europe and go to Paris, to the Paris Opera. He had heard Alban Berg's *Wozzeck* in Paris. When he was discharged and returned in 1947 he had enrolled in the Manhattan School of Music to study classical music, which he had already been studying. This became very common among jazz musicians. There was respect and awe and cross-pollination. It happened very gradually and incrementally.

"Did the G.I. Bill change the sound of jazz? I imagine it did in certain cases," Collette continued. "I think about that too. It is different. You think about the vibrato and sound of music. I think so. Once you learn why things are happening, you have to be more than a jazz musician. What I mean is I came up with more jazz in my personality because of my culture. When I was playing with my little trio with [Charles] Mingus, we didn't have guidelines. We heard records and then played them. We'd just go by what we heard. Change came by being more aware of things and being able to bring in the modern classical sound."[56]

When Bill Holman began arranging for Stan Kenton in the early 1950s he completely changed the band's sound. But Holman's formal training worked in reverse—transforming the band from a neo-Wagnerian jazz orchestra in 1950 to a swing band with brassy power by 1953. "The G.I. Bill made it easier to get the arranging knowledge I needed," Holman said. "It cut a few years out of the process. Of course, there were a lot of inspiring and competent people who never went to school. I think school under the G.I. Bill made it easier to get that knowledge, without the expense of tuition. If I had not gone to Westlake on the G.I. Bill, I probably would have picked up what I learned from other people. School sped up that process, and provided an atmosphere with a like-minded bunch of people trying to get the same knowledge. That spurred me on. Within the first few weeks I attended, I found out the answers to the problems that had been keeping me from writing. I could have found those things out on my own if I had had a little more curiosity. But I didn't. Going there was a convenient way to find out those things."[57]

Though jazz-classical fusion would never become overwhelmingly popular with most jazz fans, it was greatly aided by dramatic shifts in technology starting in the late 1940s and early 1950s. The use of magnetic recording tape in studios and the production of the long-playing record gave jazz-classical more room on records to expand while enabling other jazz artists to develop new jazz styles that had their roots in both the jazz-classical movement and rhythm and blues.

4 Speed War, Tape, and Solos

On a hot afternoon in August 1951, Zoot Sims ambled into Apex Studios on 57th Street and 6th Avenue in New York, opened his instrument case and assembled his tenor saxophone. Bob Weinstock, the owner of Prestige Records, had rented the studio for the afternoon. He had also hired a swinging rhythm section to accompany Sims—the pianist Harry Biss, the bassist Clyde Lombardi, and the drummer Art Blakey. When the session began, Sims recorded a song he had composed called "Trotting" and the standard "It Had to Be You." Then Weinstock suggested a blues, telling Sims, "Let's run it down first." Though Weinstock was recording the session for release on a 10-inch LP—a relatively new format that provided more space on each side of the disc than the customary 78-rpm did—the group assembled that day still needed to be mindful of the clock and how long solos could reasonably last. A blues had a funny way of running on and on.[1]

As Sims and the trio did a practice run, Weinstock kept track of the time on his stopwatch. When they finished, Weinstock told Sims he had room for a four-chorus solo—or about four minutes. With the duration worked out and translated for Sims into measures, the musicians were set to record. Weinstock told Sims to watch him toward the end of the solo, that he'd use a hand signal to indicate when the choruses had elapsed. But once the recording began, Sims became caught up in the music and never looked up to catch Weinstock's signal. "Zoot was on fire and had passed Bob's mark," recalled the jazz writer and producer Ira Gitler, who was in the studio that day as a Prestige employee. "Everyone in the room was digging Zoot so much that he kept going. Bob also was so excited by what he was hearing that he didn't cut him off, figuring right then and there that he'd devote the entire first side of the 10-inch LP to Zoot's blues, which meant he'd want a track nearly as long for the second side. So while Zoot was recording 'East of the Sun' and began to wind down, Bob waved him on to keep going to fill the time. Zoot hesitated for a split second, and you can hear that on the record where Weinstock waved him through. The result was pretty close to a jam session or a relaxed club performance."

Weinstock released Prestige no. 117 as *Swingin' with Zoot Sims*, featuring "Zoot Swings the Blues" on one side and "East of the Sun" on the other. The album was one of the first 10-inch LPs to feature extended solos. It was also one of the first 10-inch jazz LPs to include liner notes on the back of the album jacket.[2] "Bob was so excited about what he had heard that afternoon," recalled Gitler, "that he said to me, 'Let's say something on the back. You're the writer and you know Zoot. Write something about the music and the musicians.' So I did. This was the first liner notes in the Prestige 100 series and the first notes I had written."

If the recording session had taken place a few years earlier, the unplanned extended solo by a jazz musician would most likely have caused the session's supervisor or producer to break in on the studio speaker and halt the take. In the 78-rpm era, a disc could hold only an average of three minutes of music per side. Every element of a recording session had to be carefully timed to ensure a tidy finish. But with the introduction of the long-playing microgroove record (LP) in June 1948 and the format's acceptance by most record companies by 1951, a 10-inch LP could support up to fifteen minutes per side. The development of new technology allowed a recording stylus to cut 224 to 300 grooves per inch into a vinyl LP versus 90 grooves per inch on a 10-inch shellac 78-rpm single.[3]

When the 10-inch LP format was first introduced by Columbia Records and began to be adopted industry-wide, many labels at first used each side of the LP to hold four tracks, each a little over three minutes. In other words, they viewed the 10-inch LP as a convenient way to hold multiple 78-rpm singles.[4] But before long, jazz labels realized the value in recording longer tracks of music that featured extended solos. They also recognized that they could capture uninterrupted the musical experimentation and excitement that were normally found only at jazz clubs and jam sessions.

With the proliferation of the 10-inch LP in the early 1950s—and new phonograph equipment on which to play the $33\frac{1}{3}$-rpm discs—jazz was transformed in subtle but substantive ways. By the early 1950s LPs gave greater creative leeway to artists in recording studios. The LP also further established jazz as serious performance art, encouraging record companies to treat albums as unified concepts rather than a hodgepodge of singles.

From a marketing perspective, the 10-inch LP also provided jazz record companies with new opportunities. Since each 10-inch disc slipped into a protective cardboard jacket, covers could be used like highway billboards to grab the consumer's attention with typeface, illustrations, and, eventually, photos. These images not only gave buyers a glimpse of the featured artists and set the mood but also allowed record companies to package music for different audiences and for different experiences—such as a date, drinks, or at-home dancing and relaxing. Most important, the art direction on covers worked effectively to burnish jazz's mystique as hip, adult music. As for the back covers, they could be used variously, to list the company's other LP releases or to print a writer's essay explaining why the music and artists were special. Thanks to the LP, jazz was no longer presented on a faceless 78-rpm disc. Now there was a visual experience, an emotional component, and an opportunity to educate listeners, giving the album a new level of intimacy and creating a personal connection to the artists.

Because the 10-inch LP provided more space than the 78-rpm single, it quickly became ideal for tracks of varying lengths. From a business standpoint, recording an LP began to take on logistical challenges similar to those of publishing a book of short stories or a magazine with articles. Record companies needed a "manager," someone to oversee the project—to ensure a marketable concept, a mix of song choices that audiences would find appealing, consistent standards of musical performance on all tracks, an appropriate cover, and a finished product that met the company's standards and consumers' expectations. This recording manager became known as the producer—an expert with a sharp eye, a trained ear, and business smarts who was responsible for every aspect of an album's development, from concept and musicians to marketing and distribution.

But the introduction of the LP and its dramatic impact on jazz would have been impossible without the widespread use of another new technology—magnetic recording tape and tape recorders. Starting in 1949, tape began to replace the "mad scientist" process that had been used in recording studios to capture sound on wax platters and convert them into metal masters by means of a series of electrically charged chemical baths.[5] Tape, developed in Germany during World War II, made the recording process easier, cheaper, and much more flexible. Tape let musicians record for longer durations at little additional cost and, with the help of an engineer's steady hand and razor blade, allowed the producer to edit the result. When a soloing musician made a mistake on an otherwise sterling take, the error could be spliced out and replaced seamlessly with a better moment from another take.[6]

As the LP and magnetic recording tape became standard, jazz record companies could afford to take greater risks with artists. Tape in particular lowered a record company's overhead, reducing the pressure that labels had faced to turn an immediate profit and enabling them to record a larger roster of jazz artists. One result is that labels began capturing and releasing the musical creations and experiments of artists such as Thelonious Monk, Gil Mellé, Miles Davis, Gerry Mulligan, Elmo Hope, Bob Brookmeyer, and Sonny Rollins—many of whom might not have had an opportunity to record as leaders in the past, when the recording process was more expensive. But the rise of the LP and other important changes from 1948 through the early 1950s were by no means smooth transitions.

COLUMBIA GETS IN THE GROOVE

Prior to 1948 all jazz recordings were issued commercially on 10-inch 78-rpm shellac discs with just one song per side. You listened to these discs by placing them on a turntable spinning at 78 revolutions per minute (rpm). At this speed, your phonograph's needle could accurately reproduce the music embedded in the disc's grooves. But the relatively small number of grooves on the record meant that if it was played at the 78-rpm speed, the stylus would reach the end of the disc in roughly three minutes. Three minutes of recording time was highly confining for all forms of music, but especially jazz. In roughly 180 seconds, an ensemble or orchestra had to get to the point and tell an exciting musical story. If the record's songwriter, arranger, and musicians all did their jobs well, a listener would want to hear the record again and again, which meant that listeners would feed more money into jukeboxes and spend more at record stores. But record companies understood the limitations of the 78-rpm. The heavy needle bearing down on shellac discs ensured that the disc would have a relatively short sonic life. More important, the record's three-minute duration was inconvenient for the at-home listener who had to be ready to take the record off or turn it over.

But the LP's introduction in 1948 was not motivated by jazz or swing. The chief factor behind its research and development was classical music. Most symphonic works ran thirty minutes or longer, and the same was true of operas, concertos, and other classical works. In the 78-rpm era, a classical recording by a prestigious orchestra and conductor often required the release of more than six 78-rpms. Because the audience for classical music tended to be wealthier than jazz fans and better able to afford the price of multiple records, such multidisc efforts typically sold in a multisleeve book that resembled a photo album, which is where the word *album* originated.[7] But the inconvenience of having to turn over a classical disc every three minutes or so was a big drawback. From the record company's standpoint, a disc that could remain on the turntable longer would be able to hold more music on each side and could thus generate higher revenue.

Technologically, there were only three ways to lengthen a record's playing time: by making a record that required a slower turntable speed, which would delay the arrival of the phonograph needle at the end of the disc; by enlarging the circumference of a record so that it could hold more music; or by reducing the width of the grooves carved into a record during the recording process—allowing a disc to hold more information and giving the needle a longer spiral trail on which to travel.

The third option seemed best, since a significantly slower speed or a much larger platter was impractical. A slightly larger disc might have seemed ideal, except that a shellac record with a larger circumference would be more fragile. Larger records were already used at radio stations in the form of "transcriptions"—recordings of performances used exclusively for rebroadcast and not sold to the public. Like all records of the period, transcriptions were made on shellac and because of their larger size had to be handled with great care. Shellac was a tough, glassy material that could endure rough handling, heat, and cold, as well as a heavy tonearm with a thick needle. But the material wasn't ideal for the home market beyond a ten-inch circumference. The larger a shellac disc, the greater the risk it would crack, chip, or shatter when shipped in bulk to stores or dropped accidentally at home.

Columbia decided to pursue the duration and durability issues simultaneously for its classical line. The company had been trying to develop a longer-playing disc for the consumer market since 1939, while RCA had tried to produce a larger longer-playing record for the home market as early as 1931 by substituting vinyl for shellac. But RCA's discs had to be removed from the market because heavy tonearms were eating into the softer vinyl and ruining a recording after just one play.[8]

Columbia assembled teams to overcome the difficulties. Some company technicians worked on developing a lighter-weight needle that would do less damage to vinyl records. Others experimented with narrower grooves, so more of them would fit on each surface. But a year after Columbia began aggressively developing the longer-playing records, America entered World War II, and shellac, which was imported from countries in the

Pacific, became scarce. In addition, the American Federation of Musicians' recording ban had suppressed production after August 1942. After the war, Columbia resumed its effort to develop a longer-playing record, largely in response to steadily rising record sales. In 1945 those sales reached $12 million, up from about $1 million when CBS purchased Columbia in 1939, a trend greatly assisted by the proliferation of radios, jukeboxes, record stores, movie musicals, Broadway soundtracks, and improved methods of record distribution to stores.[9]

But as longer-playing record solutions emerged from Columbia's labs, a debate ensued at the company about what, exactly defined a "long-playing record." In 1946, when an eight-minute record was played for Edward Wallerstein, head of Columbia Records, he didn't think it long enough. He also rejected a ten-minute version.[10] As a former classical music executive at RCA, Wallerstein understood that a longer duration per side was needed to make a difference to classical record buyers. Classical music was the tail that wagged the record industry in the 1940s. Its buyers had more money and better phonographs than those who favored pop, jazz, or blues records. But more important, from Columbia's perspective, classical records were highly profitable, since there were no copyright royalties to pay to dead classical composers or their families. So Wallerstein took a stopwatch and clocked dozens of recordings in the label's classical catalog. Initially, he came up with a target duration of seventeen minutes per side, which he calculated would enable roughly 90 percent of all classical music to be put on two sides of a single 12-inch record. But soon, Wallerstein decided that seventeen minutes was insufficient.

In the fall of 1947 the Columbia R&D team brought a 22½-minute, 12-inch LP into a meeting with Wallerstein. Finally, he was ready to green-light production.[11] Once the 12-inch long-playing record was finalized, executives agreed that the records themselves would be made of vinyl, spin at 33⅓ revolutions per minute, and feature microgrooves, allowing more music per disc. Columbia set a target date of June 1948 for unveiling the radical new format to the press. But a fundamental problem still needed to be resolved. The home market did not have the equipment to play the new discs Columbia would produce. "There was a long discussion as to whether we should move right in [to the market] or first do some development work on better equipment for playing these records or, most important, do some development work on a popular record to match these 12-inch classical discs," Wallerstein said.[12] But since popular music depended largely on copyrighted Tin Pan Alley songs, Columbia decided a 10-inch disc would be sufficient for that market.[13]

Columbia began to experiment with new phonographs but quickly discovered that a lack of know-how and time made the company's entry into the record-player business impractical. Instead, Columbia outsourced the task to Philco, the country's leading maker of radios, by providing Philco with all the technology the Columbia team had developed, including the lightweight plastic used in the new tonearm's design. But Columbia still faced two problems even bigger than microgrooves and lighter tonearms and needles. By unleashing a new record format on the market, Columbia was taking a risk: consumers might not be convinced that the new format was convenient enough to warrant abandoning their current discs and phonographs. What's more, a battle was sure to result as soon as RCA found out about Columbia's innovation.[14]

In a bold move, Columbia decided to avoid this problem by sharing all its new technology with its rival RCA Victor. Behind the scenes, Columbia also began a campaign to win over the two largest international record companies—Britain's Decca and EMI—to the new format. The strategy was to sell the large foreign companies on the new LP, which would put pressure on RCA to adopt the new $33\frac{1}{3}$-rpm speed. English Decca, a major player in the classical recording field, immediately understood the virtues of Columbia's new format. But EMI balked, because the company depended on both Columbia and RCA for American recordings. To force EMI into an agreement, Columbia shared its technology with English Decca. EMI soon relented, and Columbia was ready for a meeting with RCA Victor.

But before the meeting, accountants at CBS, Columbia's parent, became greedy. Rather than give away the store, they said, why not simply show the new technology to David Sarnoff, the head of RCA, and invite him to license it, the way AT&T had leased space on NBC's phone and radio lines for years. CBS accountants told William Paley, the head of CBS, that Sarnoff couldn't possibly turn down the deal. The technology, they said, was too revolutionary and valuable even if it had to be leased.

In April 1948, two months before Columbia planned to introduce the long-playing record to the press, Paley phoned Sarnoff at RCA. Paley told Sarnoff about the LP and the new phonograph and set up a meeting to demonstrate both. On the day of the meeting Paley, Wallerstein, and the Columbia team arrived at RCA with a turntable and a stack of 12-inch $33\frac{1}{3}$-rpm records. After a Columbia LP was played for those in the room, everyone grew quiet—and uneasy. The technology clearly was a solid advantage over the 78-rpm. But it was also an embarrassment for RCA. In Sarnoff's eyes, the LP should have been developed by his team at RCA, not Columbia's. Paley broke the silence by offering to discuss a licensing arrangement. Sarnoff listened and told Paley he wanted time to talk to his staff about the offer. As the two men stood up, Sarnoff assured Paley that he'd get back to him soon. But after Paley and his team departed, Sarnoff looked around the room at the assembled RCA executives. One of them said optimistically that nothing Paley had just shown them was patentable, that they could avoid licensing the technology by developing it themselves or developing another format that was similar. Sarnoff agreed and urged the executives to move forward quickly.

As the weeks went by without a call from RCA's Sarnoff, Paley and Wallerstein at Columbia decided to roll forward. On June 20, 1948, Wallerstein held a press conference at the Waldorf-Astoria hotel that was attended by about fifty reporters. In the front of the room, Wallerstein had set up two stacks of records. As Wallerstein wrote later, "On one side of me was a stack of conventional 78-rpm records measuring about eight feet in height and another stack about 15 inches high of the same record-ings on LP. After a short speech, I played one of the 78 rpm records for its full length of about four minutes, when it broke, as usual, right in the middle of a movement. Then I took the corresponding LP and played it on the little Philco attachment right past the break. The reception was terrific. The critics were struck not only by the length of the record but also by the quietness of its surfaces and its greatly increased fidelity. They were convinced that a new era had come to the record business."

A week later in Atlantic City, at Columbia's sales convention, Paul Southard, the company's sales manager, had a clever idea. He wrote a speech that ran the length of *The Nutcracker Suite*—which took up one side of a 12-inch LP. When Southard began to speak, the stylus was placed on the record, which accompanied him softly as the speech was delivered. Just as the speech ended, the needle reached the end of the record and the manager removed the stylus. The power of the LP was clear, and the record distributors reportedly went wild.[15]

Columbia shipped its first 10-inch and 12-inch LPs to stores in the summer of 1948—the first 12-inch LP being Beethoven's *Violin Concerto*, with Nathan Milstein soloing and Bruno Walter conducting the Philhar-monic Symphony of New York. The first 10-inch pop LP shipped was Frank Sinatra's *Voice of Frank Sinatra*, which was produced by George Avakian.[16] While the fidelity of the early LPs was questionable, especially when they were played on old phonographs fitted with lighter tonearms, the new format easily bested its predecessor. LPs didn't need to be turned over as often as 78s, and record wear and scratching were minimized by the discs' new vinyl surface. In addition to longer play and better fidelity, the LP conveniently solved another basic problem. Consumers now could store more music on their shelves with LPs than with the 78s piled high next to their phonographs. The price wasn't bad either. The Ormandy–Philadelphia Orchestra recording of Tchaikovsky's Fourth Symphony had sold for $7.25 for an album comprising five 78-rpm discs. The sole 12-inch LP of the same recording sold for just $4.85.[17] But despite the marketing gimmick and hoopla in support of the LP, the risk that William Paley had taken at CBS by trying to secure a licensing deal from RCA rather than sharing the technology outright soon came back to haunt him. RCA's executives were right—the only element of the 12-inch record that Columbia could copyright were the letters "L" and "P." "I think that Paley was badly advised on the possibility of a licensing arrangement, which was the only reason he showed it to RCA," Wallerstein would say of his boss years later.[18] Columbia smugly assumed that it had the record market cornered when it began releasing its LPs and that RCA would have to capitulate once it saw the popularity of the new 33⅓-rpm format. Columbia executives failed, however, to anticipate that RCA would initially skip the 12-inch LP entirely and respond with a completely new format.

RCA FIRES BACK

When Columbia executives began shipping 33⅓-rpm long-playing records in the summer of 1948, they figured they had RCA beat. Gratified that RCA had decided to ignore the new technology, Columbia executives concluded that their company had a monopoly on the new extended record format. And even if they didn't, the executives knew they had a big head start, which was a major advantage. But deep down, something didn't feel right to Columbia's senior management. Silence from a chief rival can be at once satisfying and unnerving.

To ensure that it had the marketplace advantage and that RCA was boxed out, Columbia made its LP technology available to any record company that wanted it—no strings attached. Columbia knew that the LP's success would ultimately be measured in dollars, not know-how and technology. The faster other labels adapted the format and placed the focus on fidelity, not the science, the sooner Columbia's LP division would show a profit. "It's important to remember that the first LPs on the market were the 12-inch discs for the classical market, not the 10-inch ones for pop consumers," said George Avakian, who at the time was Columbia's director of popular-music albums. "Classical music was profitable because we earned more on multiple discs needed to hold all the music. We also didn't have to worry about royalties, since most works were in the public domain."[19]

By the end of 1948 RCA still had not produced a 12-inch LP, even though the format itself was not patented. From Columbia's perspective, RCA's wait-and-see strategy seemed ill-conceived. Columbia LPs had been in stores for six months, and already 1.25 million units had been sold.[20] What's more, Columbia's LP format had caught on with other companies. From 1949 to 1954, the number of record companies in the United States making LPs jumped from eleven to almost two hundred.[21] Then in early 1949 RCA pounced, just as Columbia executives had expected. In January *Billboard* reported that RCA was releasing a new format—the 45-rpm record. The publication said that the records would be 6⅞ inches in diameter with a 1⅜-inch spindle hole in the center, and that RCA was launching a special changer to play them.[22] As *Billboard* reported, "The record was developed by RCA engineers with the expressed objective of achieving 100 percent undistortion, or put another way, creating a record which is completely free of surface noises or distortion of any kind. . . . An important factor about the new RCA record, which must be borne in mind, is that it has no long-playing feature, as such, at all."

RCA's move at first seemed clumsy. Classical listeners would need ten to twelve 45-rpm records to listen to forty-five minutes of music, interrupted only by a second or two of clatter when one disc ended and another dropped onto the platter from the unit's changer mechanism. On the positive side, RCA had managed to produce a record that sounded good and was lightweight, making it ideal for shipping and home use. The bad news was that the 45-rpm did little more than replace the bulky 78-rpm. Consumers were still stuck with a stack of records and the need to buy a new phonograph to change them—hardly an ideal listening experience when compared with Columbia's efficient LP.[23]

But RCA's 45-rpm turned out to be an accidental stroke of genius. By releasing a format that was lighter and more durable than the 78-rpm disc, RCA had leaped far ahead of Columbia in the pop single market, which Columbia had all but ignored by focusing solely on classical LPs. RCA's 45-rpm was also more convenient for jukeboxes, newly emerging independent radio stations, and pop music listeners. RCA, when it released the 45-rpm in 1949, did precisely what Columbia executives had feared: it fired the first shot in a war focused on speed—a "them or us" conflict that forced the consumer to choose between the formats.

Naturally, the battle for speed supremacy hammered record sales. The problem both Columbia and RCA faced was that consumers couldn't tell which format was better. Rather than buy the new phonographic equipment needed for either the 33⅓- or the 45-rpm format, consumers did what they often do in such situations: They decided that their 78-rpm phonograph already sitting in their homes sounded good enough. Besides, they had their radios, and television was on the horizon, already being sold in stores. As a result, sales of all records declined precipitously from an all-time peak of $204 million in 1947 to $158 million in 1949.[24]

RCA, in an effort to gain the advantage in the speed war and boost revenue, developed an ad campaign promoting its 45-rpms to listeners of classical music.[25] Columbia didn't bother to counter, preferring to position its classical LP as the best-sounding product on the market. RCA's move initially was something of a ruse. The company realized that if it could keep Columbia focused on the superiority of its 12-inch 33⅓-rpm classical LP, RCA would have a better shot at the pop outlets the LP didn't cover—radio and jukeboxes. While Columbia boasted in ads about the superior fidelity of its classical LPs and marketed a 7-inch LP for the pop and jazz markets to compete with the 45-rpm, RCA developed a pop-single line that was easier to ship to radio stations, jukebox owners, and stores.

By the summer of 1949 Columbia's 12-inch LP was overtaking RCA's 45-rpm in classical sales. To deliver a deathblow, Columbia extended the right to its classical LP process to any company that wanted it. Three labels accepted the offer almost immediately—Cetra-Soria, Vox, and Concert Hall. By August, Mercury had joined the 33⅓-rpm movement, as had English Decca. One month later, Capitol began issuing classical recordings on 12-inch LPs as well as on 45-rpm and 78-rpm discs in a bid to hedge all bets. In November 1949 American Decca signed on, too. In the eighteen months that had elapsed since the launch of Columbia's LP, nearly every major record company except RCA had adopted the format.

Then on January 4, 1950, RCA gave up and began pressing LPs as well as 45-rpms.[26] The speed war was over. Ironically, RCA's own classical department had made the decision for the company. By ignoring the 12-inch 33⅓-rpm format, RCA had seriously damaged its classical line. With sales declining, the label risked losing its most famous classical artists, such as Arthur Rubinstein and Jascha Heifetz, to Columbia. From June 1948 to January 1950, as RCA held out, the company lost $4.5 million while Columbia earned a net profit of $3 million. Soon after ending its battle with Columbia over the 33⅓-rpm speed, RCA fired nearly every executive who had urged the label to resist Columbia and its new technology. But RCA didn't abandon the 45-rpm. Too much had been invested in the smaller, lightweight format. With its classical market covered by the LP, RCA began to promote the 45-rpm aggressively as the preferred format for pop and jazz music, stressing that it was both durable and affordable.[27]

TAPE SETS THE TEMPO

The expanded use of magnetic tape in recording studios was as important as the introduction of the LP and 45-rpm in the late 1940s. Although the development of tape occurred separately from that of the LP, the 33⅓-rpm would not have been feasible without magnetic tape, which was far more cost-effective and less cumbersome than the previous form of recording.

In the years before 1949 music was recorded in studios and processed in an environment that resembled a garage. Music that entered a studio's electric microphone passed through wires connected to a recording stylus, which engraved the music's vibrations into a wax-coated disc. When the recording was completed, the disc was immersed in an electrically charged chemical bath along with a blank metal disc, magically resulting in a metal proof. From the proof, metal masters were created and used at plants for pressing. Clearly, recordings in the studio had to be as close to perfect as possible, since there was no way to edit the music once the recording was completed. All you could do was discard an unsatisfactory disc and start again.

Tape revolutionized the recoding process. In addition to capturing more sonic information than a wax-covered disc, tape could record for thirty minutes or more without the engineer's needing to change reels. Tape could also be stopped and started at will—or even recorded over. That made it ideal for expensive classical recording sessions. A tape reel also could capture an entire performance, so that orchestras no longer had to be stopped if discs had to be replaced. Tape had other convenient properties. An engineer could play back tape immediately to listen for defects, without fear of degrading the master or compromising the fidelity.

Eventually, producers figured out that tape could be edited. Using a razor blade and tape, an engineer or producer with a careful ear could remove errors or add better musical passages in a process known as splicing. On tape, moreover, unwanted external noise could be removed and multiple tracks layered onto a single master tape, a process called overdubbing. Best of all, tape was much cheaper than earlier recording surfaces. As a result more takes could be recorded, musicians could play without interruption, and, with the rise of portable tape machines, jazz musicians playing live in clubs and at concert venues could be recorded.

Magnetic tape dates back to 1899, to Vladimir Poulsen in Denmark. But the idea that sound could be written and stored on a magnetic surface remained a laboratory experiment until 1931, when the Magnetophon tape recorder was developed in Germany by AEG and iron-oxide tape was developed by BASF for use on German radio. After World War II, John T. (Jack) Mullin—who had been a member of the U.S. Army Signal Corps and was assigned to Britain's Royal Air Force to sort through captured German technology—brought a Magnetophon back to the United States. Among the discoveries he made when he examined the workings of the recorder was that it had a frequency response not much better than that of a telephone along with a high level of distortion.[28]

Mullin made modifications to the machine and tested it. Eventually he was asked to demonstrate the capabilities of his Magnetophon to the singer Bing Crosby.[29] Crosby liked what he heard, and the singer's approval led to the development of the first U.S.-made audio tape recorder—the Ampex model 200, which Crosby and Louis Armstrong would use to tape their performances and listen to the playback.

Columbia also heard about the Magnetophon early on. "Columbia had an advantage in that we were the first people in the U.S. to use tape for master recording," Wallerstein wrote. "[Adrian] Murphy, [a CBS technician], was one of the first to see a German Magnetophon tape recorder in newly liberated Luxemburg after the war. He quickly packed it up and shipped it back to CBS. Not long thereafter both EMI and Ampex came out with machines, and we immediately placed an order for both. By mid-1947, we were using them and had discontinued direct disc cutting. The Ampex proved to be the better machine, so we sent the EMI machines back. Of the originally issued LPs, about 40% were from tape originals."[30]

Magnetic tape was developed for use in recording studios, but the LP was launched into the market quickly in 1948 for a reason. The contract that the American Federation of Musicians (AFM) had signed with the country's record labels, ensuring that royalties on record sales would be paid by record companies to a union fund, was set to expire at midnight on December 31, 1947. Major record companies balked at signing a new contract when the Taft-Hartley Act had become law, believing that the AFM was now violating the law because it controlled the fund. For their part, record companies assumed that the 78-rpm market would once again be the pressure point of any labor action, since radio and jukeboxes were dependent on singles. As a result, Columbia decided to change strategies and develop the home market, which the AFM had always favored and encouraged.

AFM STRIKES AGAIN

The LP, 45-rpm, and magnetic tape ushered in a new era of recording. But in 1948 neither Columbia—nor any other record label—could do much with the new technology. In January, the AFM had made good on its promise to launch a second recording ban in an attempt to force record companies to renew their royalty contracts. From January through October 1948, union members were once again prohibited from making recordings in studios—a ban that mirrored the 1942–44 ban.

But this time, Columbia was prepared. No matter how the ban was resolved, Columbia executives were convinced that the only way to halt future union action aimed at radio's airplay of 78-rpms was to develop records that were suitable for the living room. This approach required records that sounded better and played longer. "Part of Columbia's thinking here with the LP was to reach people who bought records to listen at home," said Avakian. "For years, the record industry was focused solely on advances in the radio and jukebox markets. The single 78-rpms were ideal for both, so the bulk of the industry's efforts was geared to getting the singles played on the radio and jukeboxes to generate sales and revenue. The home market had been an afterthought. With the birth of the LP, a new era had begun. You didn't push LPs to radio stations. You got them into stores so people would buy them for play at home. Of course, we were still interested in radio play. We were always interested in that, since it was the only way large numbers of people could hear new recordings for the first time. But the LP was no longer a radio product exclusively. We now could promote LPs directly to consumers for at-home listening based on improved convenience and fidelity."[31]

From the perspective of the AFM, the LP was in harmony with its chief concern—the displacement of musicians by recorded sound, since albums were aimed at the home market and were simply more convenient in living rooms than singles. "Albums got around the prickly issues the musicians' union had with radio," Avakian said. "The union felt that the airplay of records put its members out of work, and for years it had battled radio and the record companies over payments to a fund for out-of-work musicians. But the union didn't have a problem with Columbia or anyone else selling records to the home market, since revenue wasn't being generated after the initial fee was charged on the record sale. I joined Columbia in 1946, before the second recording ban began. I was in the right place at the right time. Mr. Wallerstein had already asked me to produce 10-inch pop albums on a big scale before the 1948 strike started. There were no pop albums of any consequence in those days. Everything was singles, singles, singles. As early as 1947, Mr. Wallerstein had told me to record anything that made sense as a 10-inch album, in anticipation of the LP's launch. The 10-inch LP for pop was an important change in the business because it altered how the mass market listened to music."

During the 1948 strike, Avakian recorded Frank Sinatra and other singers with just a choir singing in the background, since singers did not belong to the AFM. "The results were pretty bad," Avakian admitted. "We weren't getting anywhere with that. Mr. Wallerstein finally said, 'George, I love that you're constantly looking in the icebox'—which is what we called the backlog of unreleased recordings. He said, 'See if there's anything in there that might actually sell.'"

One recording that Avakian noticed was an unreleased instrumental single by Les Brown of "I've Got My Love to Keep Me Warm"—without Doris Day singing. "We put it out as a single that year, and it was such a lovely record that DJs played it and the record became a hit. So I had a million-seller with a record that had never before been released. I realized that there was enormous value in unreleased material—if you knew which recordings would connect with at-home buyers."

SPEED, TAPE, AND JAZZ

The introduction of the long-playing record by Columbia in 1948 had a profound impact on the look, feel, and sound of jazz—though the transformation did not occur overnight. Not until the second recording ban ended, in late 1948, and the speed war between Columbia and RCA was resolved, in early 1950, did phonograph makers begin manufacturing inexpensive turntables with three speeds—$33\frac{1}{3}$, 45, and 78. Once this equipment became standardized and was available at affordable prices, the demand for LPs and 45-rpms started to climb. With the establishment of the LP, smaller jazz labels and the musicians who recorded for them were quick to exploit the longer format and larger packaging. As early as 1951, the introduction of the 10-inch jazz LP resulted in longer solos by jazz musicians. Because the new, more durable vinyl LP needed only a cardboard jacket to protect it against damage, jazz labels used their covers to establish their brands. At first, illustrators and graphic designers created images in just two or three colors. But by 1952 the cost of cover production and improvements in reproduction meant that labels could feature photography. Jazz LP covers were no longer just spaces on which to list the songs and artists. They were part of the complete package—like the front of a soap or cereal box in stores. There needed to be a come-on, a promise that seduced curious buyers who may have been unfamiliar with the musicians or the music inside.

Jazz record producers and their marketers also viewed LP covers as promotional opportunities—a chance to package jazz as music played by exceptional, quirky musicians who were outside the mainstream culture. These covers began to give jazz a nocturnal feel. In time, individual jazz musicians became identifiable brands with specific fashion statements and aesthetic styles. "The LP cover let us graphically merchandise records," said Creed Taylor, who began his career producing LPs for Bethlehem in 1954 and went on to found the Impulse and CTI labels. "Before the LP, there was no graphic component, except with an album of six 78-rpm records or a rare illustrated 78-rpm sleeve. LP covers turned the whole world of jazz around. With a designer, artists, and photographers, you could convey to prospective buyers what you were offering inside. The goal was to get buyers to ask themselves, 'This looks interesting, I wonder what it sounds like.' Once they asked themselves that question, a consumer would ask the store clerk to play a track, which would be followed by a sale if the music lived up to expectations. It all came down to the cover. A great deal was riding on it."[32]

At first, record companies issued jazz on 10-inch LPs, a size that was standardized in Avakian's popular music department at Columbia Records. From the start, Columbia had made a business decision to forgo the 12-inch size for pop releases. The 12-inch LP was invented for classical music, which ran long and in most cases didn't require royalty payments. But within months of unveiling the 12-inch LP, in 1948, the company began to develop a line of 10-inch LPs for its second most profitable line—pop music, which at the time included jazz. "Logistically, pop didn't need 12 inches of space the way classical did," Avakian said. "Pop music was by definition a short form. You just needed three minutes or so for a vocalist to sing the words to a story about love or breaking up."[33]

But the biggest motivation to issue 10-inch pop LPs was, of course, to maximize revenue. "The publisher of a pop song was required to receive a royalty of two cents per record that was then split equally between the publisher and the song's composer or composers," Avakian said. "So using a 10-inch LP for pop recordings was cost-efficient because there were fewer songs needed than on a 12-inch LP—meaning lower royalty payments and greater profit."

At first, Columbia had no developed strategy for expanding its line of 10-inch LPs from pop to jazz. "The priority was to get as many consumers as possible to convert to the 33⅓-rpm format, which meant leveraging the music with the widest following—classical and pop music," Avakian continued. "Columbia was able to hold down its marketing costs with its powerful distribution network. Part of the secret of the Columbia pop album catalog was that we had a distribution system that was owned almost exclusively by Columbia Records. The only part of the country where we didn't control distribution was in a few counties in West Texas and Oklahoma. In the rest of the country, our distributors handled only Columbia Records. Other companies distributed through jobbers who handled many other labels, which divided their forces, money and interests. When you controlled distribution, you had a strong grip on the retail end."

Why did small, independent jazz labels like Savoy, Prestige, and Blue Note bother to follow Columbia's 10-inch LP lead? They had little choice if they wanted to reach the at-home market, and Columbia made it easy and affordable for them to convert from 78-rpm to the 10-inch LP. While the introduction of magnetic tape in studios made recording jazz more cost-efficient, the master tapes still had to be turned into physical LPs, which required access to a plant, raw materials, and an assembly line of workers. In the early 1950s most of the smaller jazz labels in New York turned to Columbia to fabricate their LPs, which was part of Columbia's plan to convert 33⅓-rpm buyers.

"If you were a jazz record producer in New York in the 1950s, everything was downstairs from your office and around the corner," said the producer Creed Taylor. "My office at Bethlehem Records in 1954 was on 52nd Street. So all the music publishers were two blocks away, and I could go downstairs to Charlie's Tavern and Birdland to hire the jazz musicians I needed for record dates. Most of the record studios were in Midtown Manhattan, and all the record distributors were on 10th Avenue. The big record stores were on Sixth Avenue, and the major radio stations were nearby.

"The only time I left the New York City area during the album-producing process was to go up to Bridgeport, Connecticut, where Columbia manufactured records. I went up to supervise the lacquer-masters process, to make sure the master sounded perfect before it was pressed. I also wanted to be sure that pure vinyl was used in the pressings for top-quality sound. Columbia back then was a custom fabricator. Everything at Bethlehem Records was manufactured up there."[34]

In the early days of the 10-inch jazz LP, many record companies transferred 78-rpm singles onto tape and then used the tape to transfer as many of the 78-rpms onto 10-inch LPs as would fit. At the newly formed Riverside Records in late 1952, Orrin Keepnews and his partner,

Bill Grauer, began by issuing out-of-print 78-rpm jazz recordings from the 1920s on 10-inch LPs. "Grauer had set up a low-royalty sweetheart deal with John Steiner, who owned the rights to Paramount Records, a Chicago-based label," Keepnews said. "Paramount had recorded some of the most important classic jazz and blues artists of the 1920s, including Ma Rainey, Ida Cox, Blind Lemon Jefferson, King Oliver's Creole Jazz Band when Louis Armstrong was a member, and a number of sides by Johnny Dodds, Muggsy Spanier, and Jelly Roll Morton. That gave us the right to re-release old Paramount material in the new 33⅓-rpm long-playing album format. John Hammond loaned us his perfect copies of Paramount 78-rpms for the process.[35]

"We had all of the discs transferred to tape. One benefit of magnetic tape being such a new medium was that many recording engineers were what I guess you could call 'ambidextrous.' They had learned the art of tape-recording while still retaining their skills with old-fashioned wax and metal masters. The biggest remaining problem with the disc transfers was noise reduction. There were a great many pops and clicks and crackles on the original records to begin with, and even minimal playing quickly made the sound worse. I have often pointed out over the years that the initial form of noise removal was quite literal: two close-together cuts on a quarter-inch tape with an industrial razor blade, carefully rejoined with adhesive editing tape. So that's what we did, though the results were much less than uniform or perfect. But we were helped by the limitations of early recording—there had been very little extreme highs or lows recorded in the early days. So there was some loss through compression when the final edited tape was copied and mastered on wax, but not much."

By early 1954, Keepnews and Grauer were growing weary of transferring shellac discs of traditional jazz to LPs, especially given the growing appeal of modern jazz in New York. "We did our first studio recording with pianist Randy Weston," Keepnews recalled. "The date was a duo with bassist Sam Gill—and it was something of a compromise. We felt we couldn't afford more than a solo album, and Randy had wanted a 'normal' trio date. The record was made one afternoon in April 1954, at a long-vanished mid-Manhattan recording studio. Not long after that session, we made a long-term deal for studio space. Through pianist Dick Hyman and others, Grauer become aware of Reeves Sound Studios in the East Forties. It was a big room—although easily brought down in size with screens and baffles. The studio was used primarily for radio jingles and other advertising-agency work. That meant it was rarely in use after daytime working hours. Reeves agreed to give us almost unlimited time for a very low annual flat fee, provided our recording was basically done at night. It was a real meeting of needs. That low studio rate, and the quite reasonable union scale rates in that far-off deflationary period, made it possible for us to do a lot of recording with very little cash, which was a pretty essential factor in the early growth of Riverside."

By the mid-1950s, the 10-inch jazz album began to be replaced by the 12-inch LP, largely because of cost efficiencies, George Avakian said. The 12-inch format for jazz began as a trial run at Columbia in 1950. "Columbia president Ted Wallerstein called me one day and asked me to come up to his office," he said. "When I arrived, Mr. Wallerstein said, 'I've got something we might be able to release. If you like it, we'll put it out on 12-inch LPs.' Mr. Wallerstein and I went into the engineering department and he put on a test pressing. It was the Benny Goodman Orchestra in 1938. It sounded familiar. I asked if the recording was of Goodman's famed Carnegie Hall concert. Mr. Wallerstein said it was. Someone had found the masters in a closet someplace.[36]

"So we put out the concert on two 12-inch LPs, releasing the album on our classical Masterworks label, because we charged more for the line," Avakian continued. "We had to do that for the Goodman album because of the all the extra copyright payments we had to make on the additional number of popular songs. Though Columbia charged $5.95 for the album, the LP set sold a million copies. This opened our eyes to adapting the 12-inch record for pop and then jazz. We first launched a line of 12-inch pop records in 1951, selling them for just over $4 each. The line wasn't too popular. There was no concept behind what we were doing other than the desire to issue 12-inch records."

Then one morning in 1951, Stan Kavan, Columbia's merchandising manager for pop albums, came into Avakian's office. "Stan asked me if I had watched *The Arthur Godfrey Show* on TV the night before," Avakian said. "I didn't, because I didn't care much for Godfrey's programs—even though I was recording him at the time for Columbia. Kavan told me that Godfrey had done an entire program that was perfect for a 12-inch LP. Godfrey had featured 12 songs—one for each month of the year, and each was sung by a different member of his cast. A light bulb went off. I said to myself, 'Six months on each side of an LP.' "

Avakian called Godfrey and asked him to record the songs for an LP. "Soon after we released the LP, it sold around a million copies. That was the first 12-inch pop LP, in 1951. The record's success told me two things: First, using the 12-inch format for pop could be profitable even though pop was chugging along modestly in the 10-inch format. Second, recording pop and jazz on a 12-inch LP would require a switch in the standard royalty policy for it to be cost-effective."

Avakian called his boss, James Conkling, who had replaced Wallerstein as Columbia's president in 1951, to discuss the numbers. "Mr. Conkling said that if we could get the price of a 12-inch pop LP down to $3.98 and still earn a profit, Columbia would be able to sell a ton of pop records. Our researchers had determined that this was the price break point for consumers at the time. But with a two-cent royalty rate per pop song, Columbia would be losing a fraction of a cent on every record, and a $3.98 retail price was untenable.

"We were about to call it quits when Bill Wilkins, Columbia's comptroller, said, 'Look, if you can get the copyright rate down to 1.5 cents per song from 2 cents, you'll earn a profit of 6 cents on each 12-track LP. Even more important from a profit standpoint, Wilkins urged me to explore a more efficient use of the presses when producing records. In essence, Wilkins suggested that I let the presses run longer to produce more LP jackets. He said this would help us avoid losing time changing plates. Every album should have a ten thousand or fifteen thousand press run of jackets, he said, and if we didn't sell them all, the overrun wouldn't be that big an expense to discard. Avoiding the need to start the presses again to print jackets, using the night shift to do the work since the presses typically ran all night, and not using extra electricity to restart presses, lowered the cost of manufacturing and allowed us to cut the cost of making each record."

The move contained the cost of record production but didn't address the label's copyright royalty obligations. Avakian and Columbia's president Conkling tried to convince music publishers who held the rights to pop songs to cut their copyright rate to 1.5 cents. "We offered them a deal," said Avakian. "We said, 'Lower your rate for a year. We think we will make much more money if you do this—and you will, too.' Every publisher agreed to cut the rate except one—Music Publishers Holding Corporation (MPHC), the country's largest publisher that was owned by Jack Warner of Warner Brothers. Herman Starr, the head of MPHC, had balked.

"Starr said to us, 'Why should I? I have an enormous catalog. At the time, MPHC owned the rights to nearly every standard imaginable, except the music of Irving Berlin, who had not sold his copyrights to a publisher. Starr scoffed at us. He said, 'You'll have no choice but to use my material to fill your albums.' At which point Mr. Conkling turned and asked me, 'Can we use just a little bit of MPHC's material at the regular two-cent royalty rate and still get by profitably?' I said I thought we could."

A year later, Starr asked for a lunch meeting. "Mr. Conkling and I thought we were going to get a one-cent rate on his whole catalogue," Avakian said. "But at the end of the lunch, Starr pulled out one of those accounting accordion folders and took out statements that showed he had made more money at a 2-cent royalty over the previous year than if he had agreed to the 1.5-cent rate. Starr finished by saying, 'See? I was right.'

"We said, 'Herman, you win,' which made him very happy. What Herman didn't know was that the 2-cent royalty rate no longer mattered. By then Columbia had figured out a way to hold down its manufacturing costs. Thanks to increased record sales and longer press runs, the label could more than afford the 2-cent copyright. In fact, we would have made a profit even it had been higher. The industry never knew about this because we never publicized it. We didn't want our competitors to know."

As a result, Columbia began to profitably produce 12-inch pop and jazz albums in 1955, and so did the many smaller labels that used Columbia to fabricate their records. Jazz began to change in response. The 12-inch LP almost immediately encouraged producers to have jazz artists duplicate the longer improvisational format they favored in clubs. Instead of rushing the music, musicians had time for longer solos while jazz songwriters had more room to develop compositions. Mistakes were easy to fix or re-record, thanks to magnetic tape. "I wish I had done more with splicing with longer solos at Columbia," Avakian said. "I always was concerned that longer solos could easily get dull and uninteresting. You had to be really careful. Frankly, I had to reduce the length of quite a few long solos on LPs."

Repackaging also proved to be profitable. For example, when Miles Davis first recorded twelve 78-rpm sides for Capitol Records in 1949 and 1950 with a nonet that he had assembled, the music failed to generate much interest after the initial release. Interest was equally lackluster when in 1953 Capitol issued eight of the Davis singles on a 10-inch LP as part of its Classics in Jazz series. Not until February 1957, when Capitol issued all the instrumental tracks on a 12-inch LP called *Birth of the Cool*—a title coined by Pete Rugolo, the session's original producer—did the album gain widespread recognition and generate sales.[37]

The use of magnetic tape also provided producers and artists with more leeway. In some cases, producers called for additional takes of the same song to strive for the best possible version of it. But there was another motivation—insurance against takes with flaws that producers heard only during the playback and mastering process after the musicians had departed. "The best thing about tape is that we could splice it," Avakian said. "At first we were told by Ampex, the major maker of tape and tape machines, that we couldn't splice. There was concern in the studio that anything could happen—such as tape flying apart at the spliced seams when you ran the reels through the machines, or that clicks would develop when the cuts ran through the playback heads.[38]

"No one in the business wanted to challenge Ampex's expertise, especially with so much at stake," Avakian continued. "But one day in the early 1950s, while recording a pop album by the Andre Kostelanetz Orchestra, I needed a perfect high note at the end of a score. The brass section was getting pretty tired. After the customary three-hour session with multiple takes, I still wasn't sure we had captured that high note. But union rules prohibited me from holding the orchestra any longer without running into overtime costs, so I dismissed them. When I went into the editing room, I found I did have a good high-note ending—but it was on a different take than the one I liked best. I got permission from the chief engineer to make a splice—cutting the bad note out of the master take and inserting the one I liked from another take. I used a razor blade. It was primitive, but it worked. It was the first time I had spliced, and it came out beautifully."

A couple of months later, Avakian spliced on a Dave Brubeck album. "I can't recall on which album it was but somehow word got out about what I had done, and the editor of a jazz magazine called and confronted me," Avakian said. "He asked, 'How can you do that—you're altering the artistry of the musician, and you're putting out a recording of something he didn't actually play?' I said, 'It's better that way. You wouldn't want to buy a record with mistakes in it, would you?' He said, 'Well I'd like to talk to Mr. Brubeck about that.' I said, 'Great, I'll have him call you.' About 20 minutes later, the editor called me back. I asked him, 'Well how did you make out?' He said he spoke to Dave, and Dave had no objection. The guy said that Dave told him, 'George saved my ass.' That's the last time I heard from editors questioning the artistry of the musicians and the finished product."

The producer Creed Taylor also favored splicing better solos from alternative tracks into master takes. "Starting with Bethlehem Records in 1954, almost every album I recorded required splicing," Taylor said. "You had to splice. The additional room on LPs increased the odds of error and occasional bad notes. If you had alternate takes, you had material to choose from."[39]

While Columbia dominated in the 12-inch LP market, the label had missed out on early opportunities in the 45-rpm market, which RCA had introduced in 1949. Although the 45-rpm started out as a competitor to the LP by featuring multiple tracks on each disc, the format soon found its natural niche—as a disc for single songs, replacing 78-rpms in jukeboxes, on the radio, in stores and at home. "We could have developed a 7-inch 33$\frac{1}{3}$-rpm single record for pop music and a phonograph to handle various sized discs," Avakian said. "But [CBS president] William Paley felt since we had invested $250,000 in the LP, we should stand behind it and not confuse the marketplace. So we didn't experiment with sizes. As a result, we lost the pop singles market to RCA's 45-rpm.[40]

By the early 1950s Columbia was firmly in the fidelity business. "The idea on an LP was to do something that made the listener feel he or she was in the presence of something special," Avakian said. "The goal on pop or jazz always was to create an LP that was programmed to entertain the listener—a crass word for the gripping quality of jazz and the effect it had on the listener. But you wanted that record to hold the listener's attention for the duration of the LP, not just a few tracks. Which wasn't the easiest thing in the world to do."

The LP would continue to be the dominant format for the next twenty-five years and beyond, requiring a new way of thinking about jazz, recording, and marketing. "The LP marked a dramatic change for jazz and broke the music into a much bigger art form," said the producer Creed Taylor. "Musicians in the 12-inch LP era had more space to express themselves and to make recordings more exciting, which was essential. Before LPs—and the gear you needed to play them—listeners used primitive equipment that didn't let you hear most of the music. You only heard a fraction of it. With the LP, producers could feature more complex arrangements and let solos run. There was no limit to what you could do in the twenty minutes before the needle hit the end of the record. The LP also enabled the good jazz players to step up and experiment. Thinking long became a way of life."[41]

By focusing on the LP, record companies were investing heavily in the home market just as the suburbs were evolving and new media such as television and color movies were competing for the same market. As bedroom communities sprang up around major cities and homes became affordable thanks to the G.I. Bill, the living rooms of homes became a major target market for record companies. While jazz remained primarily an urban art form, it was adapting to the new, more laid-back lifestyle of suburban consumers and conformity. Nowhere was this more pronounced than in Southern California in the early 1950s.

5 Suburbia and West Coast Jazz

In mid-1955, Dave Pell bought a three-bedroom ranch house in Encino, a suburb of Los Angeles about an hour north of the city in the San Fernando Valley. The tenor saxophonist was working six days a week and doing well—in fact, better than well. He was recording and playing concerts with Les Brown's big band, recording movie soundtracks, making jazz records, playing on local TV shows, and gigging around Hollywood at jazz clubs with his octet. Married, with three children, nine cats, and three dogs, Pell had fallen in love with the Encino house at the end of the cul-de-sac as soon as he saw it. It stood on a third of an acre, far from neighboring homes, and had a swimming pool out back.

"The first thing you had to have with a house like that was lots of cars," Pell said. "I had four of them—including a Corvette and a Cadillac. Every musician I knew had a home in the suburbs and several cars. It wasn't about car collecting or anything like that. Everyone in the music business had that many cars, because if one didn't start, you had to be able to hop into another one to get to the recording studio on time. If you weren't on time, you didn't get the call for work next time. Musicians were living the dream out here—the house, the cars, golf, the racetrack, family, swimming, the great weather. All of the top studio musicians were going through the same thing. We couldn't believe it. All you had to worry about was the traffic slowing you down."[1]

Pell, like a growing number of musicians on the West Coast in the early 1950s, was in the right place at the right time. California's suburbs were expanding at an unprecedented pace—and so was the music business. The movie industry, which needed musicians to record soundtracks, was booming, thanks in part to the end of Technicolor's monopoly over color film in February 1950 and the rise of Eastmancolor.[2] The movie industry's rush to color was a response to the equally rapid rise of television—a perceived threat to moviegoing in the early 1950s. Amid these visual diversions, the LP was catching on fast with homeowners, who replaced their old 78-rpm record players with affordable three-speed phonographs. Almost overnight, demand for the new technology exceeded supply.[3]

For the white jazz musician who could compose, arrange, sight-read perfectly, and socialize comfortably on golf courses with the contractors and producers who did the hiring for studio jobs, Los Angeles was idyllic. "We woke up happy, drove around optimistic, and ended the day content," said Pell. "It only would make sense that the jazz many of us played would sound the way we felt. We were blessed. The musicians were all playing in harmony because we were having a great time. You could say that all of that spirit and feeling came out in the music that writers called West Coast jazz. If you knew the background to what was going on out here, you could hear on those records how much fun we were having."[4]

As Los Angeles expanded in the early 1950s, jazz on the West Coast mirrored the changes brought about by the city's expansion. Although many Los Angeles jazz musicians had embraced bebop in the late 1940s and early 1950s, the frantic form championed by Dizzy Gillespie and Charlie Parker in New York made less and less sense to the white musicians who were leaving big bands and settling in Southern California. The competitive intensity and raging individualism of bebop forged in compressed urban environments was less relevant in Los Angeles—a region of sparkling newness, dreamy optimism, and open spaces.

Many of the jazz musicians who settled in Los Angeles and landed steady work in the movie, TV, and recording studios no longer had to scuffle to find work. In fact, just the opposite. Many had to organize their calendars and hire telephone answering services to field all the job offers. Home ownership, growing families, and increased responsibilities entailed some measure of risk aversion, commercial conformity, daily routines, and cookie-cutter systems for completing large volumes of work. In this intoxicating culture of long horizontal lines, rhythmic surf, lingering sunsets, prefabricated neighborhoods, curvy cars, cocky narcissism, drugstore stardom, and stubborn expectations of fame, a new modern jazz style emerged in the early 1950s. The sound suited its surroundings, placing a new emphasis on instrumental harmony, fluid execution, and polished teamwork. The level of individual musicianship, particularly in small groups, was extraordinary, and the collective results were often sleek and neatly resolved, relying less on the blues and more on new melodies and old standards cloaked in pleasing harmony and counterpoint.[5]

To the average ear, the sound of this music was less urgent and more layered, with lines coming and going in an organized flow, much like the region's emerging freeways. Horns in these small groups of four to ten musicians were the focus of attention, not the piano, bass, or drums. Early West Coast groups like the Gerry Mulligan Quartet in 1952 even dropped the piano completely. The music was often like a Bach fugue, with the instruments typically playing contrapuntally. Horns, for example, might play a melody line in tight formation and then break off into variations on the theme. Featured musicians took solos, but those tended to be short and were often exchanges with other instruments. Most important, the music was carefully arranged, with parts written out for the skilled musicians.

Instead of using the formula that had been perfected on the East Coast—where each horn in a small group played a solo accompanied only by the rhythm section—West Coast jazz increasingly featured a more scripted dialogue between the soloist and accompanying horns. By late 1952, new California record labels emerged to capture the results. The photographer William Claxton described the mood of that moment: "It was opening night at the Haig and I arrived early. After introducing myself to Gerry [Mulligan], I got permission to take pictures. The music was, of course, wonderful, and the place was packed. While I was shooting pictures, a young man introduced himself as Dick Bock. He was recording the group and he asked if he could see my pictures as soon as possible. I asked, 'Oh, do you have a record company?' He replied, 'No, but I will have one by morning.' He was so bright-eyed and optimistic. That was the beginning of Pacific Jazz Records."[6]

Pacific Jazz was soon joined on the West Coast by Contemporary, Good Time Jazz, Intro, Jazz West, HiFi Jazz, Imperial, Fantasy in San Francisco, and other small start-ups. Major labels, including RCA, Columbia, Decca and Capitol, also had offices in Los Angeles to scout and record artists while smaller labels like Prestige sent East Coast producers to the West Coast to mine the expanding pool of musical talent.

By 1955 West Coast jazz—with its emphasis on seductive melodies, counterpoint and brushy rhythms—was in full flower and attracted the attention of East Coast critics, many of whom at first expressed distaste for the laid-back sound.[7] Initially, the problem with West Coast jazz was that it looked different. Many West Coast jazz groups were made up of white musicians who had defected from big bands in California to take advantage of the weather and work. Before long, a new jazz-musician prototype emerged on the West Coast, assisted in part by the photographs on record covers and in jazz magazines. These lean, hungry-looking white musicians, clad in white T-shirts and chinos, looked more like beachcombers than struggling urban artists. Their faces were enigmatic—seemingly relaxed but with eyes that revealed an edgy impatience and a troubled disposition. Eventually, this look was romanticized and exploited in the movies. "By 1955, the rush to produce jazz LPs and their cover art became so frantic, recording day and night, that we had to constantly invent new ways to sell these jazz artists visually," wrote the photographer William Claxton.[8]

On the East Coast and in Chicago, where many of the most influential jazz writers were based, jazz editors and record companies began to frame jazz on the West Coast as they might a prizefight or professional wrestling match. The thinking was that jazz fans would take sides, stimulating interest and sales. The musicians mostly played along with the "battle of the coasts"—even though many so-called West Coast jazz artists like Shorty Rogers and Shelly Manne were from the East Coast originally, while many so-called East Coast jazz artists, like Zoot Sims and Dexter Gordon, had moved there from the West Coast. Marketing a rivalry, whether or not one actually existed among musicians, had financial benefits but also unintended consequences. By the late 1950s, the constant comparisons, faux bickering and repeated references to West Coast jazz's "lightness" in print carried negative connotations with cultural and racial overtones. In addition, the stylistic battle left many East Coast jazz fans with the false belief that California's jazz style was somehow inferior.

Yet West Coast jazz did indeed have a distinctly gentler, rounder sound that successive waves of California jazz musicians exploited with great success in the 1950s. Where did this cooler, more harmonious sound come from? Why did the jazz style emerge when it did? And why did it flourish in Southern California and not in the suburbs of Texas, Colorado, or Florida? Clues can be found in the lifestyle of Los Angeles in the early 1950s and the region's environment in general. The historian Kenneth Jackson offers a hint in *Crabgrass Frontier:* "The space around us—the physical organization of neighborhoods, roads, yards, houses and apartments—sets up living patterns that condition our behavior."[9] The same can be said for music and art, and California's jazz artists were very much a product of their surroundings. It's no surprise that West Coast jazz's relaxed emphasis had much in common with California's landscape and lifestyle at the time.

"Los Angeles was bucolic, it was great," recalled Johnny Mandel, a composer, arranger, and musician who was born in New York, moved to California in 1934, traveled back to New York after his father's death in 1938, and returned to Los Angeles in 1954. "Many guys who came out

West with the big bands in the late 1940s decided to stay and start families here. By the early 1950s, I decided I didn't like New York at all. It was too crowded and noisy, and hard to think. But when I arrived in L.A., I found that many of the tenor saxophonists were too laid back. They all were trying to sound like Lester Young and Stan Getz, emulating an alto saxophone's range rather than the tenor. I thought the sound was light and missed the edge I had favored in New York and when I had played in Count Basie's band. Back in New York, Coleman Hawkins was still the sound most players admired.

"In L.A., I also missed the kind of close proximity to friends and other musicians that I had enjoyed in New York. Out here, I lived off in Hollywood for a long time, which was probably as tightly populated an area out here that one could find back then. I liked places that were right in town but didn't have the feeling of being in town. I liked small houses. I also wanted to be near where you could go and hear music. My metabolism was West Coast but my sensibility was still East Coast. Dexter Gordon was my man, and I spent a lot of time with the black players out here. I had just finished working with Basie in 1954, and the guys here were in awe and invited me right into their groups.

"But the segregation in Los Angeles was terrible. If you were a mixed couple, you'd always get pulled over by the police. I didn't have to deal with that, but many of my black friends did. That kind of thing went on with the police long after segregation was supposed to be illegal."[10]

The growth of Los Angeles' white suburbs—with their structure, materialism, and emphasis on the automobile, self-containment, and neighborly competitiveness—had a direct bearing on the sound of West Coast jazz. Just as New York's crushing density, noisy subways, and pressures of urban living had influenced bebop's development, Los Angeles' wild-eyed optimism and resort-like environment contributed to a new, more formulaic and airy, jazz style that matched the general mood.

WHITE PICKET FENCE

In the years immediately after World War II, Los Angeles became the fastest-growing city in the country. More veterans settled in the city and its outskirts than in any other region of the country.[11] As Los Angeles' outlying suburbs expanded, they became a destination for hundreds of thousands of middle-class families from the South and Southwest seeking employment and home ownership in the postwar economy. Significant population growth in Los Angeles actually had begun during the war, when the federal government's program of military mobilization led to the rapid expansion of industrial companies.[12] The favorable climate allowed aircraft plants, shipbuilders, and other military-hardware companies to test and produce large orders year-round, twenty-four hours a day. A large percentage of the arms and soldiers needed to fight in the Pacific were then shipped out through the Port of Los Angeles.

But the rise of the defense industry worried elected officials in Los Angeles. Forecasts in 1942 predicted that after the war, military production would slow, reducing the number of employees needed, cutting jobs just as veterans were returning or relocating. In addition, waves of workers who had arrived in the area's unincorporated districts to work in military plants were severely straining public utilities and other resources such as highways and housing.

Throughout the country, the population was shifting en masse to suburban areas. Congress, fearing that mass unemployment and discontent at the end of the war would be compounded by a straining infrastructure, in 1942 provided funds for local and state governments to expand public works projects. Few cities were as ambitious as Los Angeles in embracing postwar planning. "The future position of Los Angeles among the great cities of the world will be largely determined by how we plan and how intelligently we put our plans into operation after the war," Los Angeles mayor Fletcher Bowron announced in 1943. The city's 1943 budget was increased from $77,000 to $133,000, and civic leaders began outlining a master plan for development that included surveys of population dispersal and industrial expansion, maps identifying shortages of community facilities, and land use proposals that in 1944 included a massive regional freeway system.[13]

When the war ended and the influx of job-seeking transplants to Southern California surged again, interconnected commercial interests joined to help the city adjust rapidly to physical expansion and accelerated population growth. New markets and submarkets were created in the region for prefabricated home building, car sales, shopping, construction, landscaping, and hundreds of new goods and services that offered households the promise of convenience and a comfortable future.[14] The two forces that led the way in shaping Southern California's development immediately after World War II were the real estate and auto industries. Larger populations needed affordable places to live. Once settled, they needed a way to get back and forth to work and shopping districts. The already crowded streets of downtown Los Angeles were inconvenient for housing and impractical for shopping. The vacant farmlands north, south, and east of the city were ideal for both.

There was little to contain the ballooning population of Los Angeles after World War II. With the passage of the G.I. Bill in 1944, federally subsidized zero-down, low-interest home loans were made available to millions of returning veterans. Land developers in Southern California were quick to capitalize on the demand for affordable housing by buying large expanses of farmland cheaply and holding down home costs by using prefabricated materials that standardized the look of the new homes and the plots on which they stood. West Coast equivalents of Levittown sprang up, offering residents a relaxed, modern suburban lifestyle at prices they could afford. Nearly sixty cities would be incorporated in the suburbs of Los Angeles from 1940 to 1960. In 1954 Lakewood, with its snaking mosaic of prefabricated homes, was typical of the new, primarily white and largely working-class, suburban municipality.[15]

The call for such communities began at the government level. In 1945, a state commission concluded that Los Angeles County needed to add at least 280,000 new homes from 1945 to 1949. "I appeal to you for help in connection with a critical housing shortage in Los Angeles," Mayor Bowron wrote to President Roosevelt in early 1945. "The situation is so serious that many persons including families of war workers and wives and children of servicemen and returning veterans are undergoing serious privations and many are in actual need."[16] The San Fernando Valley's population alone had jumped from 112,000 in 1940 to 165,000 in 1945. Spread over 212 square miles, the population growth burdened both public services and roads. Plans were needed for the physical and social development of organized communities. Two years earlier, in 1943, Catherine Bauer, vice president of the California Housing and Planning Association, had anticipated the problem, too, and offered a solution: "A major concern of post-war planning and housing must be the integration and protection of outlying communities and even the development of entirely new towns." The following year, the city's Housing and Planning Association called for socially desirable neighborhoods and new communities in outlying areas.

With housing development escalating after the war, the region needed roadways to ease suburban congestion and allow developers to build deeper into the regions surrounding Los Angeles. An elaborate system of freeways, supported by funds from the federal government, was planned to allow traffic to move fluidly with speed, safety, and efficiency.[17] The highways also needed to be built with room for further growth. Unlike most of the country's suburban regions, which were tied to the commercial centers of nearby cities by roads and rail, Southern California was too expansive and was growing too fast to follow that model. From a practical standpoint alone, the suburbs of Los Angeles needed to be self-sufficient, and much depended on there being freeways to connect these new outlying communities without compelling drivers to enter downtown Los Angeles. "Back then, all of the suburbs ran into each other," said the saxophonist Dave Pell. "You really couldn't tell them apart."[18]

Southern California came relatively late to constructing highways, largely because before the war, there was no need. The country's first highway—the Long Island Motor Parkway in New York—was completed in 1911,[19] and the city repeated that model over the years, with multi-lane parkways designed exclusively for cars. All led into and out of New York, and all were initially designed and landscaped to give wealthy Long Island and Connecticut suburban residents a pleasant driving experience. By contrast, California's first expressway—the Arroyo Seco Parkway (later renamed the Pasadena Freeway)—opened in 1940,[20] with the Cahuenga Pass Freeway soon to follow. After the war, the efficiency of the German autobahn was adapted as a model by California's engineers, who developed the region's highways for maximum speed and the rapid delivery of traffic to and from the region's communities, shopping centers, and business districts. The suburbs were linked to each other but not to the center of Los Angeles, creating a new ring of commercially independent communities around the city.

Much of the enthusiasm for highway development in Los Angeles came from the auto industry's decades-old efforts to promote buses and cars over rapid rail transit systems and streetcars. Beginning in 1926, General Motors operated a national subsidiary jointly with Firestone, Standard Oil, and Mack Truck that bought up failing streetcar systems nationwide and replaced them with networks of GM-made buses.[21] Nowhere was this strategy more successful than in Los Angeles in the late 1940s, where streetcars and tracks clogged already busy streets in the city's downtown area. As the construction of affordable homes around Los Angeles increased, and suburbs expanded in the late 1940s, cars and highways were needed to ease congestion. Whether or not General Motors conspired to ensure the growth of surface transportation to sell millions of cars, residents of the region's outlying areas had no way to get around except by car. A suburban rail transit system in and out of Los Angeles would have been impractical given the vast scope of the suburbs, the network of suburban employers, and the commercial self-sufficiency of the communities around the city. The car provided the convenience and privacy that a rail transit system would not have been able to duplicate.

All of this suburban growth left downtown Los Angeles struggling. Retailers lost business in the late 1940s as white suburban residents found what they needed near their homes and avoided the city entirely. Meanwhile, those white customers who remained moved away eventually as more distant communities were developed and homes became available. Los Angeles had once contemplated a mass transit system to link the suburbs to the city, but the idea was scrapped in 1949, largely because of its cost.[22] To fund an elaborate rapid rail system, the city would have had to borrow money from residents by issuing bonds. The highways of Los Angeles, by contrast, were fully financed by taxes on gasoline and tires.[23]

By 1952, millions of suburban residents in Southern California owned new homes and cars. The virtues of the lifestyle they enjoyed—a tidy home, nuclear family, large local parks, highway driving, access to the beaches—were promoted repeatedly in advertising, television shows, and movies. The whole notion of what a suburb was supposed to be—a community located within commuting distance of an older urban center where companies with job opportunities were located—was changing. Downtown Los Angeles was viewed increasingly as an urban dinosaur. Southern California's new suburban culture, by contrast, represented a futuristic, self-contained, and sanitized environment in which residents were able to commute to work, shop, and enjoy country life from their cars—without having to encounter society's problems or the disenfranchised.

From a white jazz musician's perspective, Los Angeles was more than just a constellation of small suburban communities. Hollywood and other exurban parts of the city were the nerve centers of the movie, TV, and record industries. For highly trained musicians, the studios of these enterprises offered steady well-paid commercial work during the day, and the area's jazz clubs offered plenty of work at night. The recording studios, like the suburban developers, had aggressive production goals and deadlines, all of which necessitated musical formulas, discipline, and perfection. Jazz, like the prefabricated homes and mass-produced housing developments, needed new models and systems of execution to accomplish the heavy workloads. But Los Angeles hadn't always been dominated be white jazz musicians.

JAZZ HEADS WEST

Though Los Angeles in the first half of the twentieth century wasn't a breeding ground for jazz styles the way New Orleans, Chicago, Kansas

City, and New York were, the California city had enormous enthusiasm for jazz early on. As a Pacific port, Los Angeles attracted early railroad lines, and its mild climate and open spaces lured industry and early moviemakers. Where commerce succeeds, entertainment and nightlife quickly follow, and Los Angeles was no exception.

At least one member of the Original Creole Orchestra—one of several bands that would originate New Orleans jazz and become the first New Orleans jazz band to tour outside the South—had lived in Los Angeles in 1907. What's more, the Original Creole Orchestra itself was formed in Los Angeles, giving performances there as early as 1911. During World War I, Jelly Roll Morton, jazz's self-proclaimed inventor, toured Los Angeles and promoted shows in the city. Ada "Bricktop" Smith, Edward "Kid" Ory, and Joe "King" Oliver had all performed in Los Angeles by 1921.[24]

As the California film industry grew in the 1920s, so did the popularity of jazz in Los Angeles, particularly in the clubs along Central Avenue, the main thoroughfare in the city's black neighborhood. Silent-movie stars frequented many of these clubs, patronizing establishments like the Quality Night Club to hear the blues shouter Jimmy Rushing in 1923.[25] Starting in 1927, with the advent of sound movies, the music industry in Los Angeles expanded significantly because studios needed high-quality instrumentalists to record music. Thousands of musicians displaced from movie theaters by talkies also arrived in search of movie-studio work.

During the Depression, Los Angeles' economy rebounded modestly, thanks to the movie industry and demands for entertainment. As a result, the city attracted a growing number of black jazz musicians. But musicians who were attracted to Los Angeles weren't just itinerant musicians hustling gigs. Black families with professional musician pedigrees—like the Youngs, Woodmans, and Royals—had relocated to Los Angeles with hopes that their children would become musicians and entertainers. Fresh waves of black jazz musicians from the Midwest and Southwest moved to the city once the swing era began in 1935, following Benny Goodman's successful appearance at Los Angeles' Palomar Ballroom.

Throughout the decade, the jazz-club scene flourished along Central Avenue, nicknamed the "Brown Broadway" by a columnist for the *California Eagle*, Los Angeles' major black newspaper,[26] for its dozens of clubs. During World War II, Los Angeles became a winter base for many popular big bands. Government restrictions on gas, rubber, and truck and car parts made road tours by bands more difficult and inefficient. In addition, the American Federation of Musicians' ban on recording by its members, starting in 1942, further reduced work opportunities, because there were few newly issued recordings for them to promote on the road. To keep busy, the major bands that settled in Los Angeles made films, performed up and down the California coast, and appeared often on the radio.

After World War II, as veterans settled in the area and the economy started to slow, the ballroom business declined considerably and, with it, the demand for dance-band appearances. The trend at first favored black musicians who performed at the small clubs along Central Avenue, playing mostly bebop that they had picked up by transcribing records by Charlie Parker, Dizzy Gillespie, and other East Coast artists. But in the late 1940s many of the better white musicians who had traveled to California with the big bands began to quit major orchestras rather than go back out on the road. Touring from town to town across the country had always been a harsh life, and many musicians no longer found the trips appealing. A growing number were able to find work playing in small groups, while those who had served in the war took advantage of the G.I. Bill to study formally with private teachers and at local schools.

At the same time, the demand for highly trained arrangers, composers, and musicians who could play two or more instruments and sight-read music intensified with the popularity of LPs and the movies. After Columbia and RCA settled their differences over the $33\frac{1}{3}$-rpm speed of long-playing records in 1950, new record companies emerged in Los Angeles to record local jazz artists. Smaller groups like quartets, quintets, sextets, septets, and octets were ideal for such purposes; they not only were less expensive for the fledgling labels to produce but also could sound as dynamic as a big band with the right arrangements.

But quitting a big band to live in Los Angeles didn't immediately lead to record contracts or movie studio work for new arrivals. To protect union musicians who already lived and recorded in Los Angeles from the rising tide of transplants, the union enforced work restrictions. Newly arrived musicians had to establish residency for six months before they were issued the all-important union membership card.[27] Without the card, finding work in the city's recording studios was impossible. Nightclubs were among the only places that employed these itinerant musicians. "When I decided to move to L.A. in 1954, I knew that I would have to transfer out of the New York local of the musicians' union and into the L.A. local, which wasn't easy to do," said Johnny Mandel. "When you moved to L.A., the union wouldn't let you work as a musician for your first three months. Then when that period expired, you could only work in clubs for the next three months. The studios were off limits. This system was set up to keep musicians who relocated to L.A. from taking studio jobs away from those who were already here working. So for the first three months I worked as a shipping clerk at the Southern California Music Company."[28]

West Coast jazz's contrapuntal sound is often dated to the summer of 1952, when Gerry Mulligan recorded with his pianoless quartet featuring the trumpeter Chet Baker, the bassist Bob Whitlock, and the drummer Chico Hamilton. But origins of the harmony-driven West Coast sound can be found earlier, especially in the recordings of Lester Young, whose dry, airy, and relaxed sound was the dominant influence on many West Coast tenor saxophonists. Other influences included the arrangements of Jimmy Giuffre and Shorty Rogers for Woody Herman's orchestra in 1947, Gerry Mulligan and Gil Evans' charts for Claude Thornhill in the same year, the Dave Brubeck Octet of 1949, and the Miles Davis Nonet of 1949 and 1950. All these musicians prized harmony and space as much as individual solos. The small-group sound that emerged on the West Coast was a crystallized extension of these trends. "Our music definitely had a different sound," said the bassist Howard Rumsey, who managed the Lighthouse in Hermosa Beach, one of the most popular jazz clubs in the Los Angeles area in the 1950s. "But it wasn't as laid back as most critics thought at first. The only difference between us and the bebop players was that we played at the Lighthouse and other guys were in Chicago and New York. West Coast jazz just sounded happier."[29]

L.A.'S RACE PROBLEM

In the late 1940s and early 1950s, Los Angeles was one of the most segregated cosmopolitan areas of the country. Though Los Angeles during this period did not enforce stringent segregation by law, as in Southern states, the city and its suburbs took aggressive steps to ensure that the new suburbs would be for whites only. The prohibitive mechanisms were real estate covenants and a police department that often used harassment to discourage integration and even the free movement of blacks through the largely white areas outside Los Angeles.

"In my experiences, the Los Angeles–area housing conditions for blacks and dark-skinned Latinos were the most segregated area in the western part of the country, including Las Vegas and most of Nevada," said the jazz bassist and manager John Levy, who represented George Shearing, Cannonball Adderley, Ahmad Jamal, Ramsey Lewis, Nancy Wilson, Wes Montgomery, and other jazz artists starting in the 1950s. "Black musicians who traveled from the East and midwestern cities to play engagements in the Los Angeles area could not live in the city's major hotels—no matter how popular those artists were. Even in the late 1950s, stars like Sammy Davis Jr., Harry Belafonte, and Lena Horne had to stay in hotels in the black ghetto areas of Los Angeles. Nat Cole, at the top of his career, had problems buying his home in the segregated Hancock Park area of Los Angeles."[30]

The black residents of Los Angeles had always been hemmed into a narrow zone south of the city's downtown. Although no laws on the books prohibited blacks from owning property outside their Los Angeles neighborhoods, real estate covenants—written agreements between white residents of communities to rent and sell their property only to whites—were standard practice, making it impossible for blacks to gain access to homes in white suburban communities. Such covenants had existed in Los Angeles since the early twentieth century, when black migration had increased. But when the Supreme Court, in 1919, overturned a lower court's ruling that challenged the legality of restrictive residence rules, these restrictive covenants—originally used to deny housing to Mexicans, Asians, and Jews—were used to bar blacks too.[31] Such practices forced existing black residents and the twenty-four thousand black migrants who had relocated to Los Angeles during the Depression into the few areas of the city where decent black housing was already hard to come by.

By 1940, some fifty thousand blacks lived in Los Angeles, and the clubs along Central Avenue attracted interracial audiences to the heart of the strip, from 41st Street, where the Dunbar Hotel and Club Alabam stood, to 108th Street, where the Plantation Club was located.[32] Movie stars, sports figures, and other progressive celebrities were frequent visitors, often traveling in interracial groups. Because the city's clubs in white neighborhoods during the early 1940s prohibited black patrons, Norman Granz, a white music producer and concert promoter, organized Sunday afternoon interracial jam sessions on Central Avenue.[33]

With the onset of World War II, blacks once again migrated to California, where factories operated around the clock, and blacks and women were hired to fill the shifts. In 1942, California Shipbuilding and Consolidated Steel in Los Angeles hired more than six thousand blacks to meet its production quota.[34] But unfair labor practices based on race continued. Blacks were typically denied union membership while working in manufacturing plants or were encouraged to form subsidiaries of more powerful white unions. Blacks were also routinely given the most menial and dangerous tasks. And for those blacks who achieved some level of economic prosperity, real estate covenants still restricted housing opportunities.

In 1948, the Supreme Court decided in *Shelley v. Kraemer* that real estate covenants were a violation of the Fourteenth Amendment and judicially unenforceable—meaning they couldn't be enforced by the courts. But the decision did not explicitly state that it was against the law to establish such covenants or that they could not be privately enforced. As a result, restrictive covenants continued to dictate where minorities could live. Not until 1953, in *Barrows v. Jackson*—a year before *Brown v. Board of Education*—did the Supreme Court deliver a final blow to restrictive covenants, deciding that an individual could not be sued for damages for failing to observe an illegal covenant.[35] But even the Supreme Court's decision did little to purge the practice. Here's how suburban Los Angeles realtors barred minorities from white neighborhoods in 1954, according to Becky Nicolaides's *My Blue Heaven* (2002).

"The Stevens family [a white family] lived one block below the South Gate border in Lynwood. They decided to sell their house. They listed the property with realtor Henry Beddoe, a member of the South Gate Realty Board. Soon, the Portugals, a Mexican family friendly with the Stevens, decided to buy it and commenced escrow negotiations. The Portugals and Stevens reached a verbal agreement, sealing the transaction. When word got out that the Portugals were Mexican, neighbors sent a letter to the Realty Board demanding the sale be stopped. Immediately, other realtors brought customers around to see the property and the transaction was delayed.

"Merle Stevens, who insisted on his right to sell to the Portugals, was disgusted with the practice. 'They were trying to substitute a buyer. . . . I thought they were stalling for time in hopes that the Portugals would get disgusted and not take the place.' Beddoe [the realtor] ultimately stood by the wishes of his client and sold the property to the Portugals. At this point, the South Gate Realty Board came down hard and fast. It fined both the buying and selling realtors $310.85 each and denied Beddoe his commission. When Beddoe refused to pay the fine, he was expelled from the Realty Board. The board claimed he had violated Article 35 of the National Association of Real Estate Boards, which read, 'A realtor should not be instrumental in introducing into a neighborhood a character who will clearly be detrimental to property values in a neighborhood.' The expulsion denied him access to the multiple listing service, an indispensable tool for realtors, and it tainted his professional reputation. A 'whispering campaign' against him alleged that his true intention was to 'open the gates to Negroes.' Through professional pressures like this, realtors maintained control over the local housing market and sustained racial covenants long after their invalidation by the courts."[36] Such deeply entrenched segregationist practices would not be halted until the Fair Housing Act of 1968.

In the early 1950s segregationist practices also affected Los Angeles' black and white jazz musicians. Until the mid-1950s all the musicians' unions in big cities—except Detroit and New York—were segregated. In Los Angeles, Local 767 was the black division of the American Federation of Musicians; Local 47 was the white branch. The white local had fifteen thousand members while the black local, about eight hundred, with the dues collected from those relatively few members barely sufficient to run the offices. While the pay scale for the black local was the same as that of the white local, under the AFM's national rules, the black local was dependent on its white counterpart for advice and virtually all other matters, including employment opportunities for its members. Such dependence made the black local little more than a rubber stamp for the white local's directives.[37] "How the hell are you going to do anything?" asked the jazz pianist-arranger Marl Young in *Central Avenue Sounds: Jazz in Los Angeles.* "They're out there where the jobs are; you're over here where nothing is. And besides, every time [the black union] wanted to do something, they would call the white union for advice."[38]

There even was disparity between facilities. "The white union's office was downtown on Georgia Street, and then they built a new building on Hollywood and Vine," according to the saxophonist-arranger Buddy Collette, one of the first black musicians hired in 1948 to play in a television orchestra. "The black union was on Central Avenue and 17th Street. The white union had more power. The black union had to ask the white union if they could take certain jobs."[39] In 1952 the black union proposed an amalgamation—a merging of the two unions. The officials in the white Local 47 resisted a merger, but Local 767 pushed the union's leaders to put the issue to a vote by Local 47's membership. "We had people like George Kast and Gail Robinson and others who were going to meetings and saying, 'This is the right thing to do. Why, the democratic thing to do is let the membership vote,' " said Collette.[40] In December 1952 the merger was put before Local 47's members, and the amalgamation was approved by 233 votes. After winning AFM approval, the two locals officially merged April 1, 1953.[41] Despite the merger, however, there were still unresolved issues between the black musicians and the white contractors who did the hiring for lucrative recording, movie, and TV studio work. Officials at union headquarters began making notations on the cards on file, identifying a musician as white or black. Circles appeared around black members' names, instruments, or phone numbers—ensuring that most of the studio jobs phoned in went to white musicians.[42]

Though a handful of black jazz musicians like Ray Brown, Buddy Collette, Red Callender, and Plas Johnson worked consistently in the Los Angeles studios, fewer found steady work in the lucrative movie studios, and all were prevented from moving into the newly developed and largely white suburbs. As more blacks improved their standard of living and became middle class, many began to move into previously white areas north of Wilshire Boulevard that whites had abandoned to live father away in the suburbs. The departure of upwardly mobile blacks from core black neighborhoods of Los Angeles drained leadership from the Central Avenue community.[43]

The merger of the black and white union locals also resulted in more black musicians driving to work in parts of the city and suburban areas outside their core black neighborhoods. The Los Angeles Police Department responded by restricting integration and travel by blacks through these areas. William Parker, the police chief of Los Angeles in the 1950s, stepped up the practice of racial profiling and the harassment of interracial couples and integrated clubs. The wartime economy had attracted black migrants from the South, pushing the nonwhite population of Los Angeles up by more than 116 percent while the population as a whole increased by more than 30 percent. After the war more than 170,000 blacks lived in Los Angeles, 9 percent of the city's population.[44]

Black arrests in Los Angeles after the war grew disproportionately as the police department—to support its practices—attempted to connect race and crime. From 1945 to 1949, blacks made up 10 percent of the city's population yet accounted for a third of the city's "reported" homicides, rapes, and narcotics violations; black prostitution and vice made up 40 percent of the city's "reported" total. A third of traffic violation arrests involved blacks, according to the official data. "The demand that the police cease to consider race, color, and creed is an unrealistic demand. Identification is a police tool, not a police attitude," Chief Parker insisted.[45]

"On any weekend night on Central Avenue in the 1940s, you could probably see more blinking red lights than on any other thoroughfare in the country," wrote the pianist Hampton Hawes in his autobiography *Raise Up Off Me*. "It was only cops jamming brothers—the same cops who'd come into the after-hours clubs for their cut. . . . The night Billy Eckstine came by Jack's Basket Room to hear me and Wardell Gray play, he wasn't with a white woman but he was in possession of something equally suspicious: a new Cadillac with out-of-state plates. They opened the trunk to make a search. He tried to explain the New York plates by showing them identification but they still took him away, and B. wasn't able to make it down to Central Avenue until several hours later. Those were dangerous years; it had to be dedication and love of the music that kept those people coming on the scene, subjecting themselves to that kind of abuse."[46]

Police harassment of whites patronizing Central Avenue clubs also increased in the late forties, and the number of arrests along the black entertainment strip far exceeded the number in Hollywood, a white area that also featured a concentration of jazz clubs. The bassist David Bryant said, "All the stars and all the [white] people would come over to Central Avenue and listen to the music, man. [The police] didn't like the mixing, so they rousted people around and stuff, and that's how they closed it up."[47] The trumpeter Art Farmer agreed: "The police, as far as they were concerned, the only thing they saw anytime they saw any interracial thing going on was crime. It was a crime leading to prostitution and narcotics."[48]

Little by little, Central Avenue lost its audience. Migration by middle-class blacks to more affluent black communities reduced patronage by black audiences. Police harassment, increased drug busts, and relocation by whites to more distant suburbs also took a toll. "The police started really becoming a problem," said Farmer. "I remember you would walk down the street and every time they'd see you they would stop you and search you."[49]

By the late 1940s and early 1950s, the Los Angeles Police Department and the city government had succeeded in squeezing off Central Avenue's nightlife economy. One by one, the clubs closed as jazz fans headed west to the white-owned clubs of Hollywood and the beach communities. West Coast jazz emerged into this racially charged climate. Jazz musicians and record producers of the period, for their part, were largely blind to racial differences. "The musicians had no problem with each other, although the musicians' union was segregated until 1953," John Levy said. "The segregated union system resulted in a lack of opportunities for black musicians to get work in the movie, television, and recording industries. The exceptions were a small number of exceptionally talented musicians. The same was true for arrangers and composers like Benny Carter and Phil Moore, who in most cases ghostwrote for white arrangers with big names and weren't given credit for their work."[50]

Jazz on the West Coast increasingly was leaving out many black musicians. The segregationist environment severely reduced opportunities for black musicians, many of whom relocated to New York in the early 1950s. Those who remained in Los Angeles did so because they were skilled enough to find work in record studios and had personalities that allowed them to network easily with the white contractors who controlled the movie-studio jobs. "Even when banks began loaning to blacks, the attitudes were still not welcoming," Levy said. "The social and economic climate was not conducive to most creative young black musicians of that period. Therefore new music that was created on the West Coast in the 1950s was done mainly by the large number of white musicians who remained."[51]

According to Buddy Collette, "During that period, the black players almost weren't here. They didn't make very many recordings compared to the white musicians. Most were old-school players who played bebop, a sound that was increasingly out of style. Bebop was like wildfire for a while, but then the music changed. West Coast jazz came about during a period when record companies like Contemporary and Pacific Jazz helped to establish it. One thing led to another."[52] While clubs like the Lighthouse in Hermosa Beach welcomed black artists, the number of them playing at the club south of Los Angeles began to drop off in the early 1950s. "You didn't see too many blacks around there at the time," said Collette, who played at the club. "A few would come down to the Lighthouse but most stayed away. It wasn't the club's fault. The owner and Howard [Rumsey] were great, and all of the musicians loved each other. But blacks just didn't feel comfortable going there. You were in a territory where you didn't feel you belonged, and the police were quick to pull you over. If you told your friends, 'Oh, we went to the Lighthouse yesterday,' your friends would say, 'Oh, is that okay for us to go there?' As the music developed out there, black players chose not to be included. Teddy Edwards, Dexter Gordon, Sonny Chris, Frank Morgan, Harold Land, and others used to play locally. But they all left."

When the Los Angeles police stopped blacks in white neighborhoods, car occupants had to be careful. "The police usually wanted to know what you were doing there," Collette said. "Then they'd ask if you were planning to rob someone. You had to know how to handle set-up questions like that. If you became outraged and argumentative, you got into worse trouble. All of this operated in a world separate from the white jazz musicians, who were great. All had extensive playing experience with black musicians, and for them color wasn't an issue. Much depended on your talent and disposition. The guy who hired me for TV in 1948, Jerry Fielding, was white. I personally never felt racial pressure or animosity. I grew up in Central Gardens, one of the few areas in the city where people of all races lived. So when I started working in the studios, musicians asked me if I felt uncomfortable. I said, 'No, I grew up like this.' After a while, the white musicians felt better, too. I was just likeable—a trait I learned from my mother. She didn't dislike anyone unless someone did something to her. She never referred to whites as 'those white people.' "

WEST COAST'S RELAXED SOUND

When you ask most West Coast jazz musicians about the distinct sound found in California in the 1950s, their first reaction is to deny that there was such a sound. Many also insist that there wasn't much difference between what the musicians in Los Angeles were developing and what was going on in New York. But you sense immediately that the reaction is defensive and that it comes from a feeling of being cast as creatively inferior. For years, West Coast jazz had been stigmatized by East Coast jazz writers and even some West Coast musicians who called it lightweight and lacking gut heat.

"And those writers were right," said Johnny Mandel. "Most West Coast jazz sounded like the jazz in New York but with no balls. There were a few guys on the edge—like Gerry Mulligan, Bob Cooper, and others. But most of it was too relaxed. I never got behind it. West Coast jazz didn't sound great to me. Jazz out here [in Los Angeles] was quite good when there was a large black element in South Central Los Angeles. But many of the musicians had left for New York because there wasn't much opportunity for them in L.A.

"Part of the overall problem out here was that people didn't hang out the way they did in New York," Mandel continued. "Back in New York, black and white jazz musicians always hung out together. That practice was way ahead of the laws that were eventually passed enforcing integration. All the good jazz-bar hangouts in New York performed a social and intellectual role in the 1940s and 1950s. You got your jobs there. Messages were left there for you. You shared stories, and you argued with people there. They were town centers for all musicians.

"By contrast, in Los Angeles, everyone was living in their cars," Mandel said. "You had to drive forever to get anywhere. That detachment didn't have a positive impact on you. People were by themselves too much and not communicating with each other. To produce energetic work, you have to hang. I used to be part of Gil Evans's group with Miles Davis, Gerry Mulligan, and all of those guys in the late forties in New York. To be with your mates all the time was a great thing, and I missed that social interaction when I moved to Los Angeles. By not hanging out, the only time musicians saw each other was in the studios. And those interactions were always about work and work opportunities, not socializing. As a result, little by little, jazz out here became more studied and more formulaic. Everyone who worked in the studios was in a rush to move on to the next job, which could be spaced just a few hours apart. Musicians didn't linger to catch up. It wasn't part of the culture. No one had the time or the inclination."[53]

One of the hotbeds of West Coast Jazz was the Lighthouse in Hermosa Beach, where white and black musicians played. "In January 1949 I started my Sunday afternoon jam sessions there," said the bassist Howard Rumsey, who managed the club. "I had gotten the idea from something I had seen when I played with Stan [Kenton] back in the early 1940s. There were several clubs on Central Avenue where black musicians played. In these clubs, I had seen people just sitting and listening to a small jazz group rather than dancing. Sitting and listening was a new concept out here in the early 1940s. Everything was about dancing then. The image of people listening to the music stuck in my head. I thought the concept might work at the Lighthouse in the '50s."[54]

Most of the musicians who played regularly at the Lighthouse increasingly were white veterans of the big bands. "Many musicians who came to Los Angeles came with a big band that was scheduled to play the Palladium," the tenor saxophonist Dave Pell recalled. "You'd look around at the great weather, the houses, and the lifestyle, and you quit the band you were in. On off days, we'd play golf and then go to the Santa Anita racetrack. It was heaven. Soon, full bands didn't bother traveling to Los Angeles. Bandleaders that came out here would just bring a lead trumpet player, a lead alto saxophonist, and a drummer. The rest of the band they could fill out easily with local musicians when they arrived. It was more cost-efficient for them and great for us. I must have worked for fifty bands that came through in the 1950s—and I took all the jobs."[55]

Many West Coast musicians began using contrapuntal voicings in their compositions and arrangements, especially for sextets and octets. "The musicians who played at the Lighthouse were playing a new sound— all those lines and harmonies," Rumsey said. "These musicians included Shorty Rogers, Milt Bernhart, Bob Cooper, Hampton Hawes, Jimmy Giuffre, Frank Patchen, Shelly Manne, and others. Most had left the big bands that settled here in the winters. These musicians were working off their card—meaning they couldn't work officially until they had their union membership card, which required six months of residency. Many of the new guys needed work, so I threw them casual gigs at the Lighthouse, which the union allowed. These informal gigs paid them a few bucks and kept their chops in shape while waiting for the six months to elapse."[56]

Arrangements often were a necessity, because many of the musicians were playing regularly in the studios and getting together only briefly for club dates and recording sessions. "To keep up with people, you'd either be on regular phones all the time fielding jobs or you were in studios or playing at clubs," Mandel said. "That's how you networked, as they say today. Everyone liked jazz more then, so there was plenty of arranging work available, and I was taking all the work I could get, including writing for TV and Las Vegas entertainers."[57]

Though Gerry Mulligan downplayed his role in the development of West Coast jazz, he had a lasting impact on the style during his short stay in Los Angeles. "Gerry worked at the Haig in '52," Buddy Collette recalled. "The guy working the door was Dick Bock, who eventually would start the Pacific Jazz label and recorded Gerry's band. People loved Gerry's roving baritone sound. Gerry could write that way. In a small band, the roving thing plays a trick on the ear. It fills out the empty spaces, making you think there are more musicians than there really were. Gerry also had Chico brushing a certain way. It was a quieter, cooler style. Chetty's sound on the trumpet and Carson Smith, the bass player, also was quieter. They played softer and the mikes picked them up."[58]

Chico Hamilton remembers meeting Gerry Mulligan in 1952. "Gerry used to hang out at this club where I was playing with Charlie Barnet. Gerry had just come to the West Coast, and he was on his ass, man. He didn't have nothing. He used to hang out at the bar. We met on a break and became friends. I took him home a few times and my wife made him dinner. "The next thing I knew, he called and said he wanted to start a quartet. Gerry and the quartet got together to rehearse in my living room. I thought right away that these guys were great players. We just happened to be four guys in the right place at the right time. Hell if I know how this stuff happens. When Mulligan told me there wasn't going to be a piano in the group, that wasn't a problem. But Gerry didn't want me to use my bass drum. And that's when we went to war [*laughs*]. I finally went out and got myself a small bass drum and converted it into a bass drum. Gerry didn't want any bass drum at all. But I told him I needed something there for my right foot, to keep my rhythm. My timing depended on it. I'm still using a smaller bass drum today. There was no big idea here. The small drum simply fit better on the bandstand at the Haig [*laughs*].

"I played firm and light, and Gerry loved my style. Gerry was more than happy with the sound. We got along, although we went to war every now and then. Our friction was never about the music. Mostly stuff about our different outlooks. As an African-American, there was never any friction playing with the Gerry Mulligan Quartet. I played with a whole lot of white groups before Gerry. When I left the quartet, the sound went with me. Gerry never had that sound on drums again. The group didn't have the same sound after that."[59]

In 1953, the bebop drummer Max Roach traveled to Los Angeles and played at the Lighthouse. "Max was happy in L.A.," the alto saxophonist Herb Geller said. "He wasn't getting as many gigs in New York as he would have liked at the time. It was really great to have him out there. There weren't many black musicians in the studios or at the clubs in Hollywood or at the beaches. Howard Rumsey at the Lighthouse was very liberal and would have Hampton Hawes, Sonny Criss, Teddy Edwards, and other black artists on the bandstand. The lineup would change from day to day, especially on Sundays. Everyone always tried to play their best."[60]

The new West Coast sound came into being just as record technology was changing on the West Coast. "My cousin Roy Hart co-founded Pacific Jazz with Dick Bock in the summer of 1952," Dave Pell said. "Phil Turetsky was their engineer. They didn't have a studio yet, so they made demos at Phil's house. Roy owned a popular drum store called Drum City, on Santa Monica Boulevard. When I told him about Gerry and Chet at these jam sessions I had attended, Roy got them, along with Chico Hamilton and bassist Bob Whitlock, booked into the Haig."[61]

By 1953, albums recorded in Los Angeles began to be marketed as a new West Coast sound, and record companies began to tout the distinction between the jazz recorded in Los Angeles and jazz recorded in New York. Among the first albums to stress the new jazz style was Shelly Manne's *West Coast Sound*, recorded for Contemporary in April 1953. And one of the earliest rivalry albums was *East Coast–West Coast Scene*, recorded in September 1954 for RCA. One side of the LP featured a West Coast group led by Shorty Rogers; the other side featured an East Coast ensemble fronted by Al Cohn. "Part of the East Coast–West Coast jazz feud really started with the A&R guys," said Creed Taylor, who produced jazz records for Bethlehem in New York during this period. "Back then, the major labels had an East Coast producer and one on the West Coast. Both were competing for promotion dollars, exposure, and dominance."[62]

Though many West Coast musicians had started as bebop players, the sound mellowed quickly. "Shorty [Rogers] was doing a lot of writing then," Dave Pell said. "When he decided to arrange for my octet, he wanted to write differently than the way he did for his group, the Giants, which had more of a bop feel. So we cheated. We took the sound of the Les Brown band and the style of writing he favored, and we adapted it for our octet. Les liked to have all the trumpets with mutes, trombones open and a guitar underneath playing single notes. When I was in the band, Shorty came to me and said, 'You know what you should do? Instead of the full brass section, take one muted trumpet, one trombone and a guitar and create the sound in miniature.' So we did, and it worked. We simulated the sound of Les Brown with eight pieces, but it sounded much bigger."[63]

Did East Coast musicians fit comfortably into the West Coast jazz scene? "Most New York jazz musicians who came out here told me they didn't like it," Pell said. "Life in Southern California was very different from East Coast urban living. The only one who came out from the East Coast and fit right into the scene was Ray Brown. He loved it and worked steadily here. He was a golfer and fit right in. If you weren't on a call for a recording, you were on the golf course. East Coast guys would come out and not understand why they had to play golf with the contractors—the guys who decided who would be hired for recording sessions. You had to be friends with these guys, and golf made that possible.

"Many East Coast guys who weren't used to this kind of functional, structured life didn't get it. They thought we were working just to pay our mortgages. In fact, one writer at *Metronome* called the music my octet played 'mortgage-paying jazz.' Which was unfair. What was wrong with that? Hey, not all West Coast jazz guys liked it here, either. Many moved to New York and stayed there. Zoot Sims was one, for example. He didn't like it out here. He said it wasn't metropolitan enough. There was no downtown. He wanted to be on 48th Street, right in the heart of the action.

"When you hear West Coast jazz, you're hearing the happiness we were feeling, Contrapuntal music isn't the full story. But you needed the right upbeat attitude to play it and earn. A lot of guys came to town who weren't that well known but soon found themselves working steadily for the next thirty years. You had to be lucky, and you had to be in with the right crowd. You couldn't be in with the bad boys.

"The lifestyle, of course, worked nicer with a wife, kids, and country-club membership. Everyone was doing that. All your friends were doing that. It was like the houses. Everything fit together neatly. For many musicians, especially arrangers, the workload and the lifestyle demanded formulas and patterns to get it all done. If you came up with a winning formula, the way that I did with my octet, you repeated it with the best people you could find. California, especially in the music business, was about taking as many jobs each day as possible and doing them all perfectly. Such a challenge requires self-discipline and finding systems that work. The West Coast jazz sound was like that. The music you hear is of contentment. You really felt you were blessed."

Because the sound had commercial appeal, more musicians began writing contrapuntally for small groups. "The West Coast sound featured more counterpoint—instruments assuming the lead while others played things behind them," said the alto saxophonist and West Coast leader Lennie Niehaus.[64] "With West Coast jazz, you had several different voices playing at once, which the ear likes. It gives you more to listen to than just one horn. On the East Coast, jazz musicians tended to play with a harder sound. They generally applied more air and pressure to their instruments. Our interpretation wasn't softer. It was what I would call a 'lighter loud.' Much of the philosophy on the West Coast started with Lester Young, whose family was from Los Angeles. Lester had a light beautiful sound that many tenor saxophonists out here admired and adopted. We also used more linear pieces. Much of this came from the classical classes that that many of the guys were taking. Some were studying with classical composers who wrote linear.

"In the recordings I did, I aimed for a lot of movement in the inner parts. But nature also played a role in the music. It was organic, in that what we were exposed to in the landscape and lifestyle was integrated into the sound. Out here in the early 1950s, the outdoors was a big thing. You had wide-open spaces, a lot of foliage, and the coastline and surf. Everything was easier going. It was the opposite of New York. I remember my first trip to New York. I looked out of my hotel window, and at 5 P.M. everyone was moving fast to get to the subway. It was claustrophobic. On the West Coast, everyone was a little cooler. I believe that artists are products of their environment, and out here back in the fifties, there was more horizontal space. It was a different pace that was centered on pausing and taking your time.

"Most of the jazz musicians lived on the outskirts of Los Angeles in the suburbs, in ranch houses. Some lived south toward Hermosa or Newport Beach and Orange County. Others lived north near the San Fernando Valley. I lived in West Hollywood and then moved out to the Valley in the late fifties. I wanted more space. Everyone did. Shelly Manne had a little ranch and a couple of horses. You wanted space to think. Driving to and from jobs was relaxing at first. Then the population kept getting bigger and bigger and people started moving farther and farther away and driving longer and longer to get to the studios in Hollywood. I remember the freeways only went so far but they kept being extended. You had to plan what you were going to do based on your drive.

"Black and white musicians all got along. We would play together. I never heard any complaints about recording. Most of the black musicians lived in the inner city and started moving further west later in the fifties. Les Koenig of Contemporary recorded many black artists such as Buddy Collette, Curtis Counce, Hampton Hawes, Ray Brown, and others. Les even was first to record Ornette Coleman, though he never received proper credit for that."

The East Coast tenor saxophonist Sonny Rollins may have had the most romantic view of the West Coast, having spent his youth in Harlem movie theaters watching Westerns. In March 1957 Rollins recorded *Way Out West*—perhaps the ultimate East-Coast-meets-West-Coast jazz album. The Contemporary cover features Rollins standing in the desert wearing a cowboy hat and a holster with a six-shooter. On the recording, he was joined by the white drummer Shelly Manne and the black bassist Ray Brown. "I was on the West Coast at the time and Les Koenig left the choice of material completely to me. I was out West and had all these Western songs in mind from my youth. The truth is East and West Coast musicians all knew each other personally or by reputation and were friends. The album is merely a tribute to independence and being self-sufficient, which is what the West really means—at least in Westerns."[65]

Back on the East Coast, starting in the early 1950s, jazz started to change in response to the growing popularity of West Coast jazz and the inescapable influence of R&B. While West Coast jazz was developing a more suburban, laid-back sound in the early fifties, East Coast jazz musicians began to place a new emphasis on tight horn arrangements and a bigger beat. In short, musicians reloaded the West Coast approach—keeping the horns front and center but adding a more forceful and urgent attack. This jazz style was perfectly suited to East Coast jazz labels, which were seeking more original music to fill the new LP format, hold down copyright costs, and compete with R&B.

6   BMI, R&B, and Hard Bop

On December 4, 1939, Jelly Roll Morton was riffling through the day's mail when an envelope caught his eye. Morton—a ragtime and early-jazz pianist as well as a prolific composer and charismatic showman—opened the letter. It was from the American Society of Composers, Authors, and Publishers (ASCAP).[1] Morton had been trying to join the elite performing-rights organization since 1934—without success. Formed in 1914 by musicians including Victor Herbert, Jerome Kern, Irving Berlin, and John Philip Sousa, ASCAP initially sought to collect copyright royalties from theaters and restaurants on behalf of member songwriters and publishers whose songs were being performed in public for profit. In the 1920s, ASCAP added radio and record companies to its list of royalty sources, and movie studios soon followed in the 1930s with the arrival of talkies and musical soundtracks.

Despite having written dozens of songs that had been recorded and performed with great success by other leading bands since the start of the swing era, Morton had consistently been denied membership by ASCAP and its attorneys. And he hadn't received a dime in royalties for the performances of his music in concerts, on jukeboxes, and on the radio. ASCAP's initial reason for denying him membership in October 1934 was that Morton's application needed to be proposed and seconded by an existing member. The association didn't view the flamboyant showman as serious ASCAP material.[2]

In the 1930s, ASCAP represented the country's most prominent and polished composers and publishers. Many high-profile members like Cole Porter and George Gershwin earned significant sums writing catchy songs for Broadway and the movies, which meant sizable royalties. To keep ASCAP's white-tie-and-tails image from being marginalized by black writers of blues, jazz, and other forms of "barely composed" music, ASCAP had created restrictive rules that all but barred a growing number of composers like Morton. "ASCAP sure is giving me the run-around & keep[s] collecting money from my tunes, & I am unable to collect 1 cent," Morton wrote on September 19, 1934. "I think that is terrible. It almost make[s] one lose their head when one knows much lesser important people are drawing money from their tunes."[3] To make matters worse, RCA Victor routinely sent letters to Morton for his signature, giving them the rights to his compositions.[4]

But the 1934 membership snub by ASCAP didn't dissuade Morton, who repeatedly tried to join the organization and reap royalties from his growing roster of songs being recorded by white artists. Finally in December 1939, with more than twenty swing versions of his "King Porter Stomp" on the market, ASCAP could no longer justify denying the composer membership. When Morton slid a letter-opener through the sealed ASCAP envelope and pulled out the letter, he was overjoyed to read that he had been accepted as a member. But his elation dimmed two weeks later, when ASCAP's contract arrived.

The terms of membership were appalling. Rather than pay royalties based on the number of times a song was performed, played in a jukebox, or broadcast on the radio, ASCAP instead used a tiered reward system that favored elite hit makers. Composers·in the top tier, such as Richard Rodgers or Jerome Kern, might receive $16,000 a year in public-play royalties. Morton, however, was admitted to the bottom tier, which meant $120 a year—and no payments for past activity. "The situation is very disheartening sometime[s], but I will go on trying & trying again, as long as I can have a spark of energy left in me," Morton wrote to his friend and admirer Roy Carew on December 23. But Morton was unable to convince ASCAP and Victor to pay him royalties on his music, and he died in a hospital charity ward in July 1941, with 38 cents to his name.[5] Morton's bitter fight against ASCAP and the music industry for royalties was fairly typical for composers of blues, jazz, and R&B.

ASCAP's stranglehold on the royalty-recovery business as well as its restrictive admittance policy and tiered payment formula left the organization wide open to competition, which came when Broadcast Music Incorporated (BMI) was formed in 1939. As the popularity of records climbed in the 1940s and skyrocketed in the early 1950s, many new composers of hits whom ASCAP had snubbed joined BMI. Nonetheless, BMI faced challenges as it grew. From 1940 to 1950, it had difficulty attracting top composers because of ASCAP's prestige, clout, and appeal. Early on, the American Federation of Musicians' recording ban from 1942 to 1944 didn't help BMI, nor did the shortage of shellac during World War II, which limited the production of records and thus royalties. After the ban ended in 1944, BMI's fortunes began to change, since increased recording and record production meant greater BMI royalty revenue. BMI was also helped by the Federal Communications Commission's postwar granting of licenses to a growing number of new radio stations, many of which played records. With the steady proliferation of independent radio stations, the growing capacity of jukeboxes, and rising sales of records in the years immediately after the war, BMI was able to collect royalties on an increasing number of original compositions written and recorded by jazz musicians, including Charlie Parker, Max Roach, Thelonious Monk, Miles Davis, Lionel Hampton, and Sonny Rollins.[6]

But the second AFM recording ban, in 1948—followed by the introduction of Columbia's 33⅓-rpm in 1948 and RCA's 45-rpm in 1949—presented new challenges for BMI. Record sales dropped dramatically as Columbia and RCA battled for format dominance. Confused, consumers decided to wait and see which record speed emerged the victor before investing in a new format and equipment, preferring in the meantime to stick to 78-rpms.

The turning point for BMI and jazz came in 1954, when the number of licensed independent radio stations soared and the 45-rpm became standard in jukeboxes, with machines able to hold upward of 120 discs.[7] The affordability of cars in the early 1950s also played a major role in advancing the popularity of the 45-rpm. By 1952, half of all cars sold came with an AM radio,[8] and most local stations played hit singles by regional artists. All these developments helped BMI and the composers whom ASCAP would not accept as members.

During the 1950s BMI's fortunes were aided by four other developments that occurred in rapid succession: the growing popularity of television, which required live music; the proliferation of large record-store chains that discounted prices; the rise of regional record companies; and the steady construction of the interstate highway system, which made shipping LPs and singles to all regions easier than in the past. All this activity resulted in surging sales for vinyl 45-rpms and LPs. Among BMI's largest and most profitable categories in the early 1950s was R&B, a big-beat offshoot of jazz that filled a vacuum with teens when jazz abandoned dance music in the late 1940s in favor of the club and concert hall. The commercial success of R&B and the profitability of recording original R&B material put pressure on jazz as early as 1952, when consumers began to accept the new 45-rpm and the 33⅓-rpm LP formats.

To meet the growing interest in the new speeds, jazz labels such as Blue Note, Prestige, Savoy, Riverside, Contemporary, Pacific Jazz, and Fantasy began encouraging artists to compose original material. From their standpoint, original jazz compositions offered several benefits. First, original music usually ran longer—particularly with extended solos—reducing the number of three-minute tracks that had to be featured on each side of an LP. Second, original music meant labels could save on ASCAP copyright royalties, which were required for the use of Tin Pan Alley standards. Third, jazz tastes were shifting to smaller groups, which often featured original material. Fourth, and perhaps most important, the new record labels could earn additional revenue by publishing the original compositions for the musicians. Many jazz musicians knew little about self-publishing, and those who did often couldn't afford to hire the lawyers necessary to facilitate the process. Many jazz record companies not only published the music for jazz musicians recording on their labels but also had them join BMI so the organization could track and collect royalties.

As R&B occupied more and more slots in jukeboxes, and jazz talent representatives like the Shaw Agency added lucrative R&B artists to their rosters, jazz record labels and musicians needed a way to remain relevant. On the West Coast, jazz continued to shift toward a more harmonious and swinging sound that reflected the region's environment. On the East Coast, jazz moved in a different direction, adapting the hotter high-energy characteristics of R&B. Starting in 1953, East Coast jazz labels recorded more original works by musicians who featured intricate melodies and arrangements for horns playing in unison, accompanied by a strong beat. Composers included Elmo Hope, Horace Silver, Lou Donaldson, Clifford Brown, Miles Davis, Sonny Rollins, and Benny Golson.

In the wake of these cultural, technological and business developments, a new style of jazz emerged on the East Coast that would become known as hard bop—a style that came to dominate jazz well into the 1960s and beyond. As Gene Seymour wrote in an essay on hard bop in *The Oxford Companion to Jazz,* "Instead of grasping for greater complexity, hard bop provided jazz music with an innovative way of keeping things simple. And of making simple things sound extraordinary."[9]

BMI CATCHES A BREAK

Most composers dream of writing songs that millions of people will want to hear repeatedly. This aspiration—to write addictive melodies that wind up paying handsome royalties—has motivated many American composers for decades. But royalties paid to composers based on the popularity of their creations is a relatively modern reward system. For much of European history, composing music was a work-for-hire enterprise. Gifted composers typically were commissioned by the church or courts to write works to celebrate special occasions. Authors of works often received a single payment and the promise of additional assignments.

In nineteenth-century America, this tradition continued—with stage-show producers replacing kings and cardinals. With the advent of central heating and electricity in the late nineteenth century, public entertainment in theaters became possible year-round. As the number of theaters with orchestra pits grew, more American composers auditioned songs for theater owners, show producers, and sheet-music publishers, who then bought what they liked from them. Then they used the songs in shows or printed them as sheet music and sold them for public and at-home use. If a song sold well, a producer or music publisher would request additional material from the composer. As for the songs themselves, they could be performed endlessly, free of charge, after the initial payment. Music in the nineteenth century, like a wagon or water pump, belonged to the person who bought it.

But unlike that wagon or pump, music did not come with specially designed levers or gear assemblies that were protected by patents. Music was consumed through the air and was considered notes on a page that when played created pleasant sounds—free for all to enjoy. Those musical notes didn't share the same copyright protection as words printed in newspapers and books.

In general, copyright protection for the printed word dates back to 1709, when the British parliament passed the Statute of Anne. The law was designed to enable the British government to bring order to the chaos created in the book trade when the Licensing Act of 1662 lapsed in 1694. The new law allowed for a copyright on existing and past works.[10] But the English law did not extend to the American colonies, a snub that the Founding Fathers resented, given their talent for pamphlet, almanac, and broadsheet writing. After the Revolution, the new American Congress passed the Federal Copyright Act of 1790, which allowed an initial fourteen-year period of copyright protection for the printed word and gave the owner the option of renewing the copyright for another fourteen years. An 1831 copyright act extended the initial period to twenty-eight years, with a fourteen-year renewal, bringing the total to forty-two years.[11] The new law included printed musical works, such as sheet music.[12]

The Copyright Act of 1909 extended the copyright for a total of fifty-six years and was the first law to recognize the mechanical rights of composers. By 1909 several devices, including the piano roll and phonograph, had been invented that allowed music to be recorded onto surfaces that were then replayed on machines by consumers. The Compulsory Mechanical License that was part of the 1909 act stated that once a copyright owner had recorded a song for public distribution or had given permission to someone else to record the song, anyone could record the song provided they followed certain rules. Those rules included paying a royalty of two cents per recording to the copyright owner. Music was now on par with the printed word.[13]

The law also prohibited anyone from making a recording of a musical composition without the consent of the copyright owner and without seeking a compulsory mechanical license from the government first.[14] But nothing in the new law stipulated the need to seek permission for the live performance of copyrighted material. Nor were royalties required when music was performed where no admission was charged. Victor Herbert and other composers formed ASCAP in 1914 to collect such royalties, and he sued a New York restaurant for playing his music and not paying royalties. The case was eventually heard by the Supreme Court, which decided in 1917 in *Herbert v. Shanley Co.* that a copyright's owner was entitled to compensation for a public performance of a musical composition—even if there was no direct charge for admission.[15]

At first, because ASCAP couldn't be everywhere at once, it limited its fee-collecting efforts to major cities where music was most often performed publicly in theaters and concert halls. ASCAP's representatives in those cities also could read local newspaper accounts of performances and watch for ads for bars, restaurants, and theaters that featured live music. As radio became popular in the 1920s, ASCAP had an easier time tracking royalty payments due from the major radio networks based on the airplay of members' compositions—at first by live radio orchestras and then on records.

In the 1930s ASCAP demanded ever-larger licensing fees from radio stations and movie companies, which had become highly profitable with each new technological development. The tug of war over royalties between ASCAP and radio was particularly pointed, because radio was more popular in households during the Depression than movies. The battle reached a turning point in 1939, when the radio networks formed Broadcast Music Incorporated as a licensing and royalty-collecting rival to ASCAP. Though BMI had had difficulty at first generating royalties, it soon recruited composers who had been unable to join ASCAP. Initially, the bulk of BMI's revenue came from the public airplay of its licensed music on the radio and in jukeboxes. But during World War II, BMI's revenue declined as material shortages slowed the production of jukeboxes and the FCC held off issuing radio-station licenses for reasons of national security.

After the war, however, the number of radio stations surged, and the reach of stations expanded as many were granted permission to boost their wattage. In 1947 the FCC began reviewing its backlog of license applications, doubling the number it approved during the next four years.[16] Interestingly, by the late 1940s the powerful radio network lobby in Washington, D.C, no longer opposed the granting of new licenses to smaller stations. By then, the companies that owned major radio networks were expanding into television. As independent radio grew, more stations specialized in regional forms of music.[17]

ASCAP'S WAKE-UP CALL

In January 1952 radio and jukeboxes were the primary means by which most listeners heard records. Radio was particularly important to the popularity and sale of singles because recorded music had all but replaced live performances by station musicians. The jukebox wasn't far behind. In 1951 the number of records sold to jukebox operators exceeded fifty million—up 40 percent over the two previous years, thanks to higher-capacity machines. In fact, roughly 150,000 of the first 200,000 copies of Tony Bennett's "Because of You" were sold to jukebox operators.[18]

Early on, BMI recognized that independent radio and the 45-rpm single represented enormous opportunities that ASCAP had largely missed. Jukebox operators, especially, welcomed the lightweight vinyl singles because they had to pay for the records they stocked in their machines. In the 78-rpm era, shellac discs wore out with greater frequency, requiring jukebox operators to spend more to replace them. By contrast, the vinyl 45-rpm was more durable and required a lighter tonearm needle, so it lasted longer. Jukebox operators could hold on to more of their profits, because they no longer had to dedicate 10 percent of their annual revenue to record purchases.[19]

In early 1952 BMI mounted a drive to sign music composers that brought its stable to seventy.[20] What made BMI so appealing to composers in the 45-rpm age was its payment structure. Unlike ASCAP's tiered system that rewarded bigger-name members, BMI had an "open door" policy that let all composers sign on, providing them with a minimum cash advance against royalties, which were collected by keeping an eye on playlists issued by radio stations and cue sheets from TV stations. Songwriters with BMI licensing contracts now had an incentive to write hit songs. For publishers, the stakes were growing as well. In the first six months of 1952, fourteen music publishers received $697,024 in mechanical royalties from the sale of thirty-seven million records that featured new songs published in 1950 and 1951.[21] What's more, only slightly more than half of distribution and dealer unit sales were coming from 78-rpms, while distributors and dealers reported that sales of $33\frac{1}{3}$-rpms and 45-rpms were increasing at a greater rate than 78-rpms during the first eight months of 1952.[22]

As an organization formed by broadcasters in support of broadcasters, BMI employed savvy marketers who understood what radio stations needed to turn a profit. To encourage stations to select records by BMI composers, BMI published a book in 1952 called *Meet the Artist*, featuring biographical sketches of 144 recording artists and listings of BMI-licensed songs. It was shipped to all radio stations for disc jockey use.[23] BMI also issued a monthly publication for TV stations called *TV Sketch Book*, which went so far as to suggest script ideas based on BMI's standard tunes.[24] But TV's popularity, though growing rapidly, did not exceed radio's tight hold over listeners.[25] Radio's future looked bright as the FCC granted more licenses to new stations in cities that did not yet have television stations. In August 1952 there were 2,353 AM stations on the air nationwide, and 303 applications for new stations pending, notably in the new suburban markets of California and the South.[26]

Another reason for radio's growing influence was that 70.5 percent of automobiles on the road in August 1952—some 27.5 million cars— were equipped with radios. As *Billboard* noted at the time, "Cars alone accounted for greater [consumer] reach than the combined circulation of the four largest weekly magazines or even all the morning newspapers in the US put together."[27] In America's expanding suburbs, the car offered its owner escape, control, freedom, and the exhilaration of speed. And the radio enhanced all these benefits. With a dial tuned to a station, the driver and passengers were a captive audience for music and advertising messages. According to an Advertising Research Bureau survey in 1952, radio was so pervasive that it was able to influence its audience more effectively than newspapers.[28]

During radio's resurgent rise in the early 1950s, BMI continued to sign up new songwriters and win away major publishers from ASCAP with payment guarantees. BMI also forged new alliances with jazz record labels, many of which were now acting as profitable middlemen for jazz composers eager to publish and license their songs. BMI's gains were even stronger in R&B and country—so much so that ASCAP began holding regular internal meetings to address BMI's inroads. To forestall those efforts, ASCAP began offering BMI defectors $100,000 per year over five years to return to the organization.[29] ASCAP's willingness to fight BMI with cash signaled its growing unease about the upstart organization's expanding power and growing stable of new composers and publishers.

In the fall of 1952, ASCAP came to the realization that its tiered payment system favoring established members was antiquated and in need of review and overhaul.[30] Its decision was fortified in November, when BMI reported that in the fiscal year ending in July, it had had a record annual income of $5.6 million, with $4.97 million coming from radio and television licenses alone. Even more important, BMI-licensed songs during that same fiscal year comprised 51 percent of the fiscal year's no. 1 hits and 66 percent of the all positions on the *Hit Parade* chart, without an end in sight.[31]

Despite the battles between ASCAP and BMI, the year 1952 ended on an upbeat note for the entire music industry, with growth in excess of the $200 million it had earned in 1951. The two new record speeds continued to gain favor with consumers, with the $33\frac{1}{3}$-rpm LP devoted to classical and jazz, and the 45-rpm committed mostly to pop.[32] BMI was closing the gap between its revenues and those of ASCAP. At the end of 1952 ASCAP finally abandoned its tiered royalty classification system and replaced it with a royalty plan similar to BMI's, which was based largely on the play of records on the radio and jukeboxes. As *Billboard* reported in December, "Within ASCAP, radical changes occurred in the publishers' and writers' classification system. The systems were streamlined with more emphasis placed upon performance. Old, traditional concepts such as availability, seniority and the components parts—[such] as vogue, prestige, etc.—have been eliminated for all practical considerations."[33]

Part of ASCAP's rush to rethink its payout system was the rising sales of new phonographs. In 1952 Columbia and RCA, for the first time, had begun producing units that could handle all three speeds with the flip of a switch. Columbia also manufactured a low-price three-speed attachment that fit onto existing turntables while RCA launched a new line of changers that featured a removable spindle that could stack and play 45-rpm discs in rapid succession.[34] From 1951 to 1952, the number of records pressed had increased from 169 million to 176 million, and income from sales, from $156 million to $164 million.[35]

At the start of 1953 the record business was experiencing extraordinary sales. Record-pressing plants reported their strongest months since 1945. Particularly noteworthy and beneficial for BMI was a report from the independent record labels stating that the growth of pop, country, and R&B had been unprecedented.[36] As record sales soared, so did radio's appeal—even in homes with television sets. Radios could be heard in any room of a house by moving the unit. Radios could also serve as background for other activities or tasks. The same could not be said at the time of television. Portability also helped the appeal of radio and records. Half of all respondents to an industry study in 1953 said they owned a portable radio or listened to the radio in their car.[37]

Despite TV's growing popularity, radio sales continued to climb in 1953, with the production of radio-set units predicted to exceed fourteen million by the end of the year, reversing the downward radio-manufacturing trend of the preceding two years. In the fall, more than 110 million radio sets were in use in the United States, a gain of over five million in a little more than a year. The trend was greatly helped by the nation's growing number of radio stations and the increased number of dealers that sold radios.[38] Meanwhile, car radios in 1953 accounted for 50 percent of the fourteen million radio sets of all types produced.[39] The radio airplay of records not only enchanted audiences but also sent them off to stores to buy singles and new phonographs. In New York, Liberty Music Shops, a major chain, reported more than $1 million in record sales and a 25 percent jump in phonograph sales thanks to the stocking of models that sold for seventy to a hundred dollars each. The majority of Liberty's sales were for new table models with three speeds rather than the quirky speed-adaptor attachments.[40] By late 1953, phonograph makers were using the term "high fidelity" in ads to emphasize that their new equipment, designed for the new records, could deliver truer and more dynamic sound.

Naturally, the registration of music copyrights jumped in 1953 in tandem with record and phonograph sales. By November, the number of music copyrights registered hit nearly 8,259, with pending registrations at 40,773—a substantial increase over the previous year.[41] Radio as a medium also experienced historic growth. At the beginning of 1953, for the first time in broadcast history, 2,550 AM stations were on the air, with the FCC granting licenses to an average of more than nine stations a month. Although most of the new licenses were for daytime-only radio broadcasting, the FCC authorized round-the-clock broadcast operations in a range of markets, including such small communities as Grand Island, Nebraska, and Wallace, North Carolina—though stations like these broadcast with just 1,000 to 5,000 watts.[42] By the close of 1953, radio was experiencing unprecedented growth, thanks to its convenience and its appearance in cars, as well as the proliferation of station licenses granted by the FCC. The same was true for jukeboxes, which featured better speaker systems, smoother changers, and a larger and more diversified inventory of records and music styles.

As 45-rpms grew more popular, new markets for music developed along regional and demographic lines. In the South, blues and country were popular. In the West, a more energetic form of R&B, popularized by the saxophonist Big Jay McNeely and the drummer Johnny Otis, was gaining ground, along with a cooler form of jazz. In the Northeast and Midwest, vocal groups were popular, along with a newly emerging jazz style, ideally suited to the $33\frac{1}{3}$-rpm LP. As in the swing era, teens had once again become obsessed with music. But now they had their own records, portable phonographs, and radios.

THE LP HEADS HOME

In 1952 there was a jump in the number of jazz albums released and in the grosses of top jazz artists at nightclubs. *Billboard* called it "the most successful year experienced by jazz since the late 1930s." In addition to an increase in the number of new releases, record sales were also up. Though jazz records did not sell as well as R&B and pop, some jazz artists had sold as many as thirty thousand records in 1952. Jazz artists such as Illinois Jacquet, who leaned toward R&B, and George Shearing, who recorded jazz-pop, each sold more than a hundred thousand units. Increasingly, jazz record companies sought small groups that sounded big and could complete recording sessions quickly and cost-efficiently. There were many reason for the renewed interest in jazz, among them the promoter Norman Granz's Jazz at the Philharmonic concerts and records as well as other jazz concert tours,[43] such as Billy Eckstine and Nat King Cole's "Biggest Show of '52."

The LP was another factor in jazz's resurrection, since the long-playing album made it possible to record longer selections of music and re-create the excitement of clubs for listeners in newly purchased homes. The pirating of out-of-print traditional-jazz recordings by a number of labels helped convince the major labels to reenter the jazz market with their older catalogues, and the demand for reissues accelerated.[44]

Smaller jazz labels were greatly helped by the willingness of major labels such as RCA, Columbia, Decca, and Capitol to press other labels' records when they weren't manufacturing their own. The additional business allowed the major labels to avoid the cost of shutting down plants and starting them up again. Custom pressing, moreover, meant additional revenue, especially if the smaller labels had a radio and jukebox hit that required additional pressings.[45] The majors found that fostering competition was much more profitable than attempting to stamp it out—a shift in strategy that became a necessity as independent pressing plants emerged to compete for the small-label record-pressing business. In April 1953 more than fifteen hundred record labels were operating, with the independent labels in New York paying musicians more than twice as much for recording dates as they had paid in 1952 to meet the new demand. As a group, those New York independent labels were holding ten recording sessions for every one by the six largest labels as a group.[46] The major record companies were especially irritated by an independent label's ability to produce a raging hit without much investment of capital up front, thanks to magnetic tape. For example, a small company such as Imperial Records in Los Angeles could discover an R&B pianist in New Orleans, record him there on a portable recorder, and have the tape reels sent to Los Angeles for mastering and pressing. Thanks to independent radio and jukeboxes, a 45-rpm like "Goin' Home," by Fats Domino, could become a huge hit in 1952. Smaller labels could earn huge profits because they didn't need to buy a recording studio, a record plant, or even trucks to distribute the records. Nor did they need to do much marketing initially, given the strong word of mouth and radio airplay in local markets.

BMI benefited most from the transformation of the record business and shifts in music tastes nationwide, particularly as smaller labels registered original R&B, jazz, and country compositions with the organization. The greater the proliferation of records, radio stations, and jukeboxes, the greater the copyright royalties to collect.[47] What's more, the increase in the number of 45-rpms led quickly to more diverse selections in jukeboxes. Record companies preferred that jukebox companies feature the widest possible range of music tastes. Doing so not only provided a greater variety for fans of different types of music, resulting in more coins inserted into slots, but also increased the odds of a crossover hit—a record originally intended for one market that gained favor with another. The more varied the mix in a jukebox, the more likely it was that someone new to the music spinning would want to hear it again, buy the 45-rpm, and tell others about it.[48]

While the proliferation of radio stations and jukeboxes spurred the growth of the 45-rpm, the 10-inch $33\frac{1}{3}$-rpm LP was in a rut in the early

1950s. Record labels were able to promote LPs in stores in major markets, but they had trouble reaching the rest of the country, because radio and jukeboxes played 45-rpm singles. In late 1953, however, Columbia landed on a solution. The company began testing a mail-order record club in Ohio—advertising in magazines and newspapers and by direct mail. Customers were told that if they signed up, they would be able to choose one LP free of charge if they agreed to buy six records during the twelve months that followed. For every three records purchased, the buyer would receive a special record at no cost. Members were also told they could quit the club at any time after buying the initial six LPs.[49]

The record club was a stroke of marketing genius, and RCA soon copied it. Through its club, Columbia also marketed a three-speed phonograph attachment for $9.95 and portable player at $19.95—both offers reflecting a savings of 30 percent on the retail price.[50] As the quality of phonographs improved and phonographs were sold at record stores, sales of both record changers and records increased. Successful sellers offered tips to phonograph makers for publicity that included in-store advertising, window displays, extensive use of promotional materials, and setting up a phonograph corner where models could be demonstrated for curious shoppers.[51] The home phonograph was creating new demand for improved convenience and finer fidelity.

HARD BOP CATCHES UP

With the introduction of new affordable phonographs, increased use of magnetic tape in recording studios, and the greater rollout of 10-inch LPs in 1952 and 1953 by a wide range of record companies, the pressure was on for jazz to change. Bebop was no longer fresh and exciting by the late 1940s, jazz-classical appealed to a smaller, more sophisticated market, and West Coast jazz was still a regional phenomenon. At the time, the jazz market was saturated with bebop singles, many of them sounding indistinguishable and interchangeable. Even bebop artists were drifting toward pop by 1952. For example, Charlie Parker was recording Tin Pan Alley standards with a big band and strings, and Dizzy Gillespie recorded with strings in Paris. With R&B's expanding popularity in the early 1950s,[52] jazz needed to adapt if it was going to survive.

Part of the problem for jazz had been its explorations beyond the blues and its lack of a big, steady beat. Some jazz musicians had dismissed the blues as too formulaic and rudimentary, viewing it as the music of Southern fieldworkers, not cosmopolitan sophisticates. Others were determined to pioneer new styles in an effort to stand out. By the end of 1952 the blues belonged squarely to R&B—a more commercial form of dance music with enormous youth-market appeal. All of which left jazz musicians and small jazz record labels with a dilemma: If they distanced themselves from the blues, they risked becoming irrelevant to larger portions of the marketplace just when the 33⅓-rpm LP and 45-rpm were transforming listening habits and tastes. If they embraced the blues, they would sound similar to R&B artists. "As hip and as great as bebop was, there was a period when musicians had kinda . . . not totally, but somewhat . . . eliminated the blues, you know?" the pianist Horace Silver told Gene Seymour in a 1993 interview. "They got so sophisticated that it seemed like they were afraid to play the blues, like it was demeaning to be funky."[53]

R&B, however, with its relative simplicity and its mandatory repetition, presented a creative problem for many jazz musicians, who knew firsthand its stultifying sameness and limited possibilities for improvisation. When jazz recording had slowed because of consumers' hesitation to embrace the new record speeds, many up-and-coming jazz musicians took jobs playing in R&B bands and recorded with them. The list included Benny Golson, Tadd Dameron, Jymie Merritt, Freddie Redd, Tommy and Stanley Turrentine, Teddy Charles, Blue Mitchell, and John Coltrane. Few relished the experience, for the rigidity, sameness, and clownish novelty of R&B ran counter to their self-image and advanced skills. And the jive element of the music could be grating.

"In Tiny Grimes's band in 1950, we played the same tunes every night, but we never knew what key they would be in," said the tenor saxophonist Benny Golson, who played in several R&B bands, including ones led by the guitarist Grimes, the alto saxophonist Earl Bostic, and the vocalist Benjamin Clarence "Bull Moose" Jackson. "The key was wherever Tiny's hands fell on that darn guitar. So I had to learn to play in all keys. Tiny would play a short intro to let everyone know the key. You had just a few notes to pick it out. I was a nervous wreck. We had to wear kilts, because the group was called Tiny Grimes and His Rockin' Highlanders. In one club I had to walk on the bar to get off the bandstand. At first I'm stepping over drinks, and the women sitting at the bar are picking up my darn kilt. And I've got my boxer underwear on. After the first night, a friend said, 'No boxers, man, you have to wear a tight bathing suit.' "[54]

What R&B lacked in inventiveness it more than made up for in sheer stamina and showmanship. Early R&B saxophonists like Big Jay McNeely, James Von Streeter, Paul Williams, and others created blues riffs and played long and hard in an effort to distract and captivate integrated audiences. Unable to improvise as deftly as jazz musicians, R&B artists used the blues and endurance as a platform. "I didn't play with a real legit jazz sound," McNeely said. "For that sound, you'd use very little lip, what they called a nonpressure embouchure. Just enough pressure on the reed to make it vibrate. I took the same principles I learned in vocal lessons and applied it for a good, big soulful sound on the saxophone. That's why when I played, people recognized it was me. People have criticized me for playing one note over and over, but they never criticized my sound."[55]

As a gimmick to attract and excite teens, R&B artists increasingly added theatrics, which jazz musicians disparaged as vaudeville. Stagecraft might feature a choreographed line of dancing saxophonists or a soloist who pretended to throw his tenor saxophone into the audience. McNeely, who pioneered playing the sax while laying on the stage, recalled one night's performance: "When we played Clarksville, Tennessee, in 1950, the audience didn't respond. They just sat there. I couldn't understand that. The music usually got people going. So on the next set I did something different. I got down on my knees to play. Then I laid down on the stage and played from there. People went crazy. After the concert, I said to myself, 'I'm going to try this again.' So I did it in Texas. And again, everyone went crazy. Back in L.A., I did it, too. The kids went nuts. They loved that I was on my back blowing like that, and my energy fired up theirs."[56]

With R&B record sales strengthening rapidly by the early 1950s, the jazz producers Alfred Lion and Francis Wolff of Blue Note Records had to make a choice. They realized that unless a new form of jazz could generate jukebox singles and excite jazz LP buyers, jazz might soon shrink to a point where there were no profit margins. Blue Note had few recording sessions in the early fifties: six U.S. dates in 1951, nine in 1952, and fifteen in 1953. To scout new music, Lion traveled to clubs all over New York City looking for a new jazz sound.[57] In 1952 he hired Rudy Van Gelder to engineer his recording sessions. Van Gelder had reduced his overhead by using magnetic recording tape. "The first record session Rudy recorded for Blue Note was with my husband, [the baritone saxophonist] Gil Mellé," Denny Mellé recalled. "Gil often liked to tell a story about Blue Note's Alfred Lion and Gil's early association with engineer Rudy van Gelder. Gil said that when he first told Alfred about Rudy and how blown away he was by the new form of recording Rudy was using called 'tape,' he wanted Alfred to come over to Rudy's studio to take a listen. Alfred, with that thick German accent said, 'Vas ist tape?' Of course, the rest is history."[58]

From Rudy Van Gelder's perspective, the three-minute format of the 78-rpm was too confining. "The Gil Mellé recording on tape, which ultimately went to Blue Note, was my first project to result in a commercial release in the 10-inch LP format," Van Gelder said. "I had a Scully lathe and I was able to make masters in that format. My Scully was capable of making 78-rpm masters, too, the standard format for commercial release in the 1940s. But three minutes of music was not sufficient for the kind of music I was interested in. I was also working for Savoy Records at the time, and I wanted to quit making 78s. Savoy objected. Producer Ozzie Cadena said, 'What about all our customers in the backwoods of the South who only have 78-rpm players?' That was their market. Ultimately I prevailed and stopped making 78s altogether."[59]

As Blue Note's business picked up with the advent of the 10-inch LP, Lion and Wolff needed a steady flow of newly recorded material.[60] Blue Note had to come up with a formula for these new albums that could be repeated, but without ever making the music sound repetitious. With more space available on the LPs, solos were increasingly important, which meant more room for original material. But if Blue Note recorded only long tracks, it risked becoming tiresome and dull. The label needed a style that was distinctly jazz but also shared some of R&B's knack for generating excitement. The music's energy level had to be high and forceful—with horns and a big beat—if it was to be heard and bought. The music had to be the instrumental equivalent of Dinah Washington, whose voice had enormous snap and soul—and was crystal clear coming through small radio and jukebox speakers.[61]

One of Lion's first new horn-heavy, big-beat discoveries was a group assembled for a recording session on June 9, 1953. On that date, Lion united Clifford Brown, Lou Donaldson, Elmo Hope, Percy Heath, and Philly Joe Jones. "In 1953, I recorded what's considered the first hard-bop studio date, with Clifford Brown and Elmo Hope," said the saxophonist Lou Donaldson. "Then in February '54, I was with Art Blakey and Clifford Brown on the album *A Night at Birdland* for Blue Note. That was probably the greatest live jazz recording ever made. But it wasn't a Jazz Messengers date nor was Blakey the leader. It just happened that way. Art was leading a band in Brooklyn at the time that he called the Jazz Messengers. The quintet we had at Birdland was a studio band that Blue Note had put together for the live recording. Art owed a lot of money to someone. Blue Note made it his date so he could get paid more money as the leader and pay off his debt. It was just a blowing session. We didn't have a lot of time together and it was all new music, much of it written by me and Horace Silver. The band sounded different than anything else out there because of the blues sound. We wanted to keep the blues sound firmly in the band. R&B was coming on strong, and the blues had to be a part of what we were doing so the music would stand out. Blues gives jazz its identity."[62]

Though the band borrowed heavily from bebop, it had a harder, more unified sound. "Charlie Parker was one of the greatest blues musicians who ever lived," Donaldson said. "Early hard bop musicians just played what he played—but with more conventional, standardized structure. We also were swinging more. Our rhythm was more definite and predictable than bebop's. The bebop drummers were always trying things, adding this and that. What many people don't realize is that Art Blakey wasn't actually a bebop drummer in the purest sense. He was first and foremost about a strong beat and a strong rhythm. He was a swing drummer. Enormous rhythm. The effect or impact was different. Art's style, and the style of all good hard-bop drummers then, is that his sound would project out more to the people listening. The hard-bop drummer was less about nuances and more about a big, driving beat."[63]

Alfred Lion and Francis Wolff also realized that to grow their Blue Note business, they'd need to give their recordings more visibility. The best way to do that, they decided, was to proceed on two tracks—releasing both 10-inch LPs and 45-rpm singles. As late as 1954, Blue Note continued to issue singles on 78-rpm discs. But when newer and larger jukebox mechanisms could handle the 45-rpm format, Blue Note switched, recording its first 45-rpm in November 1953 (Art Blakey's "Message From Kenya," backed with Blakey and Sabu's "Nothing But the Soul").[64] Hard bop's signature sound—as evidenced by its earliest recordings with Donaldson, Brown, and Silver—was marked by a driving beat, blues and gospel influences, catchy melodies, and an ability to make songs in a minor key sound upbeat and urgent.[65] Where bebop's focus was on fast compact solos, hard bop shifted the emphasis to the beat and a tight unison sound featuring a trumpet, a saxophone, and often a trombone. "Our hard bop thing on the East Coast was the opposite of jazz on the West Coast," Donaldson said. "We consciously tried to do everything that they didn't do. We tried to swing hard, not cool. They had a light touch to their music. We had a heavy touch, with a swinging feel underneath. We knew that was going to be the only way to stand out."[66]

Hard bop echoed bebop's pace and embrace of minor-key songs and leveraged R&B's catchy riffs with original melodies played by tightly arranged horns and extended solos. Hard bop also added a backbeat—a strong accent on the second and fourth beats of each measure.[67] The return of the steady, swinging beat was significant because when jazz largely abandoned it in the late 1940s, R&B took the opportunity to exploit it and fill the vacuum. By then, many jazz labels like Savoy also were recording R&B, to generate jukebox sales. "I started out playing jazz but I didn't have a perfect ear, like Sonny Criss did," said the R&B saxophonist Big Jay McNeely. "Guys like Sonny could pick up their horn and play anything. They heard things once, and they could go off on it. At the end of 1948 [when the second AFM ban ended], Ralph Bass, an A&R guy at Savoy Records in California, asked me if I wanted to do a record. I said yeah. He told me to put a tune together. A kid I knew in Watts had a record shop. He gave me a record by Glenn Miller that opened with a drummer playing the sock cymbal. I can't remember the name of the song, but I built a blues off of it called 'Deacon's Hop,' which became a big hit. ['Deacon's Hop' hit no. 1 on the R&B chart in early 1949.] I always thought of myself as a jazz musician who was playing for people who wanted to dance. I wanted to become a jazz musician, but when I recorded 'Deacon's Hop' in 1948, it became so big they wouldn't let me record anything else but more of it."[68]

The way the engineer Rudy Van Gelder recorded the hard bop sound for Blue Note, Prestige, and other record labels made it particularly attractive in the LP era. Van Gelder's recordings had a new clarity, warmth, and urgency; they didn't sound distant or sonically flat. When Van Gelder recorded, he set up microphones in creative ways so that the sound of both the group and individual players was captured realistically on magnetic tape and then mastered into microgrooves. The trick was to maximize the warm tones of the collective sound without minimizing the nuanced personalities of the soloists.

"All my technical efforts were directed at recording and processing the sound for a consumer product, which in the early years just happened to be the new 10-inch LP format," Van Gelder recalled. "I was recording in Hackensack, N.J., at my parents' home. The new LP format was almost capable of reproducing the sound of the original tape, which was important. I might add that great strides were being made in plastic molding techniques during this time for vinyl records. My motivation was always to record jazz music. I liked that music and I wanted to record it in the best way that I could, better than the big companies. The essence of jazz is improvisation, and a three-minute recording span could hardly be described as adequate for creative musicians. Three minutes hardly gets through the intro. There was usually adequate time on the recording tape, but it couldn't be translated to a consumer record product lasting about three minutes. For a consumer product, the advantages of the LP were obvious: higher quality, a wide frequency range, longer playing time, and the capability of being reproduced in large quantities so it could be sold at a reasonable price. I could transfer the original tape to a master disc with minimal degradation of the sound."[69]

Van Gelder's self-described goal was to capture the mood of the musicians and their music. But magnetic tape allowed the editing of the finished product, a process that was impossible in the 78-rpm era. "I developed a good technique for editing out music and technical noise," Van Gelder said. "I had to, since I often was the only one working on the tape. Editing involved actually physically slicing the tape with a razor blade. There was only one tape, no backup. I had to cut it up. On Blue Note sessions, the producer was reluctant to let the musicians leave the studio after the session until he knew that all the edits I made worked. I remember cutting tape late in the evening, being surrounded by musicians watching me edit, hoping it would work so they could go home. There was a lot of pressure."

When cost efficiencies made possible the replacement of the 10-inch LP with the 12-inch jazz LP in 1955,[70] longer original compositions were needed along with extended solos. "The adoption of the 12-inch LP didn't make that much difference with regard to studio activities," according to Van Gelder. "The 10-inch LP contained about 15 minutes per side, while the 12-inch had about 20 minutes per side. The difference was that more music was needed, which meant longer recording sessions. Artwork and liner notes also made the product more attractive."[71]

The 12-inch LP also allowed musicians like Benny Golson to branch out into more elaborate compositions. "When I was with Earl Bostic, we used to play up in Massachusetts at towns like Holyoke, Peabody, and Revere Beach," Golson said. "We'd spend our days off in Boston. There was a nice elegant restaurant off Copley Square. If you went to the back of this restaurant and down the steps, you'd be in a jazz club called the Stable. Herb Pomeroy, the trumpet player, was there, along with Varty Haroutunian on tenor, John Neves on bass, and others. Herb and I became friends, and I would sit in and jam with them. One of the first compositions I wrote for the group was a crazy tune because of the number of bars it had—fourteen bars followed by an eight-bar bridge, then fourteen more bars. This was most unusual. I didn't have a name for the tune and wondered what I would call it. As I thought about it, I said to myself, 'I'm sending it to Herb Pomeroy. Well, he works at the Stable. Hey, stablemates means good friends. We're stablemates. I'll name it "Stablemates."' And that's how that song happened."[72]

As more companies issued the 12-inch LP, composers like Golson were in greater demand. As Golson recounted it, "About a week after John

Coltrane left [the band he and Colson had played with in 1955 in Phila-delphia], I saw him on Philadelphia's Columbia Avenue. I asked him how it was going. 'It's going great,' he said, 'but Miles needs some music. Do you have any?' Did I have any? All I had was music. When I look back now, it was embarrassing. I gave everyone I met back then a lead sheet from one of my compositions. You had to do that if you wanted your songs played. But nothing had ever happened. So when John took the tune I gave him, I didn't think any more of it. About a month later, I ran into John Coltrane again. John said, 'You know that tune "Stablemates" you gave me? We recorded it.'"

As a growing number of jazz musicians composed and recorded their own songs, royalties were generated. But a significant cut of those royalties often went to record companies that set up publishing units and licensed music to BMI. "Gigi [Gryce] and Lucky Thompson were the only black musicians who had their own publishing company in those days," the hard bop pianist Horace Silver recalled in his memoir. "Gigi turned me on to publishing, and I immediately started my own company, calling it Ecaroh Music Inc. Whenever I had a publishing or copyright problem, I'd call Gigi, and he'd tell me what I should do. . . . I don't own any masters. I own the copyrights to the compositions but not the master recordings themselves—'the masters,' as we say in the business. The recording com-panies paid me for the recording sessions, they paid me composer's royal-ties through my publishing company, and [they paid me] artists' royalties, but they own the masters. I didn't care if the label leased this project for three years or seven years, so long as they gave me a fair deal. I wanted them to make a profit, because if they didn't they wouldn't have wanted to take my next album."[73]

Jazz musicians had long struggled with copyrights and publishing com-panies and in some cases wound up being cheated by fellow musicians. In 1944 Thelonious Monk shared the credit for some of his original composi-tions with Teddy McRae, a tenor saxophonist, arranger, and songwriter with ties to several publishing houses. Monk hoped that McRae would find him a publisher. "McRae's only contribution was to submit the copyright registration forms and arrange for Regent Music Corp. to publish them, which he did in early February 1944," wrote Robin D. G. Kelley in *Thelo-nious Monk: The Life and Times of an American Original*. "In exchange for his services, McRae took co-composer's credits and listed himself as a claimant on both tunes."[74] The two songs were "The Pump" and "Well, You Need 'Na," which Monk later reworked as "Little Rootie Tootie" and "Well, You Needn't."

Hard bop musicians often let the labels for which they recorded publish their original material, because they knew little of such legal matters. "Yes, I did that," Lou Donaldson said. "When you did record dates, you filled out these contracts. I figured out what BMI was, and when I got to Blue Note, I filled out the contracts they had for composers. The original tunes were licensed to BMI. You weren't making money off of the music then, but at least it was out there and protected. And if eventually there were royalties, you would see a piece of them."[75]

Hard bop musicians who took control of their business affairs had more freedom. Gryce, who self-published, resented record companies taking 50 percent of an artist's publishing royalties for preparing the forms. Gryce established Melotone Music Incorporated, in the mid-1950s with Benny Golson, and they affiliated with BMI to handle the publishing rights and royalties for their compositions. The attorney who helped Gryce incorporate was William Kunstler.[76]

But in most cases, hard bop musicians weren't well versed in such matters. "In those days, the option musicians had to form their own companies wasn't so well known or sought after," Sonny Rollins said. "Every time you recorded, the record company would automatically take your music and put it into their record company's publishing company. No one was really aware of that. Gigi Gryce was one of the first who tried to change that, tried to get musicians to take care of their own music. I didn't know anything about publishing and that stuff. Prestige would publish my music and take 50 percent in royalties."[77]

Little by little, musicians during this period began to realize that record companies were reaping a significant profit based on their efforts in exchange for a small amount of paperwork. "Early on, recording companies were routinely and expectedly claiming ownership of all recorded material," Golson said. "Eventually this just did not seem right, not equitable concerning any composer. Thus, Gigi Gryce, my partner at that time, and I ambitiously set out to change all of this. We set up our own publishing company and hired a Fifth Avenue legal firm to enforce our rightful pursuits and decisions. This made us very unpopular in the music business."[78]

Soon, Melotone began publishing other musicians' compositions. Eventually, other musicians set up their own micropublishing companies that often did little more than register a new song with the Library of Congress in Washington, D.C., hold on to those copyrights, and receive a two-cent statutory rate for each use.

Golson continued. "Later on, I hired Liberace's attorney, the fantastic and extremely talented Joel Strote, in Los Angeles, where I had moved in

1967 to work in film. I paid him quite a sum to go to New York and reclaim everything I had ever written. And did he ever! The time was epochal. Musicians had become tired of being used and taken complete advantage of by the insatiable and possessive tactics of the music industry and the companies that represented it."[79]

Changes in the record industry—both on the technological and business sides—allowed hard bop to take hold and grow in popularity among musicians and audiences. The ability to publish hard bop compositions, either on one's own or with a record company, meant that more original works were being recorded and properly credited. But as the number of jazz labels and jazz LPs grew, jazz artists were under increased pressure to deliver original works. To become more prolific, many jazz composers tapped into personal experiences and their struggles to overcome professional obstacles and racism. Silver, Rollins, Donaldson, Golson, and others drew upon their childhood, their ongoing experiences with their church and spirituality, and their dreams of equality and fairness. Their spiritual fervor only deepened with the acceleration of the civil rights movement, which would profoundly affect the sound of jazz in the second half of the 1950s.

7 Bias, Africa, and Spiritual Jazz

Sonny Rollins doesn't recall exactly how the riot started at New York's Benjamin Franklin High School on September 27, 1945. What he does remember vividly is the high level of tension in the largely Italian neighborhood on East 116th Street and Pleasant Avenue that fall. Rollins's junior high school class was the first to be sent to Franklin High in the fall of 1945—part of an early outreach program by progressive city officials determined to integrate the public school system.[1]

The high school's principal, Leonard Covello, was known for his "community-centered" educational vision that hailed the contributions of immigrants and respected their need to preserve their language and culture against the pressures of assimilation.[2] He had also made the integration of community and school a career mission, inviting students from all parts of the city—including blacks, Hispanics, Jews, and the children of immigrants—to attend Franklin High.[3] But the neighborhood, one of the most tight-knit Italian communities in the city, was caught off guard by Covello's progressive approach to integrated education. About sixty thousand Italian Americans lived there in 1940—in an area bounded on the south by East 96th Street and on the north by East 125th Street, from Madison Avenue to the East River.

In the fall of 1945, classes began at the all-boys Franklin High just after Labor Day. But as the neighborhood's Italians watched large numbers of black and Puerto Rican students arrive for school in the weeks that followed, worry turned to grumbles and then to open resentment. The school enrolled 1,162 students that fall—50 percent of them Italian-American and 30 percent of them black.[4]

"We were happy to go to Benjamin Franklin—it looked like a nice place," Rollins recalled. "I had no idea, and no one who I knew was aware, that our arrival was going to cause any kind of trouble. Some of my friends went to the High School of Music and Art and other specialized schools in New York for students who already knew what they wanted to do. My friends and I played jazz, but we were still just kids who were going to go through high school and then figure out what we wanted to do after that"[5]

Each night during those weeks in September, Italian-American students returned home and heard fearful parents complain aloud over dinner about the invasion of their neighborhood and the perceived threats, When Italian-American students left for school each day, they carried with them their parents' fears and anger, which grew more intense. Because school officials rarely heard much about the everyday social drama of high school students, they knew little about the escalating tensions between the Italian-American and black students. Toward the end of September, all that was needed to trigger a much larger physical confrontation was a bump, a shove, a remark, or a glare.

That event occurred on September 27, when an argument over a basketball in the high school gym spilled into the locker room. Although the coaches averted a melee, the groups arranged to fight after school. When school officials caught wind of the conflict, they took steps to ensure that black and Italian-American students left the school separately that afternoon and in an orderly fashion. But the school's best efforts weren't enough. Two blocks north of Franklin High, at a bus stop, a mob of Italian-American students caught up with black students and attacked them with sticks. Within ten minutes, the police arrived to break up the disturbance, but the damage had already been done. The next day, new racial incidents flared up. Black students who chased a white boy on 116th Street were stopped by the police, who arrested two of them for carrying weapons. Other black students from the same group were searched later in school and also arrested for carrying concealed weapons.[6]

Covello, the school's principal, tried to reach out to the community to tamp down the hostility and violence. But the neighborhood could do little after the fact, and grudges became entrenched. As newspapers reported on the "race riot" and published editorials, Mayor Fiorello LaGuardia asked the singer Frank Sinatra to speak to school's students.[7] On October 23—just weeks ahead of the release of Sinatra's short film *The House I Live In*, which featured a plot similar to the real-life drama that had unfolded in East Harlem that September—the singer traveled up to the school's auditorium to "lay it on the line, as the *Daily News* described his mission."

When Sinatra took the stage, he told the students that hate groups had sent "delegates and agents" to mingle among the teens and stir up racial prejudice. He told the students: "This country was built by many people of many creeds, so it can never be divided. . . . No kid is born and two days later says: 'I hate Jews or colored people.' He's got to be taught." The *Daily News* also reported that Sinatra insisted there are no discernible "biological differences between races." He asked the students to serve as "neighborhood emissaries of racial good will,"[8] and then he sang "Aren't You Glad You're You?"

"We didn't know we were going to be met with this kind of stuff when we first got to the school that September," Rollins said. "For us, we were just going to a nice new school. Of course, if I had thought it through, it did look as though we were invading their neighborhood. When Sinatra came, we were in the auditorium—all the kids. He was Italian, and everyone knew and loved him. Sinatra said, 'Don't fight, be friends, get along.' It was great. I was a Sinatra fan. Soon after, the Nat Cole Trio came to the school. Nat gave a similar speech and played and sang. In just two weeks, we had a chance to see two of the country's top entertainers. After they came, things changed. There was no more fighting. After that, I knew Italian people, and they knew black kids. Everyone got along. Only music can do this."[9]

In the events of that fall, Rollins experienced firsthand the racial tensions he had known only from the accounts of his grandmother, who in the 1920s was an admirer of Marcus Garvey. Rollins's grandmother had talked for years about the need for black self-determination and African repatriation. The seeds she had sewn at home about justice and an African homeland echoed in Rollins's mind as he matured as a jazz musician in the late 1940s and early 1950s. Rollins wasn't alone with these thoughts. For many black jazz musicians growing up in New York and other major cities, Africa held a mythic significance and appeal during the civil rights movement. Though the countries of Africa had long been controlled by colonial occupiers, European domination of the continent was easing by the 1950s as more nations pushed for independence. After World War II, more American magazines, newspapers, and television networks sent reporters to African countries, and stories and images depicting a peaceful people who loved music and dance turned up in publications, particularly those in America's black communities. These magazines confirmed what blacks had been taught for years in the homes of their parents—that Africa was a cultured homeland and that a permanent return to their countries of origin was always a possibility.

Hope for integration and civil rights in the United States may have grown brighter after Jackie Robinson and Larry Doby began playing for major league baseball teams in 1947 and President Truman ordered the army desegregated in 1948. But after the U.S. Supreme Court handed down its *Brown v. Board of Education* decision in 1954, rendering states' segregation laws unconstitutional, little changed on a local level, especially in the South. Many communities and institutions used loopholes and intimidation to avoid or delay integrating public facilities and institutions, determined to keep the status quo. As blacks attempted to claim the rights the Supreme Court had extended to them, they were often met with beatings and worse, making equality seem to impossible to achieve, and the African ideal became all the more appealing.

In the minds of a growing number of black jazz musicians, Africa represented a positive spiritual force, a place where fairness, respect, nature, justice, and culture were paramount; in America, by contrast, they experienced commercial pressures, racism, business trickery, and violence. Musicians such as Duke Ellington, Dizzy Gillespie, Sonny Rollins, Yusef Lateef, Buddy Collette, Randy Weston, Max Roach, John Coltrane, Mary Lou Williams, and many others began to incorporate their feelings about Africa, the Middle East, and the Caribbean into their music. To black jazz artists of the 1950s who were fully aware of their talent and self-worth, these areas of the world represented a spiritual oasis, free of the hostilities faced in America.

For some black jazz musicians, spiritual awakening had begun in the black church—where fairness, justice, and self-worth were common themes. For others, it was fostered at home by older family members and their friends who had been exposed to Marcus Garvey's Return to Africa movement in the 1920s and the separatism of the Black Muslim Movement in Detroit and Chicago in the 1930s. In the 1950s, images of heightened racial tensions and impending liberation of African nations from European rule created feelings of elation among many blacks. During this period, a new form of jazz emerged that was both spiritual and political, evoking expressions of protest, self-determination, and inner peace. Along the way, many highly influential jazz musicians found their own creative and intellectual liberation through these expressions, in effect leaving America culturally by integrating ancestral homelands into their music.

"Civil rights was very much at the heart of this shift," said Dan Morgenstern, a jazz historian and the former director of the Institute of Jazz Studies at Rutgers University. "The Newport Jazz Festival and other jazz gatherings played a major role in helping jazz musicians unify their thinking about civil rights and focus globally on places like Africa. What I found fascinating about these festivals is that musicians had an opportunity to get together and exchange ideas. In the days before cell phones, texting, e-mail, and all of the other communication technologies we take for granted today, musicians were largely isolated. They spent much of their time in clubs or touring but weren't together long enough to share their thoughts, experiences, or philosophies on a wide range of topics. It was fascinating to observe all of the musicians gathering in Newport and hugging each other and talking. You also had so many foreigners who were there and had access to backstage areas and could interact with the musicians. There were journalists from all over the world as well—from Europe, Japan, and South America. So jazz was becoming increasingly internationalized by the mid-1950s, particularly with the start of the State Department's global jazz tours. All of this external input had an enormous impact on black jazz musicians' consciousness and their spiritual awakening."[10]

JAZZ-AGE MOTIVATION

In the first half of the twentieth century, Africa was perceived as a promised land by many American blacks. Blacks who had migrated from rural areas of the South and the Caribbean to the North found a much harsher environment in their new communities than they had expected. The weather was bitter in winter, tenement conditions were cramped, and racism was still pervasive, albeit in subtler and less menacing ways than the places they had come from. They also found that the relaxed, polite customs of the rural South had little currency in the hustling industrial North. Blacks who had skills that white businesses needed found better jobs. Those who lacked connections at factories or the necessary skills to find such employment scrambled to find work in their own neighborhoods. In many cases, these opportunities included drug-peddling, numbers-running, and other forms of vice that worked against marriage and family unity.

After World War I, as black soldiers returned from Europe with stories of heroism and fair treatment by white residents of France, they rapidly grew to resent the denial of access to advantages and opportunities enjoyed by whites in the U.S., even in northern cities. Many disenchanted blacks in the early 1920s gravitated to the speeches and writings of Marcus Garvey, a Jamaican immigrant who argued passionately for self-determination and the return to Africa by American blacks seeking fairness and dignity.

Garvey had arrived in New York in 1916 from Jamaica, moved to Harlem,[11] and by 1917 set out on a speaking tour of American cities. He established in New York the first chapter outside Jamaica of the Universal Negro Improvement Association (UNIA) and African Communities

League. The UNIA's mission was to promote social, political, and economic freedom for blacks. Many blacks in northern cities connected immediately with the organization's call for blacks to take charge of their lives economically and return to Africa. Many of Garvey's followers felt trapped in America, and their migration from the rural South to the urban North years earlier had hardly been deliverance. Cities that experienced large influxes of blacks and the economic challenges that followed had responded by passing Jim Crow laws, meant to keep blacks and whites separate, and blacks disadvantaged. As blacks competed with whites for jobs in the South and the North, lynching and other forms of organized terror led to race riots in major cities in 1919.[12]

Garvey's message of self-determination, a return to Africa, and the unification of all black people worldwide resonated with many who found themselves economically powerless and spiritually lost. But Garvey's movement extended beyond self-motivation talks and writings to entrepreneurship. He founded the Black Star Line in June 1919 with the intent of buying ships to transport goods and, eventually, black passengers to Africa.[13] By August 1920, the UNIA had four million members, and a UNIA rally at New York's Madison Square Garden on the first day of that month attracted twenty-five thousand to hear Garvey speak.

On 135th Street and Lenox Avenue, just a few blocks from where Sonny Rollins's family settled after they emigrated from the West Indies, was a space once known as Speakers' Corner. There, street scholars would mount stepladders and talk about injustice and liberation. When Garvey arrived in New York, he began speaking there as well. Colin Grant writes, in *Negro with a Hat: The Rise and Fall of Marcus Garvey*, "Unexpectedly, [Garvey] found the Harlemites, especially the West Indians, twitching with pride and excitement as he spoke. Though the immigrant West Indians and native black Americans shared a much-prized possession in the shape of Harlem, a current of suspicion and competition lingered just beneath the surface. The Caribbean migrants' boldness stemmed from the fact that they did not recognize the lesson, learned by every African-American in the cradle, that the more distinguished jobs were off limit."[14]

For Harlem residents of Caribbean descent after World War I and in the early 1920s, Garvey was a bold motivating force in voice and in print. Garvey's training as a printer and his experience as a journalist enabled him to start a series of newspapers. He published the *Watchman* in Jamaica; *La Nacion* in Limon, Costa Rica; and *La Prensa* in Colon, Panama, and he was also involved with the *Bluefields Messenger* in Costa Rica. In New York, Garvey published the *Daily Negro*

Times in Harlem from 1922 to 1924.[15] But the most influential Garvey publication was the *Negro World*, published weekly in Harlem from 1918 to 1933. This newspaper played a crucial role in promoting black self-determination and the abolition of colonialism in Africa and the Caribbean.[16] Expectations of civil rights were folly, according to Garvey, and only repatriation and global black unity could provide black Americans with the pride, safety, and power they sought.

The *Negro World's* scope and influence widened when it included French and Spanish sections. Circulation, which varied over the years, was estimated at 200,000 at its highpoint. A single issue of the paper was likely to be left behind and read by many others in bars, barbershops, salons, and restaurants. Issues of the *Negro World* were generally ten to sixteen printed pages and typically featured a statement by Garvey on page one addressing "Fellowmen of the Negro Race" and was signed, "Your Obedient servant, Marcus Garvey, President General."[17] As Garvey wrote in the *Negro World* in October 1923: "The Universal Negro Improvement Association teaches our race self-help and self-reliance . . . but also all those things that contribute to human happiness and well-being. The disposition of the many to depend upon the other races for a kindly and sympathetic consideration of their needs, without making the effort to do for themselves, has been the race's standing disgrace by which we have been judged, and through which we have created the strongest prejudice against ourselves."[18]

Ultimately, Garvey's potent writings and speeches failed to motivate American blacks to relocate en masse to Africa in the 1920s. But whether or not such a wholesale migration occurred isn't important. What matters most is that Garvey gave millions of American blacks a new sense of self-esteem, and he raised a new level of consciousness about their treatment and rights. He also articulated what many blacks already knew and believed. Garvey's steady drumbeat of self-worth influenced a generation of Harlemites, particularly women, who formed the UNIA Women's Brigade in 1924. These women were the mothers and grandmothers of sons who needed a finer understanding of their dignity and pride. Sonny Rollins credits his grandmother for instilling in him a high level of self-confidence: "My grandmother had been a strong follower of Marcus Garvey and had served in several ancillary back-to-Africa movements," Rollins said. "When I was a boy, I went with her to many rallies in our Harlem neighborhood for a range of different causes. I remember one in the mid-thirties where we went to implore people to get involved in the early civil rights struggle. One of the slogans I remember on signs was

'Free Tom Mooney and the Scottsboro Boys,' in support of the union activist and the black teens wrongly jailed in Alabama.

"In my grandmother's heart, she wanted to get some kind of justice for black people. I loved my mother and father, but kids seem to have a special thing for their grandmothers, and that was true of me. My grandmother was fearless. Fortunately, I began getting successful in my musical career before she passed away, so she had a chance to see that I didn't turn out to be a bum, that her strength and resolve made a difference for the next generation. What my grandmother taught me was to always fight for justice and never back down. Interestingly, Miles Davis told me his father was a Garveyite."[19]

West African countries—depicted in the black press as a place where readers would feel at home—loomed large as a haven, particularly in the 1950s. For some jazz writers, this spiritual connection made perfect sense. Quite a few jazz writers were particularly sensitive to injustice and the struggle to be treated as an equal and a valued member of society. They had faced their own share of beatings and torment in schools and neighborhoods. "As a Jew who grew up in a Boston neighborhood that was highly anti-Semitic, we knew all about yearning for a homeland that could protect us," said the jazz writer Nat Hentoff. "When I was a kid we collected coins for Palestine, which became Israel. So I know firsthand that there's a thrust of self-confidence and comfort that comes with knowing you have roots, that you're from someplace dating back centuries and that you always have the option of going there to live if things become impossible here. There's an inescapable dread that you're not wanted. Many blacks facing prejudice here in the 1950s yearned for the same thing—a haven where they no longer felt subliminal."[20]

THE LURE OF AFRICA

Marcus Garvey's deportation in the late 1920s created a vacuum and opened an opportunity for the Nation of Islam (NOI). Founded in 1930 in Detroit by Wali Fard Muhammad, a Saudi Arabian immigrant, the NOI was leveraged and expanded by Elijah Muhammad in the 1940s. The NOI promoted Pan-Africanism globally—arguing that blacks in America weren't really a part of the American experience and never would be. Instead, the NOI believed that blacks throughout the world needed to unite, and that Afrocentricity should become the cultural basis for blacks' view of themselves and their art.[21]

In the 1920s Detroit experienced enormous growth with the arrival of thousands of blacks from the South, seeking employment and escaping injustice and the ever-present threat of violence. Detroit's automobile industry was expanding, along with related rubber, glass, steel, and auto-parts businesses, and all were in need of labor. But after the stock market crash in 1929 and cascading bank failures through 1933, black unemployment soared. During this period, the Nation of Islam replaced Garveyism as one of the most influential political-action groups in black communities, particularly in Detroit and Chicago. After World War II, when the economy tightened with the return of servicemen seeking employment, racial tensions increased. But blacks who embraced Islam weren't a monolithic group. Among the Islamic sects was Ahmadiyya Jama'at, which believed that by modernizing many of Islam's customs, practices, and ceremonies and by adopting aspects of Western culture, they could improve Islam's image and convince potential converts that being Muslim and modern was possible.[22] In the 1950s, the Ahmadiyya movement attracted a number of black jazz musicians,[23] including Sahib Shihab, Yusef Lateef, Ahmad Jamal, Art Blakey, and McCoy Tyner.[24]

Yusef Lateef was born William Emanuel Huddleston in Chattanooga, Tennessee, but moved with his family to Detroit in 1925. "My embrace of Islam came about in 1946 while I was working with the Wally Hayes Band in a club on the west side of Chicago," Lateef wrote in his autobiography. "One night a trumpet player named Talib Dawud sat-in with us. He told me that he was an itinerant musician and that he was practicing Islam as a member of the Ahmadiyya Movement. . . . I expressed an interest in learning more about it. Reading about another religion was nothing new for me because from a very early age, I was interested in religions and the concept of God. My understanding of Islam at the time was that God could be an earthly helper, and that He was alive and He speaks to those He chooses. It was clear to me that Islam, through prayer and doing good deeds, could direct one's life in a proper way."[25] After his conversion, Lateef found himself striving for spiritual development. "My music, like my religion, is supposed to take you from this life and into the next. I believe this and try to express that belief in my music."[26]

JUSTICE AS GOSPEL

The term *black church* has come to mean the political and social power of American black religious institutions. In truth, however, there is no such all-encompassing umbrella institution. Instead, there are seven independent black-controlled denominations that share a religious worldview, which originally took into account congregants' African heritage and conversion to Christianity after slavery. Through religion, the black church created a distinct culture that cut across denominational lines and ran in line with the broader American culture.[27]

Since the nineteenth century, the black church has been the paramount institution in black communities, playing a significant role in congregants' political, economic, educational, and social lives. In urban communities of the North, as had been the case in rural areas of the South, it has served as a cultural force and a collective conscience, stressing right from wrong and standards of behavior, especially in regard to how blacks treated one another. The church's stake in the civil rights movement deepened in 1951, when Oliver Leon Brown, an assistant pastor at St. Mark's AME Church in Topeka, Kansas, and twelve other plaintiffs, aided by the NAACP Legal Defense Fund, sued the state board of education on behalf of his nine-year-old daughter, Linda Brown, and other black children in an effort to desegregate the public schools. The U.S. District Court decided in favor of the local board of education. But the Supreme Court agreed to hear the case, and in 1954 agreed to review the decision. That year, the court found separate but equal public facilities and services unconstitutional. The Supreme Court's decision gave the civil rights movement and the black church enormous momentum. In 1955, the Reverend Martin Luther King Jr. began a yearlong boycott of the Montgomery, Alabama, transit system for violating the Supreme Court's decision. Black churchwomen in Montgomery played a crucial role in the boycott, until segregationist rules and laws were abolished.[28]

The black church has also served as a community cultural center where oratory and music have played essential roles. The black congregations have always prized dynamic preaching and impassioned singing as fundamental to illustrating and celebrating the black experience in America. In the early days of the black church, worship services commonly featured the spontaneous creation of spirituals during the preaching, as members of the congregation called out in response to the preacher's sermon. Little by little, this exchange between authority and audience became a song. Eventually, a shift occurred in the performance of spirituals, from an expression of the collective to the showcasing of individual soloists and ensembles.[29]

Gospel, in contrast, was an urban form more relevant to the needs of common people in rapidly growing cities. Gospel songs grew out of revival meetings that were held in huge temporary tents erected in urban settings by touring evangelists. Some in the black church complained that gospel was little more than blues and jazz disguised as spirituals. Certainly, the blues-like gospel music of Thomas A. Dorsey, the so-called Father of Gospel, was heavily influenced by the music emerging in the cities. When gospel first appeared in black churches, it was not immediately accepted. It differed, moreover, from denomination to denomination. For example, the Holiness-Pentecostal gospel songs featured a prompted "shout," an individual's emotional testimony of sanctification. By contrast, the tradition in black Methodist churches featured the minister's reading of a stanza or two of a hymn and then asking the congregation to stand and sing with the choir.[30]

Ultimately, music performed in the black churches was a recruiting tool—a way to attract and hold congregants, both young and old, and influence their spiritual development, morality, and sense of justice. As music became a means of upward mobility and even celebrity with the rise of radio and the recording industry in the 1920s, the black church became a master class for future instrumental and vocal talent, further enhancing the institution's status and role in the black community.

The music of the black church—from gospel singing to call-and-response exchanges between sections of a congregation—played a significant role in the development of jazz and had enormous influence on musicians. "Charles Mingus and I were talking once, and he said his mother and father went to different churches," Nat Hentoff said. "One was a Roman Catholic black church. The other was a Pentecostal Holiness church. Mingus said the Holiness church was the one that excited him. There was a call-and-response between the preacher and the congregation that became one of the strongest elements of the jazz idiom. This came from Africa, Mingus said. Preachers were responding to the audience and the audience was responding to them."[31]

Horace Silver was deeply involved in the Catholic Church, an experience that had a lasting impact on his music. "I was raised a Catholic because my dad was a Catholic," Silver said in his autobiography. "I remained in the church until I was in my mid-twenties, when I became involved in the study of metaphysics and Spiritualism. The Catholic religion didn't seem to have the answers to a lot of spiritual questions that I was asking myself. I became and still am a dabbler when it comes to religion. I investigate as many religious concepts as I can, use what I can accept from each, and discard the rest. My mother was a Methodist. I attended her church occasionally and enjoyed the black gospel singing."[32]

JAZZ EMBRACES SPIRITUALISM

The concept of a better life outside of the United States wasn't a new one for black jazz musicians. From the time they first toured Europe, between World War I and World War II, black artists were exposed to white societies with differing racial histories. One of the first black jazz bands to undertake an extensive tour of Europe was Will Marion Cook's Southern Syncopated Orchestra. Cook had been a member of James Reese Europe's Clef Club Orchestra in New York, which had performed at Carnegie Hall in 1912, exposing a white cosmopolitan audience to black band music for the first time. Cook's band departed for England in the spring of 1919 and spent three years in Europe.[33] The young saxophonist Sidney Bechet, who played in Cook's band and remained behind when Cook returned to the United States, became one of America's earliest jazz expatriates.[34] During the 1920s and 1930s, a growing number of jazz bands toured Europe, a trend that continued after World War II. Some of the musicians chose to take up residence there for extended periods, relocating in Europe for reasons as varied as escaping the need to pay alimony and finding greater audience appreciation and racial respect.

In the United States before World War II, Africa was viewed largely as an exotic prop. The Cotton Club in the late 1920s, for example, sported a jungle motif to satisfy the expectations of white patrons who had traveled uptown to hear uninhibited music. White and black bands used Africa for novelty emphasis. Tiny Parham and His Musicians recorded "The Head Hunter's Dream (An African Fantasy)" and "Jungle Crawl" for the Victor's Bluebird label in 1928. There also was "Shakin' the African" (Don Redman) in 1931, "Harlem Congo" (Chick Webb) in 1937, and "African Jive" (Slim Gaillard) in 1941, to name a few. In the late 1920s Duke Ellington had developed what is known as his "jungle sound," using rich textural effects and harmonies that featured growling trumpets and trombones. The sultry, exotic sound could be heard in Ellington's "East St. Louis Toodle-Oo," "The Mooche," "Jungle Nights in Harlem," and "Echoes of the Jungle." For most other bands during these prewar years guided by white promoters, Africa was a cartoonish theme used to stir up images of the continent's wild and primitive nature while unfairly positioning jazz and black jazz musicians as comical, casting them as less threatening to white record buyers and audiences.

After World War II black and Hispanic jazz artists began to interpret African culture with more seriousness. Machito and His Afro Cubans had been leveraging Cuba's African cultural heritage in recordings since 1941, while Dizzy Gillespie, Charlie Parker, and Stan Kenton featured Afro-Cuban rhythms in the late 1940s. By the early 1950s black jazz musicians viewed ancestral African homelands as an inspiration and a means of expressing their feelings about American social injustice and the slow progress of the civil rights movement. As jazz in the late 1940s and early 1950s became the music of individualists rather than the collective, the music reflected the new social and political consciousness of artists and composers. One of the first postwar jazz compositions to make a sociopolitical statement about Africa was Sonny Rollins's "Airegin," which was Nigeria spelled backward.

"Back in the early 1950s I was going through an issue of *Life* magazine at a barbershop or someplace like that and came across a photo of Nigerians dancing in their traditional costumes," Sonny Rollins said.[35] "To me, those people were struggling for their dignity. When Miles [Davis] called me in June 1954 to play on a Prestige record date, which eventually was released as *Bags' Groove*, he asked me to bring along some original songs. One was a tune I hadn't yet finished. But Miles needed it for the session and wanted to put it in there. At that time, I was a recording neophyte, and the idea of Miles's using my compositions was a big thing for me. I was a composer but hadn't had a track record yet in the recording studio. So I didn't really know too much about how it worked. In this case I was writing a song off the top of my head, and I didn't want to do that. I wanted to make it complete, like the rest of my songs, composing at a leisurely pace. These things take thought and time. But that was how it was that day. There was time pressure.

"As I struggled to complete this new song in the studio, Miles took it and contributed the last four bars. He probably should have been the song's co-composer. Even though the song was finished in the studio, I already had the title in mind. When the producer asked for the name, I told him 'Airegin.' No one asked me what the word meant. They probably figured it was the name of someone I knew. Miles probably assumed that, too. But if Miles had known it was Nigeria spelled backward, I'm sure he would have been sympathetic and said, 'Oh, cool.'

"Why did I spell Nigeria backward? I guess it might have been too controversial to call a song *Nigeria* at the time. Perhaps that would have been too blunt and too blatant. Perhaps I wanted to make my message incomprehensible to white-owned record companies. I don't recall. But spelling Nigeria backward was an act of incredible subtlety. *Airegin?* Who, what—what's that? Eventually those in the know figured it out.

"When we were done recording, I felt I had tossed my hat into the struggle. To me, 'Airegin' was a consequential thing. I thought that it was a chance to instill racial pride in my people. With my usual trickery, I had spelled Nigeria backward. Seeing that photo in *Life* was deeply moving and important for me. I thought it would be an excellent way to instill civil rights and pride in blacks who listened to my music. I'm thinking, this is something to be proud of, because the American history of black people was nothing to be proud of in terms of treatment and lack of humanity. The photo of the dancers instilled in me a certain pride. The dancing was happening in Nigeria, where many American blacks had come from.

"Was there solidarity among musicians about the political statement that the song's title made? I don't know if solidarity among musicians is an oxymoron or not [*laughs*]. I know how tenuous jazz musicians' livelihoods are. It's hard to be a musician whose livelihood depends on not making waves. Many guys were beholden to their managers and agents, and they didn't want to compromise that. Hey, it's controversial enough playing jazz.

"Most people [in jazz] knew I was an activist. I had a reputation among promoters and other musicians for being someone who wasn't compliant. I already had some run-ins over working conditions and royalties. But given my background—with my activist grandmother and what had happened at Benjamin Franklin High School—I felt that I was contributing something to the struggle."

Rollins's self-confidence and political views also played a role in the distinctive sound of his tenor saxophone and music, which encouraged other jazz musicians to take similar creative risks. "I never thought to myself, 'Gee, am I going to be good enough?'" Rollins said. " I always knew I was going to be significant and didn't care or worry about being compliant or what was going on in the music. My grandmother, with her Garveyism, instilled that in me. When I took my occasional sabbaticals from performing and recording jazz, other musicians said, 'Well, gee, man, you can't get away from the music business like that. You'll lose your status and foothold.' But I never thought about that. I always did what I had to do. Great musicians had invited me to play and record with them when I was very young, in the late forties, so I was secure that I had enough there that I could go away and return better than when I left."

Growing up with Garveyism also instilled in Rollins a finer sense of self and justice as well as outrage when fairness was compromised. "Many people are unaware that I was blackballed by promoters in the fifties because of my attitude and comments about conditions for jazz musicians," he said. "I was able to survive that period knowing I had great mentors. People said, 'Why are they blackballing you?' There was no answer that made sense. I knew I had a certain power in my music. When I wrote 'Airegin,' I hoped that greater consciousness for equality and freedom would be raised."

Other jazz musicians adapted the music of the Middle East to express their feelings and disapproval of American segregation. In October 1957, Yusef Lateef recorded *Jazz and the Sounds of Nature* and *Prayer to the East* for Savoy, albums that reflected his spiritual feelings and religious conversion. "After I embraced Islam in 1948, my goal was to try to be a good person," Lateef said. "When you're good to mankind, it has an effect on whatever you do. I was introduced to Eastern culture in the early 1950s, when I lived in Detroit. I would go to the local public library and spend hours listening to the music of different countries. This broadened my thinking and made me realize that there were many different approaches to music than the ones we were using here. The librarian helped me a great deal to research Indian flute players and other forms of music from around the world. Hearing that music was a complete change for me."[36]

Lateef's extensive listening to recordings of music from different cultures freed him creatively to explore new approaches on his saxophone. "I began playing more spiritual music in the early 1950s, when I tried to advance my concept of music," he said. "I was drawn to the music of Eastern culture but Western culture, too, like Stockhausen, Russian composers, even pygmy musicians of the rain forest. Exploring this music took effort and was a challenge, but it was exciting. The purpose was to seek knowledge."

Lateef also had interactions with John Coltrane, who was beginning a similar artistic and spiritual Afro-centric journey. "John and I were friends. Every time we'd meet, John would ask, 'What are you doing now with your music?' We were both trying to develop our spiritual concepts, and we shared ideas—though I didn't hear myself in John's playing later. We each had developed our own voice and views, just as Coleman Hawkins and Lester Young did. My objective was to share whatever I had developed with others. I remember when I moved to New York in 1960, I went by John's apartment on 103d Street. As I approached the door, I heard him practicing. I rang the bell, and he welcomed me in. I took a seat, and he started to practice again. I listened for fifteen or twenty minutes before getting up to tell him that I was leaving. I went home and started to practice with John's intensity. John developed quite a practice habit that helped him find ways to learn more about himself. I began to do the same."

Lateef came to realize that developing a more spiritual approach to jazz was an enormous undertaking. "John was very introspective. I remember in the late 1950s, when critics began to call his arpeggios 'sheets of sound,' I knew where that was coming from. When I'd visit John uptown, he had a harp in his apartment that his wife Naima had bought for him. By pressing the pedals, you could create a glissando that was like sheets of sound. John told me he was interpreting that harp sound on the tenor saxophone and was fascinated by how different those runs sounded on the saxophone compared with the harp. He integrated the harp's sound into his music. The harp was a spiritual instrument in a religious sense. This music we expressed was part curiosity but also a reaction to what was happening. You couldn't avoid the civil rights movement back then. The scenes were in the newspapers and on TV all the time. Of course I was sympathetic with anyone who suffered. My music was an expression of my feelings toward life and toward that struggle."

Africa, for jazz musicians, wasn't a place to be viewed and interpreted only from afar. In May 1956 Louis Armstrong made a trip to the British Gold Coast Colony that became independent Ghana a year later. Edward R. Murrow, the producer of CBS's *See It Now,* Arranged the trip. The point was to collect footage for a CBS documentary called *Satchmo the Great.* Murrow's mission was to "send Armstrong to Africa, the land of his ancestors, and film the result."[37]

The U.S. government in the 1950s was also quick to recognize the value of sending jazz musicians abroad. Willis Conover's Voice of America jazz broadcasts to countries behind the Iron Curtain were successfully and subversively advancing democracy's cause in oppressed countries. In the spring of 1956 the State Department began sending jazz musicians on international concert tours as ambassadors of democracy. The irony, of course, is that the black jazz musicians dispatched to South America, Eastern Europe, and other parts of the world were hardly enjoying equal rights at home, despite the Supreme Court's *Brown v. Board of Education* decision.

In 1957 Armstrong was asked by the State Department to embark on a fall tour of the Soviet Union and South America. But after the Arkansas governor Orval Faubus summoned the state's National Guard on September 2, 1957, to prevent the integration of Little Rock's Central High School and President Eisenhower delayed in ordering the desegregation, Armstrong canceled his concert trip. Armstrong found Eisenhower's lack of outrage and initial indecision reprehensible. Armstrong said to a reporter, "It's getting almost so bad a colored man hasn't got any country." He called Governor Faubus "an uneducated plow-boy" and denounced Eisenhower as "two-faced" on civil rights and lacking "guts." Uncharacteristically enraged, he said he would not tour the Soviet Union for the State Department, adding, "The way they are treating my people in the South, the Government can go to hell."[38]

Armstrong's response was particularly pointed for a leading entertainer whose perennially upbeat stage persona had come to symbolize self-restraint, good humor, and moderation. For many jazz musicians, however, Armstrong's blunt and vociferous response to Faubus's action and Eisenhower's hesitation was a sign. Armstrong's comments held a message for black musicians who had long faced indignities while touring cities all over the country and for their white musician advocates who had watched with disgust. If a jazz giant like Armstrong could risk everything by speaking out on the lumbering pace of desegregation and even go so far as to insult the president, many black musicians wondered, why weren't they doing more?

In February 1958, Sonny Rollins recorded *Freedom Suite.* "Little Rock wasn't a direct influence for me but it was there, like everything else," Rollins said. "Racial injustices were constant throughout the 1950s. Naively, I thought I'd be able to live anyplace—maybe not on New York's Park Avenue, because I couldn't afford it. But I had thought black people had achieved a little more freedom. But this wasn't the case. So *Freedom Suite* really comes from all of these things, not just one incident, and it comes to a head for me by early 1958."[39]

Unlike Billie Holiday's brazen "Strange Fruit" in 1939, which set off no immediate swell of jazz songs with protest themes and titles, *Freedom Suite* encouraged other jazz musicians to make their own political statements. Protest recordings that followed on the heels of Rollins's album included Charles Mingus's "Fables of Faubus" (1959), the pianist Don Shirley's recording of "Freedom" (1960), Mingus's "Cry for Freedom" (1960) and Max Roach's album *We Insist! Freedom Now Suite* (1960). "I had recorded 'The House I Live In' in 1956 on *Plays for Bird* with those same progressive thoughts in mind," Rollins said. "I don't know if *Freedom Suite* inspired other jazz musicians. If it did, I'm extremely humbled. *Freedom Suite* wasn't slapped together as some have suggested. It may have been pieced together from multiple takes, but it was a completed piece intellectually on my part. I do think, however, that *Freedom Suite* gave Max Roach [*Freedom Suite*'s drummer] the strength to compose his *We Insist! Freedom Now.*"[40]

When Roach recorded *We Insist!* for Candid Records in August 1960, the album's producer was Nat Hentoff. "Sometime in 1960, someone told me that Max was performing *We Insist!* at Art D'Lugoff's Village Gate in

New York," said Hentoff, who was head of A&R at Candid Records at the time. "So I went to see the performance for myself. I was thunderstruck. Afterward, I called Max to see if he'd record it for Candid, with the assumption that my call would be futile. I figured that a major label already had contracted with him for the work. When Max came to the phone, I asked him to record *We Insist!* and waited for the bad news. But on the other end of the line there was this sardonic silence. No one had called, he said. I asked if he wanted to record it. He said, 'Sure.'

"On the day of the recording, Max brought in Coleman Hawkins, who had always had big ears for new music. He was on top of every music trend. Hawk had been just as awed as I was by what we had heard. At once point Hawkins said to Max, 'Did you write this?' in disbelief. As with Duke Ellington's premiere of *Black, Brown and Beige,* I was uplifted by Max's music at New York's Nola Studios that day. It was spiritual and stunning. It was music, but it was more than music. There was self-identification, both collective and individual. Max told me that his motivation for recording the album had been the lunch-counter sit-ins in Greensboro, North Carolina, in February 1960. For years since *Brown v. Board of Education,* there had been virtually no change in the progression of desegregation. Finally, with the sit-ins, here was a sense that there could be a revolution.

"As the recording went on, you had a sense in the studio that they were in the music all the way—vocalist Abbey Lincoln being a prime example. There was a political overlay. It was a protest. The musicians were saying, 'We stand with these freedom riders, we're with the lunch-counter sit-ins.' As we recorded, it was evident that the musicians were on a spiritual, political high. It was a celebration and an insistence of their identities as blacks in their country and that they were no longer accepting what it had been to be black here. It was an artistic breakthrough, and they were actively proud of who they were despite the American culture at the time telling them who they were supposed to be and how they were supposed to act. Afterward, when we found out that *We Insist* was banned in South Africa, we were very pleased."[41]

The civil rights movement in the United States in the late 1950s coincided with the winning of independence by a succession of former colonies in Africa, including Ghana (1957) and Guinea (1958), followed by seventeen additional nations in 1960. This independence movement, coupled with the U.S. civil rights struggle, made Africa even more appealing to many black jazz musicians as a continent of hope and a homeland of potential refuge. Recorded tracks and albums by many jazz artists during this period reflect on the wave of national independence: Randy Weston's "Zulu" (1955), Buddy Collette's *Tanganyika*

Jazz (1956), Milt Jackson's "Ghana" (1957), Machito's *Kenya: Afro-Cuban Jazz* (1957), Wilber Harden's *Jazz Way Out* (1958), Sun Ra's "Africa" (1958), and Jackie McLean's "Appointment in Ghana" (1960).

In April 1957 John Coltrane recorded *Dakar,* the first of many recordings that reflected his own spiritual identification with Africa. (Dakar is the capital of Senegal.) But the big creative turning point in his feelings toward Africa was *Africa Brass.* Recorded for Impulse in May and June of 1961, *Africa Brass* was a pure cultural embrace of Africa and African music. On the album, Coltrane elevated the spiritual concept to a new level, devoting an entire side of the album to his impressions and feelings toward the continent. The sessions were recorded at the Englewood Cliffs, New Jersey, studio of the engineer Rudy Van Gelder, and he and the producer Creed Taylor gave Coltrane free rein to use the studio not only as a workshop but also as rehearsal space, something Van Gelder customarily didn't allow given his relentless recording schedule.[42]

"After hearing Coltrane at the Village Vanguard, I called him to see if he was willing to switch labels, from Atlantic to Impulse, which I had just started at ABC-Paramount," Taylor recalled. "John said he was, that he was ready to move up. As soon as he signed, we met at my office at ABC with saxophonist Eric Dolphy. Oliver Nelson was supposed to arrange the album but he couldn't do it because of a schedule conflict. So Eric took on the assignment. John wanted the album to have an African theme. I suggested adding the brass concept. All of John's albums up until that point had featured just a rhythm section. Brass would add dimension and texture. He agreed. Eric took the concept a step further and arranged the orchestra to depict wailing humanity, that sort of thing. Wailing required a special kind of instrumentation that captured sadness and blues. Eric did this brilliantly."

Taylor also realized that something artistically special was taking place, since the album's lengthy tracks and repeated riffs made this recording different from any Taylor had produced in the past. "I gave John and Eric as much studio time as they needed," he said. "The recording was pretty much a Coltrane show, and I sensed it was going to be a monumental recording. I finished editing the album with John after I had switched jobs and become the head jazz producer at Verve in 1961. John and I were in my new office talking about how the final version should sound and the things he wanted in there. John wanted to include the tribal sound effects of Africa. Eric [Dolphy] thought it should be the other way around. He thought Coltrane had gone too far with the effects. But I agreed with John, that all of the African percussive effects were really great and added drama and texture. In retrospect, I would have liked to have heard more of Eric Dolphy's bass-clarinet solos. But the date didn't require much of my input. What was I going to say anyway? 'John, uh, let's cut back on those long solos.' That was what John was about. There was a religious quality about him, and you either recorded John that way or you didn't."

During the sixties, black jazz artists would continue to be inspired by Africa and their African heritage. A partial list includes Randy Weston (*Uhuru Afrika*, 1960), Cannonball Adderley (*African Waltz*, 1961), Art Blakey (*Afrique* and *The Freedom Rider*, 1961), Oliver Nelson (*Afro-American Sketches*, 1961), A. K. Salim (*Afro Soul Drum Orgy*, 1964), and Wayne Shorter (*Juju*, 1964). In 1967 Weston, a pianist, moved to Morocco and traveled throughout the continent. "My whole life, I have been reading about and immersing myself in Africa," Weston wrote in his autobiography. "I have been forever fascinated by and deeply interested in the history of Africa, the current problems of Africa, the triumphs of the African people, the political situation in Africa. . . . and that interest came long before I made my first trip there. I was always in tune with Africa, and I was always upset about the separation of our people, the separation of those people who are considered part of the African diaspora from the Motherland itself."[43]

Weston's passion for Africa began with his parents. "My big awakening to Africa came as a result of my mother and father," Weston said. "Our entire neighborhood in Brooklyn was Pan-African. Many of the people who were here never felt they had left. I visited Africa for the first time in 1961, when I traveled to Nigeria. I instantly felt completely at home. I didn't speak the language, but the spirit of the continent was in the sky. I felt in my heart that I had never left. African Americans have always been a freedom-loving people, and it goes back to the music. The music is a spiritual force and a healing force. My father said to me, 'You have to go back to when Africa was great. You never hear anything about the African empires.' He told me to look for truth, which is what I've tried to do as a musician all my life. I wanted to find out why I played the way I played, so I went to Africa and discovered that I had never left the continent, spiritually. If I had been born in Canada, I would still want to return to my ancestral home because my relatives were torn from there during slavery. For me, Africa is about a spirit, like the music. Any people that has been oppressed feels this. When you feel oppressed because of the way you look, that's doubly upsetting. I consider myself an African born in America, but I'm a human being first. When I play music, I see all the colors of the rainbow."[44]

But if Africa played such a dominant role in spiritual development and America offered so little, why didn't John Coltrane, Yusef Lateef, Art Blakey, and other black jazz musicians relocate to Africa, the way Randy Weston did? In all likelihood, their travels and readings had exposed them to what was happening in other cultures, and they saw their limitations. Deep down, many probably decided against relocating to Africa because the move would have been hard on their families, and they would have been unable to earn a sufficient living performing jazz there. Many may have realized, too, that a good number of newly independent African countries suffered from their own economic and political problems. A large percentage were ruled by dictators who had either seized power or were put in charge by Western nations eager to retain control over valuable natural resources and cheap labor. The suppression of dissent, the perpetual violence against black citizens and exploitation of minority clans certainly would have made optimism, hope, and creativity more difficult.

Clarinetist Garvin Bushell offered such a sentiment when talking to writer Bill Moody in *The Jazz Exiles:* "I thought about [moving to Africa], but after I'd been there, I said with all the segregation and prejudice we have [in America], this is home and I feel better because there are more of my people here. Although [Africans] are black people, we don't understand each other. We don't relate to each other at all except for skin color. The background, the culture, the attitude, the philosophy is altogether different. I've been all over Africa from top to bottom, including South Africa, 49,000 miles for the State Department. I remember when we were leaving Nairobi, an East African waitress sarcastically asked, 'How does it feel going back to your big, wonderful, strong country?' I said, 'Baby, it feels just fine."[45]

The artistic shift toward a more spiritual form of jazz in the late 1950s was a product of many social and political pressures and forces. The most influential factors were musicians' personal experiences with the black church and a range of Pan-African movements as well as the frustratingly slow pace of civil rights and desegregation. Compounding the sense of injustice among black musicians was a growing sense of isolation and detachment from American mainstream culture and commerce. With the rise of R&B and rock and roll in the second half of the 1950s and their enormous commercial appeal, jazz grew increasingly introspective and abstract. As more black jazz artists looked to Africa and the Far East for rhythmic and compositional inspiration, young musicians in Britain who had grown up listening to records by America's blues and early rock-and-roll artists began eyeing the U.S. market. Within a few years, jazz would have to change again if it wanted to survive and thrive.

8 Invasion and Jazz-Pop

On the evening of August 15, 1965, the jazz vocalist Carol Sloane climbed into a car driven by her friend Bob Bonis, and they headed out to New York's Shea Stadium. Bonis was the Beatles' American tour manager, and he had prized dugout seats for the British band's much-heralded outdoor concert. When the concert began, Bonis took his place on the field just below the stage behind Ringo, while beefy members of the security detail stood behind the other members of the Fab Four. The rule was that if fans jumped onto the field and rushed the stage, the four Beatles were to drop their instruments and jump off the back and into the arms of the security team. During the last tour, in the summer of 1964, Bonis had to catch Ringo several times when mobs of teenage girls pressed forward.[1]

Alone and settled into her dugout seat, Sloane watched the stadium fill with more than fifty-five thousand fans. She also noticed something else. "There was this steady primal screech from thousands of kids that just wouldn't end," she said. "As a jazz singer, I became nauseous. I could see the writing on the wall with the Beatles. The kids had been drifting away from jazz for years. But by this concert in 1965, they were completely gone, and I knew they were never coming back. You could see it. You could hear it."

In the years that followed, Sloane had to work harder to find gigs and record dates as the Beatles and a new form of pop-rock emerged and dominated radio stations and record stores. "I'm convinced that much of jazz's decline was directly a result of the Beatles and other rock groups," she said. "The record companies just didn't put any promotion behind jazz records by instrumentalists any more. And for a singer, it was doubly hard to get a recording gig. I still had a great time, though. In the late 1960s I was on the *Tonight Show Starring Johnny Carson* quite a bit. I also was singing regularly at San Francisco's Hungry I and at Mister Kelly's in Chicago. I was very lucky to have been able to sing at these wonderful venues. But the club scene had changed."

The trend by teens to pop-rock had started in the 1950s with the rise of small record labels and independent radio. By 1960 baby boomers—7.4 million of them—were turning thirteen and fourteen years old and gravitating toward music that more closely reflected their anxieties, aspirations and sexuality. In the years that followed, about four million boomers would become teens annually through 1970.[2] High-energy rock and roll that was unleashed in 1955 and 1956 by Little Richard, Chuck Berry, Elvis Presley, and others, had mushroomed into a national craze by the late 1950s. Radio and 45-rpms became increasingly popular and personal, and competition among record labels increased.

To ensure their singles would be played repeatedly on the radio in the 1950s, record companies and their agents commonly plied disc jockeys with cash and gifts. Throughout the decade, disc jockeys most often decided which records were played on the air, how often, and at what time of day. With a little imagination, influential disc jockeys in major markets could add $50,000 to $150,000 to their salaries in payoffs.[3] Soon, disc jockeys came to expect sizable payoffs and favors when record company promoters handed them new 45-rpm singles. After Berry Gordy formed Tamla Records in 1959 and Motown in 1960, disc jockeys routinely demanded cash and favors from him for airplay. At one point, according to Berry, a white Detroit disc jockey who was moving from one home to another agreed to play Motown's records if some "big black bucks" could help him move his furniture. Gordy sent his songwriting team of Brian Holland, Lamont Dozier, and Edward Holland Jr. to do the heavy lifting.[4]

But by late 1959 the untaxed secret cash economy of the record and radio industries had caught the attention of the IRS and Congress. In November 1959 the House of Representatives opened formal hearings on record-company payoffs to disc jockeys, revealing what went on behind the scenes in the record and radio industries.[5] When the hearings were completed, in mid-1960, the House developed antipayola legislation, and the bill made its way through the Senate and then to the White House, where President Eisenhower signed it into law in September.[6] But by that time the legislation had been watered down and didn't exactly outlaw gifts, which would have hamstrung many other industries if all had to follow suit. The law merely said that stations needed to let the public know about any gifts and favors they received.[7] In addition, penalties for violation were comparatively insignificant, with the government's will to enforce the law all but nonexistent.[8] Before long, payola resumed under the guise of "independent promotion."[9]

But rock and roll's reputation took a beating. In the wake of the scandal and ASCAP's public charges that rock would not have been possible without payola[10]—a direct shot at its rival BMI, which had signed many of the genre's artists—rock was thought to be inherently corrupt, with radio in serious need of policing to prevent pay-for-play advances. Radio networks and individual stations realized they had to institute measures on their own to avoid the risk of runaway payola in the future. At stations, program directors replaced the disc jockeys in selecting which records to play, and playlists based on national sales determined what would be played and when. Once a week, after packages of 45-rpms from record company representatives reached the desk of a station program manager, the manager would meet with the staff and disc jockeys to decide the mix that would best attract and hold listeners and advertisers.[11]

In 1960, after the payola hearings, rock needed to clean up its act. The music industry did this by relying less on the blues and lyrics loaded with sexual innuendo, and more on songs with sweeter stories and catchier hooks to capture an ever-younger record-buying market. The songs that became national hits were increasingly less menacing and more innocent and endearing. Almost overnight, an entire industry emerged to write, produce, and even record hit songs of this pop-rock genre. Young songwriting teams like Jerry Leiber and Mike Stoller, Carole King and Gerry Goffin, Neil Sedaka and Howard Greenfield, Jeff Barry and Ellie Greenwich, Cynthia Weil and Barry Mann, and Burt Bacharach and Hal David did their work in New York's Brill Building—which some in the trade press called Teen Pan Alley—creating a new young American Songbook. Studio musicians also were being used more routinely and extensively in Los Angeles, Detroit, and New York to execute arrangements perfectly and provide innovative hooks.

"By 1961, the number of teens demanding rock 'n' roll in Southern California exploded, and radio stations there had to scramble to keep up with the demand," said Hal Blaine, a studio drummer in Los Angeles who recorded on many early pop-rock hits along with other musicians who became known informally in the Los Angeles recording studios as the Wrecking Crew. "The record companies quickly figured out what made a hit. You needed a dramatic song with lyrics that connected with teens and their lives. You also needed a good-looking group of young people to sing the songs so teens could relate to them and would demand cash from parents to buy records and attend their concerts. And then you needed skilled musicians behind the scenes who could add excitement and punch to the melody lines and background textures that would build the drama and stir teens' imaginations. That's where we [the Wrecking Crew] came in. Record companies in Hollywood called us to turn average songs into Top 40 hits."[12]

The first national hits to roll off this pop-rock assembly line were by girl groups like the Shirelles ("Will You Love Me Tomorrow") and the Crystals ("He's a Rebel"). Solo artists like Connie Francis, Brenda Lee, Little Eva, and others followed, along with teen idols like Frankie Avalon, Bobby Vee, Bobby Rydell, Chubby Checker, Paul Anka, and Marvin Gaye. It's no surprise that Motown's Berry Gordy modeled his Detroit company after an auto plant's assembly line, or that he groomed the label's black artists to appeal to white record buyers. To become a national hit in the new era, a song had to cross over and woo multiple markets at once.

From 1962 to 1964, *Billboard's* Hot 100 pop chart was dominated by pop-rock artists who crowded out traditional pop-jazz singers like Nat King Cole, Frank Sinatra, and Peggy Lee. For example, a random look at the week of August 3, 1963, Billboard's Top 10 featured the Tymes' "So Much in Love"; Little Stevie Wonder's "Fingertips (Part 1)"; Jan and Dean's "Surf City"; Elvis Presley's "(You're the) Devil in Disguise"; the Surfaris' "Wipe Out"; Peter, Paul and Mary's "Blowin' in the Wind"; the Essex's "Easier Said Than Done"; Lesley Gore's "Judy's Turn to Cry"; Rolf Harris's "Tie Me Kangaroo Down, Sport"; and Doris Troy's "Just One Look."

By the mid-1960s, the pop-rock market was so lucrative that many record companies shifted their resources away from less profitable divisions, like jazz. In the early rock era, the youth market increasingly viewed jazz as overly sophisticated and glum, played by musicians who tended to be puzzlingly temperamental and withdrawn. Jazz's market now was found in cities, among introspective intellectuals who seemed to revel in the music's rarified and exclusionary status. Jazz just wasn't connecting with large numbers of teens. By the early 1960s, a jazz album typically generated sales of fewer than five thousand copies. As a result, record companies limited the budgets for their production and promotion.[13]

Unlike teens of earlier generations, many in the early 1960s lived in houses, where they could escape their parents to listen to music. In their bedrooms, paneled basements, or cluttered attics, teens found the privacy they needed to play music on portable phonographs and develop their own tastes in music. As the audience for jazz declined, jazz artists explored different approaches, some with enormous creative success. Miles Davis, John

Coltrane, Wayne Shorter, Ornette Coleman, Eric Dolphy, and Andrew Hill were among the jazz innovators on the cutting edge in the early and mid-1960s.

But the shrinking marketplace for jazz forced a growing number of excellent jazz artists with families to take jobs with commercial orchestras at television networks and mood-music companies like Muzak. Those who continued to record had little choice but to explore pop-rock radio hits to remain relevant. This survivalist trend by jazz musicians began in earnest after the arrival of the Beatles and other English bands in 1964 and 1965—an invasion made possible by a realignment of the record industry nine years earlier.

CAPITOL CHANGES HANDS

The American music industry went through unprecedented changes in the 1950s. More licenses were granted to regional radio stations in markets that didn't have television, the number of independent record labels soared, and the rise of BMI as a home for R&B composers resulted in extraordinary competition. The stampede of new activity also broke the tight grip held by the four major record labels. With their control challenged, the four majors—Columbia, RCA, Decca, and Capitol—searched for new markets and partners. In addition to facing competitive pressures from radio and smaller record labels, the record industry had to compete with the growing popularity of television and color movies for consumers' dollars. To sustain profit levels, the four labels forged new distribution alliances with foreign record companies—particularly in Europe—where American pop artists were well received.

Exasperated by Britain EMI's slow adoption of the LP, Columbia, in 1953, severed its international licensing agreement with the British company in favor of a deal with Dutch Philips. RCA retained its international distribution agreement with EMI,[14] while Decca had an agreement in place that gave EMI ninety days to distribute its releases or Decca could pursue other foreign distribution arrangements.[15] Capitol, however, had no such global partner at the dawn of the LP era and needed one.

When Johnny Mercer co-founded Capitol Records in 1942, he did so with Buddy DeSylva, a movie producer, and Glenn Wallichs, who owned Music City, the largest record store in Los Angeles. The plan called for Mercer to be the creative force, DeSylva the financial muscle, and Wallichs the management, retail, and distribution whiz. Mercer's goal was to commit the label solely to pop music and songs written by the great

American composers, himself included. But in 1950 DeSylva died, and Mercer quickly found himself overloaded with recording and songwriting duties as the label grew. Day-to-day business and management matters had already been ceded to Wallichs when Capitol expanded in 1947.[16]

But Wallichs faced a new challenge with the rise of the 45-rpm and 33⅓-rpm record speeds. Though the 45-rpm at first was marketed exclusively to the at-home consumer, the lightweight, durable format quickly became a natural replacement for the 78-rpm in jukeboxes and at radio stations. The 33⅓-rpm LP, by contrast, was ideal for use at home, since it offered convenience, extended play, and improved fidelity. Wallichs hedged by embracing both formats.

Once the market accepted both new speeds, the next step by the major record labels was to sell American music abroad by means of foreign distribution relationships. But Capitol was slow to seek international partners. In 1954, when Wallichs finally traveled to London to meet with executives of Britain's EMI, he was taken by surprise. Instead of finding a partner willing to cut a distribution deal, he came face to face with a hungry suitor. EMI wasn't interested in teaming up with Capitol to press American records in Europe. The company wanted to buy the label outright and secure an American presence.

From EMI's standpoint, owning Capitol would give it several advantages over its European rivals. In addition to reaping profits globally from Capitol's roster of top-shelf pop artists—who at the time included Frank Sinatra and Nat King Cole—EMI also would be able to promote touring American artists in worldwide markets where it had a presence. At the same time, EMI would also have the option to launch British artists into the American marketplace. Wallichs had little choice but to accept EMI's purchase offer. The only issue was whether Capitol's major shareholders would be willing to go along with the acquisition.

Upon returning to the United States, Wallichs easily convinced a stretched-thin Mercer to sell his share of the company. DeSylva's estate also agreed to sell its stake. So in January 1955 EMI proposed to buy Capitol for $8.5 million.[17] Wallichs, in an announcement, said, "We feel that the new majority ownership will substantially increase Capitol's ability to operate effectively in the United States and the rest of the world. It will offer our artists a strong and well-organized distribution system and will make available important additions to Capitol's catalog from abroad with the result that we will become a more effective and expanding force in the record market."[18] Under the terms of the deal, Capitol's American senior management team would remain in place.[19]

In May 1955, with the deal finalized, Wallichs was named to EMI's board. In an effort to minimize artist defections at Capitol, Wallichs stressed the new concert component of the deal. "Such global coverage not only assures attractive royalties for the artist, but also builds a demand for highly paid personal performances."[20] Soon after the Capitol deal was finalized, Britain's EMI began building a new cylindrical office tower and state-of-the-art studios on Vine Street in Hollywood to match the technological prowess of its Abbey Road Studios in London. Capitol's annual report of 1955 quoted Wallichs: "The world-wide resources of EMI, as a majority shareholder, stand firmly behind Capitol's position as a major record label nationally and internationally."

For the next seven years, American Capitol had enormous success on the pop side reinventing the big-band sound for a generation of adults undergoing a midlife crisis. Sinatra, Cole, Peggy Lee, Dean Martin, and many other artists were repositioned in the LP era as swinging adults who hadn't lost their spark or charm. Although EMI remained true to its word and took a hands-off stance with its American management team, Capitol by the early 1960s clearly needed fresh blood in its recording studios. Frank Sinatra had departed to form his own label, Reprise, and Capitol's pop stalwarts were becoming all too predictable, raking the American Songbook for hits. In October 1962 Alan Livingston, the Capitol operations executive who had signed Sinatra to the label in 1954, was elevated to company president, with Wallichs assuming the title of board chairman.[21]

When Capitol's core jazz and pop stable began to age in the early 1960s, EMI started pressuring American Capitol executives to listen to Britain's young pop artists. The first hints came in packages of singles sent to Capitol in Los Angeles by EMI with "What think?" notes, floating the idea of their possible release in the United States. The response in Hollywood was usually indifference, and the contents of the packages were sent back with memos explaining that the recordings were not appropriate for the U.S. market. This pattern of suggestion and rejection became routine, probably because corporate executives in the States resented being told what to do by executives in a country that just fifteen years earlier needed American help defeating Germany in World War II.

By late 1962 the packages that EMI sent began to include singles by a new group called the Beatles. The group had been exciting audiences in Europe, and sales of its records in the U.K. were on the rise. But Capitol's U.S. executives exercised their first right of refusal and sent the Beatles' singles back. Livingston would later shift blame for his early brush-off of the Fab Four to another executive: "I gave one of my producers the assignment of listening to every EMI record that was sent to us. His name was David Dexter. And Dave was a good musicologist, he was a writer, he was a producer, and I trusted his ears and was not concerned about it."[22]

When Capitol turned down the singles, EMI was contractually free to send the Beatles' records to the producer Jerry Wexler at Atlantic in early 1963. But Wexler passed. Next, EMI tried Columbia, RCA, London, Mercury, and United Artists. All waved off EMI's offer. Finally, EMI found a willing partner in Vee-Jay, a label owned by a couple named Vivian and James Bracken. Vee-Jay signed the Beatles in January 1963.[23]

But Vee-Jay lacked strategic thinking or corporate maturity. Ewart Abner, Vee-Jay's company president, gambled away a significant portion of Vee-Jay's operating budget in Las Vegas in 1963, dealing the label a severe blow.[24] With a shortage of promotional dollars, the Beatles' first Vee-Jay releases, "Please Please Me" and "From Me to You," went unnoticed in the American market. The group's manager, Brian Epstein, was baffled. In November 1963 Epstein flew to New York to meet with Ed Sullivan about booking the band. Much to Epstein's delight, Sullivan agreed to two consecutive Sunday nights in February.[25] Unknown to Epstein, Sullivan had been delayed at London's Heathrow Airport a month earlier, when the Beatles had returned from a tour of Sweden. Sullivan had witnessed the teenage pandemonium when the Beatles deplaned.[26]

Back in London, EMI began an aggressive campaign to change U.S. Capitol's thinking about releasing the Beatles' singles. Len Wood, EMI's managing director, flew to New York to meet with Capitol's Alan Livingston. Wood politely and firmly told Livingston that he had to release the Beatles' forthcoming single, "I Want to Hold Your Hand." He told Livingston, "You *must* take it."[27] Then on December 10, 1963, Walter Cronkite aired a four-minute news segment documenting the teenage audience's excitement about the Beatles at a concert in Bournemouth.[28] Marsha Albert, a teenager in Silver Spring, Maryland, was watching the news that night. Moved, she wrote WWDC, a Washington, D.C., radio station, asking, "Why can't we have music like that here in America?"[29] Station executives asked themselves the same question, since there were no copies of the single in stores. Livingston still hadn't set a release date for "I Want to Hold Your Hand" in the United States. So the WWDC disc jockey Carroll James asked a friend in the Washington, D.C., office of British Overseas Airways to ask a flight attendant to bring a copy of the Beatles' 45-rpm back from London.[30]

When the disc arrived, James played the record on the air, triggering a rush of requests to hear it over and over again. The single was placed in heavy rotation, and the weekly numbers caught the attention of Capitol executives in L.A. Capitol had originally planned to release the single in mid-January but the date clearly had to change. The release date of "I Want to Hold Your Hand" was moved up to the day after Christmas, when teens were still on their holiday break. Two weeks after "I Want to Hold Your Hand" was released, more than a million copies had been sold. From January 17 to February 6, Beatlemania spread throughout the United States, stoked by anticipation of the group's February 7 arrival in New York from England.[31]

After Capitol learned that the Beatles were to appear on Ed Sullivan and at Carnegie Hall in February, the label put up a solid $40,000 to promote the group's first tour.[32] By Sunday February 9, 1964, the night of *The Ed Sullivan Show*, Capitol's record people and publicity team had done their jobs well. Teens were on edge of their seats in anticipation of the Beatles' performance. So were their parents. That night, a record audience of 73 million viewers tuned in to see the group's first appearance on *The Ed Sullivan Show*. The total represented more than 40 percent of the U.S. population at the time.[33] As the months wore on, the English group became a gold mine for Capitol and EMI. Other American record labels quickly rushed to sign their own versions of the Beatles.

Within a year of the Beatles' arrival, recording opportunities for new jazz musicians had shrunk. Already small, jazz budgets at record labels were trimmed further as jazz producers were shifted to rock departments or asked to double as scouts for new rock and folk artists.

JAZZ AND BEATLEMANIA

The Beatles' "I Want to Hold Your Hand" entered *Billboard*'s Hot 100 chart at no. 45 the week of January 18, 1964, jumped to no. 3 a week later, and hit no. 1 the week of February 1—remaining in the top spot for seven consecutive weeks.[34] When the group arrived in New York, on February 7, after a big buildup, record sales skyrocketed and the industry began to change steadily in response. Before 1964, only two singles by British artists had ever topped *Billboard*'s Hot 100 chart—Acker Bilk's "Stranger on the Shore" and the Tornados' "Telstar," both quirky instrumentals that hit no. 1 in 1962. The following year, only three singles by British artists reached the Top 40. But in 1964, sixty-five did, and in 1965, sixty-eight made it.[35] "Solo artists had a very rough time after the Beatles arrived," said Bruce Morrow, a New York disc jockey, in an interview with *Vanity Fair*. "Suddenly, everybody was putting their money and attention

behind the British groups. Suddenly there was a flood of British groups—
a flood."[36]

Jazz artists made early attempts to jump on the British bandwagon, but
only the English rock acts, with their youthful appeal, infectious optimism,
and electric charisma, could credibly deliver the songs. Jazz covers of their
songs at first seemed antique and sullen. This shift to pop only accelerated
as Motown's black artists had hits on R&B and pop charts simultaneously.
Meanwhile, some jazz producers were asked to hunt for teen groups. "In
the late 1950s and very early 1960s, I produced Benny Golson and Art
Farmer's Jazztet, Woody Herman, Ramsey Lewis, Ahmad Jamal, Roland
Kirk, Buddy Rich, and Gerry Mulligan," said Jack Tracy, a producer at
the Mercury, Argo, Limelight, and Liberty labels. "The Beatles were just
part of what changed jazz in the sixties. Pop-rock, in general, soaked up
so much of the cultural atmosphere that it changed everything. Radio stations changed their formats from a mix of different types of music to just
rock. But chasing after hot singles was perilous. When Chubby Checker's
'Twist' hit in 1960, record companies spent millions of dollars trying to
find artists to record it. But by the time those records came out, the Twist
was already passé."[37]

Tracy worked as a producer at Mercury Records in the early 1960s but
was sent to Los Angeles in the fall of 1962 to open the label's West Coast
office. "So much of what was available in promotion budgets was spent
frantically trying to find new rock groups," he said. "And so much was lost,
since most efforts failed. I think jazz lost its market when it lost the support
of radio. Before the Beatles, we had no problem getting jazz played on
stations. Not the far-out stuff by artists like Ornette Coleman, of course,
but Gerry Mulligan, Quincy Jones, and Dave Brubeck. The Beatles' arrival
was a huge game changer. By the mid-sixties, it was almost mandatory
for jazz artists to record Beatles songs. But most of their efforts were
hopeless."

To Tracy, a jazz producer on his way up in the record industry, the
Beatles and the groups that followed delivered a sharp blow. "I'll be honest—I resented the Beatles," he said. "They were just so overwhelming. I
had been busy making records with Sarah Vaughan, Dinah Washington,
Woody Herman, and Terry Gibbs. All of sudden this 'I Want to Hold Your
Hand' crap came out, and my teenage son wanted a different haircut. I'm
not blaming the situation on the Beatles, though. It was me. Rock was a
whole new element. I would go out to clubs like Whisky a Go Go to see
what was going on. But the music was beyond me. As the months pro-
gressed, more and more jazz producers were expected to do things for the

rock side of labels. Jazz producers tried to do the best they could with what they had. But as time went on, there were fewer and fewer jazz producers. The problem was that we didn't quite know how to produce rock records. We didn't know where to find the groups, what was good or bad, or what would sell. It was no longer about the musicianship. It was about things we knew nothing about."

The financial stakes compounded the problem. Rock was too lucrative to be ignored, and jazz singles sold nowhere near the same volume. The financial numbers on the LP side were even worse. "Either I didn't know how to produce rock records or the people I found just didn't have the stuff," Tracy said. "After the Beatles, the Rolling Stones and other English groups came here, the labels began to panic, especially the smaller ones. You couldn't believe the rush of success. The whole recording industry was taken aback by how fast things were changing and happening. Labels moved the best jazz producers over to the rock side, and they tried to use their rock producers to energize the jazz side. It was hell out there for us older guys. Then younger executives came in and it was a whole different world. The whole transition was rapid and puzzling. The industry wanted us to change in a heartbeat, and the pressure kept mounting. Frankly, I didn't do a good job of it. I wish I had been able to. I wish I had tried harder. But I just didn't get it. It was an explosive time in the record business, and jazz fell by the wayside."

From the jazz and pop record promoter's perspective, convincing disc jockeys to air records grew more difficult as slots were increasingly filled by Top 40 pop-rock and R&B artists—leaving less room for traditional pop and jazz. "At the time in 1964 I owned a leading record-promotion firm, and my biggest client was Nat King Cole," Dick LaPalm recalled. "An average day would be spent on the phone calling radio stations to ask them to feature my clients' records. My next calls were to all the stores where those stations broadcast to make sure they were well stocked with the discs. If they weren't, I'd call the record label to be sure they put more copies in local stores. It was a labor-intensive job. For the first six or seven years of my marriage, I was on the road seventy percent of the time.

"After the Beatles arrived in 1964, there was more competition for airplay, which meant having to work harder to get my clients on the radio. I'd do almost anything to make that happen. I'd invite radio guys to Nat King Cole concerts with an opportunity to go backstage to meet him. I'd send booze—whatever it took we would do, except cash. After Capitol released "I Want to Hold Your Hand," sales of Beatles records were enormous. It's hard to imagine this kind of sensation today. Not long after this initial frenzy, Carlos Gastel, Nat King Cole's manager and a friend of mine, happened to call Capitol Records in Los Angeles. The receptionist answered, 'Capitol Records, Home of the Beatles. How can I direct your call?' Gastel hit the ceiling. He went to [Capitol chairman Glenn] Wallichs and said, 'Nat [King Cole] built three floors of this tower. Home of the Beatles?'"[38]

During 1964 and into 1965, jazz musicians largely ignored the Beatles' music. The melodies in their early songs were so singular and repetitious that they were uncoverable by jazz musicians—or considered too far below their abilities and training to bother. Jazz artists who recorded them early on tended to sound woefully out of character. But LaPalm noted, "The British rock musicians loved the American blues artists they had been listening to in England growing up. For whatever reason, the blues moved them and jazz didn't. For example, when I worked at Chess Records in Chicago, Minnie Riperton was our receptionist. One day she called me in my office to tell me that there was a skinny white guy standing there asking to meet blues singer-songwriter Willie Dixon, who recorded for Chess at the time. I told Minnie to tell him that Dixon wasn't there. About a minute later, Minnie called back to tell me that another person was there with the first guy, also asking for Dixon. It turned out the two guys were Brian Jones and Keith Richards. They and the rest of the Rolling Stones were at Chess to record the album *12 by 5*. I don't know whether they ever met Dixon while there were at the studio, but that's how passionate they and other groups were about the blues. Jazz for many of those guys was too fancy or not direct enough."[39]

DETROIT REINVENTS R&B

In January 1959, five years before the Beatles appeared on *The Ed Sullivan Show*, the songwriter Berry Gordy formed Tamla Records in Detroit with an $800 family loan. Gordy already had experience as a songwriter, having composed several hit compositions. He had begun his music career by founding 3D Record Mart, a Detroit record store that sold jazz records. "My little group of friends were into Charlie Parker and Miles Davis," he told the writer Harvey Kubernik in 1995. "I really did love jazz, you know. I thought, I'm gonna help these people with their life. I'm gonna teach them about jazz. But they just kept saying, 'You got any Muddy Waters or Jimmy Reed?' I said, 'If you want that stuff you'll have to go down Hastings Street.'"[40]

When his record store started losing money, Gordy began stocking R&B records. But it was too little, too late. His store soon filed for bankruptcy. The experience, however, wasn't a complete loss for Gordy, who came to realize that his heart wasn't in jazz but with what he had heard in local churches, what he called "music with a funky beat."[41] Unemployed, Gordy took a job at the Ford Motor Company, trimming chrome on Lincoln-Mercury's assembly line. On the factory floor, Gordy marveled at the fluid choreography of production and efficiency, learning lessons that would come in handy when he began to build Motown Records on the same principles of production.[42]

Detroit was crowded with small independent R&B labels, but few had bothered to make records that resonated with white audiences. Gordy realized that the only way his company's music was going to break out of the jukeboxes at corner bars was for his singles to reach *Billboard*'s Hot 100 chart. To do this, he had to micromanage the entire package—from the artists and their stage style to how they dressed. "The goal," Gordy said, "was to be light." Marv Johnson's "Come to Me" (Tamla 101), released in May 1959, was certainly lighter and inviting to both black and white audiences, and it reached no. 30 on the Hot 100 chart in early 1959. Gordy knew that to reach a critical mass and make money, he would also have to lease Tamla's hot artists to larger labels. So after the success of "Come to Me," Gordy leased Johnson to United Artists, where he delivered nine consecutive hits.[43]

In the years that followed, Motown worked steadily to produce a new type of refined R&B that would come to be known as soul. Gordy put his assembly-line experience at the Ford Motor Company to bear on Motown's production, enforcing the same discipline and quality control. Instead of cranking out everything and anything in hopes of landing a hit, Gordy released only polished recordings by a limited number of artists. Fewer artists meant less opportunity for writers and producers and increased competition among them. Hooks and elaborate arrangements resulted, as writers created winning identities for artists and themselves. The result was a "Motown sound."[44] Gordy also favored a folksy pragmatism when selecting songs to record and promote, using colorful phrases to challenge company decision makers, such as, "It sells or it smells" and "Would you buy this record for a dollar, or buy a sandwich instead?"[45]

Even more important, Gordy understood that in the age of teen concerts, television, and album covers, Motown's artists had to look glamorous and polished to appeal to a wide range of record buyers. Motown's Artists Development Department instructed young vocalists on body movement,

elocution, grooming, choreography, and performance. Even hand movements were choreographed for maximum impact during TV close-ups.
The Supremes' lead vocalist, Diana Ross, was given special treatment,
particularly as the group's hits raced up the charts. She was taught how
to climb in and out of a limousine and how to curtsy in mermaid-tight
gowns. The goal was to position her and everyone at the label as refined
Las Vegas acts and supper-club entertainers.[46]

But Motown was more than an enterprise and launching pad for talent.
It was a label with a formula and a signature brand—much like Blue
Note, whose jazz records Gordy had sold in his record store years earlier.
Motown groomed artists and kept valuable artists out of the social and
financial trouble that typically ruined successful artists. "There's nothing
worse than having a person become a star and not grow mentally," he told
Mick Brown in London's *Sunday Times* in 1984. "The first thing they're
going to do is get into all sorts of problems, drugs and so on. Sometimes
you can't stop that, but you can do what your conscience and morality
tell you should do. We tried to play heavily on artists paying their taxes,
for example. I used to make Smokey Robinson take a certain amount of
whatever he earned and put it aside."[47]

To extend this sense of paternalism and corporate belonging, Motown
even had a company song, written by Smokey Robinson: "Oh, we have a
very swinging company, working hard from day to day / Nowhere will you
find more unity than at Hitsville USA."[48] In 1961 Motown had just one
no. 1 *Billboard* Hot 100 pop hit—the Marvelettes' "Please Mr. Postman."
The label had another pop hit in 1963, with Little Stevie Wonder's "Fingertips–Part 2." But in 1964, the year of the Beatles' arrival, Motown landed
four no. 1 pop hits, and in 1965, five. In that same year Motown also had
forty-five Top-20 hits on the chart.[49]

As Smokey Robinson told Michael Lydon of *Rolling Stone* in 1968:
"I think that anybody who records somebody approaches it with the idea
of being in the Top Ten because it's the only way to stay in business,
and let's face it, this is the record *industry*, one of the biggest industries
going nowadays. So we're just going to try to stay abreast of what's on
the market. This is what hangs a lot of jazz musicians up. I've seen cats in
little clubs who are jazz musicians through and through. They would not
play a note of rock and roll ever, nothing. And they're starving to death.

"Now this gets to the point of ridiculousness to me. I don't think that
they love jazz anymore than I love what I'm doing, but it just so happens
that right now what I'm doing is more in demand than jazz. But you can
believe if it came to a point whereas jazz was what was happening and

nobody was buying this type of music and I was starving to death, I'm sure I'd write some jazz songs. The market, man, the market is people. It is the kids who are buying the records. This is the people you're trying to reach. I think that satisfying people on the whole if you're in business is more important than self-satisfaction."[50]

Robinson also shared Gordy's passion for brevity and star packaging: "A lot of the things you hear by [the Miracles], we had to splice down for radio time. Like 'Second that Emotion.' It was 3:15 when it was done and Berry—who has an ingenious sense of knowing hit records, it's uncanny—he heard it, he told us, 'It's a great tune, but it's too long, so I want you to cut that other verse down and come right out of the solo and go back into the chorus and on out.' So we did and the record was a smash. He's done that on quite a few records, and he's usually right, man. I've just geared myself to radio time. The shorter a record is nowadays, the more it's gonna be played. This is a key thing in radio time, you dig? If you have a record that's 2:15 long it's definitely gonna get more play than one that's 3:15, at first, which is very important. But it's no hang up because I'm going to work in it and say whatever I'm going to say in this time limit. It would be a hang up if I wrote five minutes of a song and then had to cut it up. But cutting 30 seconds or a minute doesn't make that much difference."[51]

The irony, of course, is that jazz had created the single-record model to begin with. From the 1920s through the 1940s, jazz had to make its point in about three minutes—the length of a 78-rpm record. This was as true for Louis Armstrong, Duke Ellington, and Bix Beiderbecke as it was for Coleman Hawkins, Charlie Parker, and Dizzy Gillespie. But with the introduction of the $33\frac{1}{3}$-rpm long-playing record in 1948, first in the 10-inch format and then the 12-inch LP in the mid-1950s, jazz had more room to stretch out. Artists were encouraged to replicate the longer improvised solos they performed at nightclubs, to re-create the excitement and feats of endurance and innovation. By 1960 LP producers had given jazz musicians increasing freedom to stretch out. Jazz's shift away from singles to albums also freed artists from the whims and commercial tastes of disc jockeys and the mechanical requirements and musical repetition of R&B.

While jazz singles were released throughout the 1950s, they were generally designed to promote album sales. Jazz by then was less about jukeboxes and dancing and more about at-home listening and fidelity—which would turn out to be a costly marketing and positioning error. By the late 1950s and early 1960s, the singles market rapidly became the primary means of introducing younger listeners to music. The 45-rpm concept was largely lost on many jazz producers and artists whose budgets for marketing and promotion were already limited, especially in the years when payola played an integral part in securing airplay.

WHAT "ALFIE" WAS ALL ABOUT

In the years immediately after the launch of Motown in 1959 and before the arrival of the Beatles in 1964, many smaller independent pop-rock labels emerged and captured a slice of the ever-growing teen market. California producers like Jerry Leiber and Mike Stoller, and Phil Spector of Philles, and New York label owners like Florence Greenberg of Scepter began packaging young black R&B artists for crossover appeal. Among the new writers hard at work at New York's Brill Building were Burt Bacharach and Hal David. Older than most of the other writers toiling away in the building's warren of offices, Bacharach and David seemed to bridge the two decades, bringing an American Songbook sensibility and sophistication to Teen Pan Alley.

Starting in 1951, seventy-three of Bacharach's compositions were recorded by leading pop artists, including Jo Stafford, Johnny Mathis, Mel Tormé, Perry Como, Margaret Whiting, Tony Bennett, and Vic Damone Then from 1960 to 1962, Bacharach's name appeared on ninety recordings, by traditional pop singers and pop-rock and soul singers like Dee Clark, Chuck Jackson, the Wanderers, and the Shirelles.[52] In 1961 Bacharach discovered Dionne Warwick at a Scepter recording session, where she was a backup singer on the Drifters' "Mexican Divorce," one of his compositions.[53] Warwick was soon signed to Bacharach and David's production company.

From 1963 to 1970, Warwick turned more than thirty Bacharach-David songs into *Billboard's* Hot 100 pop chart hits, including "Walk on By," "Message to Michael," and "I Say a Little Prayer." In addition to writing for Warwick, Bacharach and David wrote for the movies (the title song for *Alfie*; "The Look of Love," for *Casino Royale*; and "Raindrops Keep Falling on My Head," for *Butch Cassidy and the Sundance Kid*), for a Broadway show (*Promises, Promises*), and for other solo artists and group acts.

Born in Kansas City, Missouri, in 1928, Bacharach moved with his family to Queens, New York, when he was four years old. He studied music at McGill University, in Montreal, and attended Mannes School of Music, in New York, and Music Academy of the West, in California.[54] In the 1940s, he was overwhelmed by the excitement of bebop, especially the music's complex, hyperactive sound. "It was like a window opening," he told the writer Bill DeMain in 1997, describing his first hearing of Dizzy Gillespie and Charlie Parker.[55]

After serving in the army, Bacharach studied music at California's Music Academy of the West with Darius Milhaud, who had a fine appreciation for jazz. "We all had to write a work for our summer project, for Milhaud's composition class," Bacharach said. "And I wrote a sonatina for violin, oboe, and piano. The middle movement was very lyrical and very melodic, and I was almost ashamed of it. We all were doing things like extreme, heavy stuff. But when I played my sonatina for Milhaud, we didn't even talk about it. Maybe he sensed my discomfort with the second movement. He said, 'Never be afraid . . . of something . . . that is melodic . . . and can be remembered.' "[56]

Like Berry Gordy and Smokey Robinson at Motown, Bacharach and Hal David had ten years on many other songwriting duos composing teen songs in the fifties and sixties. In the complexity and structure of their songs, the duo had more in common with Rodgers and Hart than King and Goffin. But Bacharach quickly found the Brill Building's conveyor-belt production system stifling. "The company A&R men used to be really omnipotent," he told *Newsweek* in 1970. "They'd say, 'That's a three-bar phrase. Make it a four-bar phrase and I'll get so-and-so to record your song.' I ruined some pretty good songs that way, because I believed them."[57]

Unable to cover songs recorded by British bands and Motown groups convincingly, jazz artists in the 1960s increasingly gravitated toward Bacharach's more traditional melodies. Songs by pop-rock and Motown writers worked magic only for the groups that recorded them. Once songs became hits, they became fingerprints, inextricably identified with the original groups and almost impossible to duplicate successfully, especially as instrumentals. A jazz saxophone playing "Baby Love" or "My Guy" would invariably sound painfully silly and commercial. Bacharach's melodies were different for jazz musicians, and proved convincingly adaptable in the 1960s.

Unlike the arch and repetitive compositions of American and English pop-rock acts, Bacharach's melodies were customized for instrumental treatment, largely because Bacharach himself orchestrated many of them with a jazz feel. Songs like "Don't Make Me Over" and "Message to Michael" featured a large orchestra with strings; "Anyone Who Had a Heart" featured a fat guitar; "Walk on By," "I Say a Little Prayer," "Do You Know the Way to San Jose," and "Promises, Promises" had trumpet or flugelhorn solos—or entire trumpet sections added for jazz flavor. "Those songs by Burt and Hal were difficult to sing and play," said Dionne Warwick, who unlike many pop-soul singers of her day had received training on the piano and could read music. "Every recording session was like taking an exam— impossible time changes and tricky melodies. Most of my peers thought I was insane for singing them. You had to be able to read music with Burt. He was a perfectionist. We recorded each of those songs twenty or twenty-five times. And they all were difficult, *Promises, Promises* probably the hardest. Try singing along with the record and see how you do."[58]

As early as 1963, jazz artists such as the pianist Dick Hyman and the guitarist Joe Pass began recording Bacharach's "Wives and Lovers." As more singles by Bacharach and David became hits, more jazz artists covered them. For example, Jimmy Smith and Grant Green recorded "Wives and Lovers" (1964), Sarah Vaughan sang "Make It Easy on Yourself" and "What the World Needs Now" (1965), Stan Getz recorded "The Look of Love" (1966), and Sonny Stitt, Vaughan, and Bill Evans recorded "Alfie" that same year. By 1967 jazz artists were devoting entire albums to Bacharach and David's music, but no Bacharach-David song was recorded more often by jazz artists than "Alfie."[59]

Although "Alfie" held enormous melodic appeal, the story behind the song's development and placement in the movie crystallized jazz's declining influence in the 1960s. When the British film about an English cad was in development in 1965, its director, Lewis Gilbert, visited Ronnie Scott's jazz club in London to hear Sonny Rollins. Gilbert was so taken with Rollins's playing that he asked the tenor saxophonist if he would write the movie's score. "I was playing with three other English jazz musicians," Rollins recalled. "Lewis Gilbert asked me to write sketches [incidental music] for the film. We recorded the sketches with a small group. For the soundtrack, Oliver [Nelson] arranged a beautiful score for eleven pieces based on my sketches. Oliver fleshed out what I wrote. He was a beautiful arranger."[60]

At about the time Rollins was working with Oliver Nelson on the score to *Alfie*, the Paramount executive Ed Wolpin asked Bacharach and David to write a theme song for the film. Wolpin felt the release in the United Kingdom needed a vocal radio hit, which didn't exist in Rollins's planned instrumental pieces. Bacharach and David almost passed on Wolpin's initial request, fearing they would have trouble writing a convincing song about a man with such a silly name. But after Bacharach saw a rough cut of the film in California, he persuaded David that they should give the song a shot.[61]

The English pop singer Cilla Black was chosen to record the song. Bacharach liked the shrill urgency of Black's pop voice, and her accent would add authenticity to the lyrics and the film's London setting. Bacharach particularly liked how Black, two years earlier, had interpreted his song with David, "Anyone Who Had a Heart." Black's rendition had mirrored Dionne Warwick's hit and sparked a transatlantic feud between the two singers. "If I had coughed on that song, Cilla would have coughed, too," Warwick said. "I never forgave her for that."[62] When Bacharach expressed interest in using Black for "Alfie," Black played hard to get, largely out of fear that she would be in over her head. Bacharach had a reputation for being a commanding perfectionist.

"When Burt Bacharach first wrote to me from New York to tell me that he and Hal David, inspired by the film *Alfie*, had written another song especially for me, I was very excited," wrote Cilla Black in her autobiography. "Because I didn't really want to record the song, but didn't want to say an outright 'no,' I thought I'd be really difficult for a change, and start putting up barriers. So first of all I said I'd only do it if Burt Bacharach himself did the arrangement, never thinking for one moment that he would. Unfortunately, the reply came back from America that he'd be happy to. So then I said I would only do it if Burt came over to London for the recording session. 'Yes,' came the reply. Next I said that as well as the arrangements and coming over, he had to play on the session. To my astonishment it was agreed that Burt would do all three. So by this time, coward that I was, I really couldn't back out."[63]

The "Alfie" recording session at London's Abbey Road studio was set for the fall of 1965. A forty-eight-piece orchestra plus three backup singers were assembled. The producer was George Martin, probably because Black and the Beatles shared the same manager, Brian Epstein. Martin had also produced Black's earlier Bacharach hit. Bacharach not only arranged and played piano on the date but also conducted. And perhaps as payback for Black's earlier petulant demands or simply to extract perfection, Bacharach was demanding.

"I put her through about thirty takes," Bacharach said. "I was so caught up pushing forward for something magical that I never bothered to stop and ask Sir George [Martin], who was in the booth producing, whether he thought an earlier take was acceptable. He finally came on the speaker and said he thought we had what we wanted on a much earlier take."[64]

Why work so hard? "Control, I guess," he said. "I've always tried to get the best performance from everyone. And sure, sometimes I've gone way too far." Bacharach was quick to add that his desire for creative control has never been about power or ego. "Look, I'm very nice. When I walk into recording studios, I stay nice. But I get very confident in there. Nervous and confident. Then I start doing all kinds of things musically to ensure I get a heart-grabbing performance."

Shortly after Black recorded "Alfie," in late 1965, Parlophone released the single in Britain, in January 1966. Paramount's English marketers intended the single to stir up interest for the movie prior to the film's planned London opening that March. But Black's single exceeded expectations, inching up the U.K. charts for three months, topping out at no. 9 shortly before the film opened in London at month's end. The contrast between Black's girlish innocence on the song's softer moments and impassioned crescendos attracted listeners who knew nothing yet about the film.

But as Paramount geared up for the film's U.S. release, in August 1966, its plans to include Black's song in the film hit a snag: Lewis Gilbert, the director of *Alfie*, didn't care for the song and felt the Bacharach-David hit trivialized the film and undermined Sonny Rollins's swaggering saxophone and Oliver Nelson's brash score. Gilbert, a jazz fan, didn't understand why the film even needed a pop theme when it had Rollins's "Alfie's Theme." But Gilbert's view mattered little to United Artists, the company tasked with marketing the film and distributing it in the United States.[65]

United Artists knew only too well from its recent experience distributing four James Bond films and two Beatles movies that a pop theme with radio support would translate into an enormously lucrative bonus. UA also knew that such a tie-in could be doubly valuable if that pop tune was released on one of its record labels. So UA turned to Liberty Records, which had just completed a deal for worldwide distribution and owned Imperial Records, which had Cher under contract. When Liberty's president, Alvin Bennett, visited London in April 1966, he told *Billboard* that he had received a copy of Cilla Black's "Alfie" and had planned to cover the song using a Liberty artist.[66] Cher in 1966 was a red-hot property. In 1965 she and her singing partner, Sonny Bono, had had seven charted hits, and Cher had had one on her own. In 1966 Sonny and Cher had four pop hits, and she had three performing solo.[67]

So UA convinced Liberty to have Bono write an arrangement for "Alfie." Bono then wrote an ersatz "wall of sound" backdrop reminiscent of Phil Spector's recordings at Gold Star Studios in Los Angeles, many of which Bono had attended. Unfortunately, the melody of "Alfie" was more demanding than Cher's talk-sing style could manage, and the result was a detached, pitchy version that paled in comparison with Cilla Black's blowtorch rendition. Now UA was in a bind. The studio knew it couldn't simply add Cher's version to the movie without upending Sonny Rollins's score and incurring director Lewis's wrath. So it compromised by placing the song at the tail end, when the credits rolled. To create buzz, Cher's version was released a month before the film's U.S. release. But her single reached only no. 32 on *Billboard*'s Hot 100 chart.

Meanwhile, Cilla Black's manager, Brian Epstein, was furious that UA had robbed his singer of her shot at the American market. Capitol Records in the United States tried to make good by releasing Black's version in the States just before the movie premiered in New York in August 1966. But Black's version managed to reach only no. 95 on *Billboard*'s pop chart. Black would never have another U.S. hit. Ironically, Dionne Warwick's recording of the song was the best-selling U.S. version, hitting no. 15 on the pop chart in early 1967.

As for jazz and Sonny Rollins, "Alfie" would become proof that pop-rock was far more commercially viable than jazz—even if the artist was a giant in the jazz field. Though Rollins had recorded edgy, rollicking solos on top of Oliver Nelson's *Alfie* score, Rollins's instrumental music was largely eclipsed by the Bacharach-David hit. Rollins, naturally, was disappointed. As he told the writer Eric Nisenson: "I enjoyed writing and playing the score for *Alfie* very much. However, if I were offered another opportunity such as this, I would only do it if the film highlighted the music rather than the story itself."[68]

BIRTH OF THE MOD

By 1966 the only way for many jazz artists to compete for record sales with the British groups and their spin-offs was to find ways to climb on the bandwagon—or at least try. Most early attempts by jazz artists to take on songs by John Lennon and Paul McCartney sounded awkward or slick. Early jazz recordings that hoped to capitalize on the Beatles' success, with fair or middling results, included Gary McFarland's "She Loves You," "And I Love Her," and "A Hard Day's Night" (June 1964), Duke Ellington's "All My Loving" (January 1965), Grant Green's "I Want to Hold Your Hand" (March 1965), and Count Basie's *Basie's Beatle Bag* (May 1966). Perhaps the title of Gerry Mulligan's pop-rock effort—*If You Can't Beat 'Em Join 'Em* (June 1965)—best summed up the frustration many jazz musicians were feeling. Singers faced the same struggle. "Sarah Vaughan wouldn't let her Beatles album, *Songs of the Beatles*, come out when it was ready for release," said the producer Phil Ramone. "Initially, she didn't care much for her interpretations of the Beatles' songs, and the album only surfaced in the late '70s. Sassy's issue was similar to the discomfort many jazz artists felt at the time about recording pop-rock covers. They believed they were reaching too far across the fence, drifting away from their comfort zone—jazz. But there were other hurdles: Pop-rock was designed for a generation that was considerably younger than most jazz artists. The American Songbook didn't have this problem since there was no age restriction. In addition, pop-rock hits were so firmly identified with the artists who recorded them that covers by jazz musicians risked stretching credibility and compromising reputations."[69]

A producer who figured out how to marry jazz and pop was Creed Taylor. After arriving in New York in 1954, Taylor had joined Bethlehem Records, recording the label's first 10-inch album with the singer Chris Connor. After moving to ABC-Paramount in 1956, Taylor produced jazz and pop records, occasionally merging the two, as in the case of Billy Taylor's *My Fair Lady Loves Jazz* in 1957. After starting Impulse Records in 1960 for ABC and producing the label's six albums, including John Coltrane's *Africa Brass*, Taylor left to join Verve in 1961. There he produced *Jazz Samba*, a 1962 album that launched the bossa nova in the United States and the world-music movement. *Jazz Samba* was followed by *Getz/Gilberto*, which featured "The Girl from Ipanema." The 1964 album won Grammys for Best Album of the Year, Best Jazz Instrumental Album (Individual or Group), and Best Engineered Album (Non-Classical). "The Girl from Ipanema" also won a Grammy for Record of the Year. After Taylor signed the guitarist Wes Montgomery to Verve in 1964, he began to think of ways to leverage Montgomery's exciting swinging sound—making it more popular without losing the jazz groove. Recording American Songbook standards and Broadway hits was a no-brainer. Getting Montgomery to try taking on pop radio hits was another story, particularly because Montgomery didn't read music. "Wes also didn't listen to the radio so he didn't know any of the new music," said John Levy, Montgomery's manager in the sixties. "That was unusual. Most jazz musicians back then did listen—just out of curiosity. Not Wes. He didn't care."[70]

One of the earliest successful jazz adaptations of a pop-rock hit was Montgomery's "Goin' Out of My Head." Recorded in November 1965, it marked Montgomery's first attempt at infusing pop-rock with a soulful, hip jazz flavor. Creed Taylor recalled the effort needed to convince Montgomery to give the song a try: "Back then I listened to all of the pop and R&B stuff that came out on the radio," Taylor said.[71] "I heard Little Anthony and the Imperials rehearsing 'Goin' Out of My Head' for a show they were going to do at New York's Paramount Theater. I thought the song could be great for Wes. He was playing at the Half Note at the time with Miles Davis's rhythm section—Wynton Kelly, Paul Chambers, and Jimmy Cobb. So I took a copy of the Little Anthony 45-rpm and a portable phonograph down to play it for him. On a break, Wes listened to the song and said, 'Creed, you must be going out of *your* head. I can't do that kind of stuff.' I told Wes, 'Listen to the chord changes and the melody, and you'll find there's something there that's going to be very useful for you in a recording studio.' I also told Wes that Oliver Nelson was arranging and that Oliver already had the chart in his head. I said, 'Forget the vocal and performance. Just listen to the chord changes.' That was the only time I had to talk to Wes in a somewhat uncomfortable situation.

"But Wes still wasn't buying it. So I told Oliver that I needed his help. I said, 'Wes is turned off about the source of the song. I don't think he's hearing the arrangement and chord changes that you have in mind.' Oliver made a demo on a Fender Rhodes [electric piano] because Wes didn't read music. When Wes heard what Oliver had come up with, he loved it. He rehearsed the song based on Oliver's tape recording. Then he and Oliver came up with a hit. After that, everything went smoothly between us. Wes trusted me. As soon as Wes heard the recording, he knew it sounded great. I certainly would never have given him a song to record that wasn't top quality."

After Taylor signed a label-distribution contract with A&M Records for his newly formed CTI Records at the end of 1966, his first project in 1967 was the album *A Day in the Life*, with Wes Montgomery. "I picked up the Beatles' *Sgt. Pepper* as soon as it hit stores in June and called Wes and [the arranger] Don Sebesky to my offices at A&M," Taylor said. "When they arrived, all three of us listened to the entire album. We agreed that the last track on the second side—*A Day in the Life*—was appropriately bluesy and would be ideal for the title track of Montgomery's new album. Don recorded Wes playing the song almost immediately and finished an orchestral arrangement within a week."

When the record was released, nearly the entire album was devoted to Montgomery's covers of pop-rock hits, signaling the start of a new mod era for jazz. "I saw that there was room for jazz that didn't completely ignore other successful types of music that had merit," Taylor said. "I liked what Blue Note Records had been doing in this space earlier in the 1960s. Lee Morgan's *Sidewinder*, for example, made a lot of noise. So did Jimmy Smith's *Back at the Chicken Shack*. Blue Note had placed one foot in R&B and one foot in improvised contemporary jazz.

"However, the boogaloo wasn't the direction in which I was interested in going. I thought Blue Note was restricting its reach by having long improvised solos on albums. I had similar ideas about mixing jazz, soul, and R&B—but without the imposition of elongated passages. These would be where the bass had maybe two choruses and drums would then do a trade. It's hard to verbalize what I knew and what I wanted to do that no one else was doing yet. I felt there were great music themes out there that weren't being packaged in a way that large audiences would connect with them."

But simply recording pop hits with jazz stars wasn't enough to sell records. There was work to do on the business side. "My many years in the record business had resulted in a close relationship with independent record distributors as a group," Taylor said. "They were almost like a fraternity. As long as you didn't cross into their territory, you were part of this club. I got to know them, and we had a direct line of communication. When the Beatles hit, the music was amazingly popular. But it was nothing I could identify with. When I heard them in the early days, much of what they had recorded sounded tongue in cheek and lighthearted, lyric-wise. I couldn't hear a great deal of substance there. I just thought that Paul McCartney was a really good-looking guy and that the drummer was a little odd and rushed the beat a lot. But I wasn't captivated. As with all great musical talents, at some point the Beatles' image dropped off and they started thinking seriously about the music. I had initially looked the other way. But when I started listening to their music—without the image and screaming fans—I realized there was some amazing stuff there.

"Popular music is music of the moment. If you can use it as a vehicle for what you're doing, then a lot of songs can be turned around. That was my thinking at CTI. I was listening to pop, R&B, folk, Debussy, Cole Porter, Rodgers and Hart, and just about everything else. Everything in the music business was intertwined. I'll give you an example: One day I met the Beatles' producer George Martin in the reception area of my attorney's office. My lawyer represented him and me at the same time. After Wes Montgomery's *A Day in the Life* came out, I gave George Martin a copy. He obviously shared it with Paul McCartney, because Paul liked it so much that two years later he sent me an advance copy of his song 'Let It Be' on cassette and told me I could cover it with whomever I wished. I recorded it with Hubert Laws in July 1969, with a Bobby Scott arrangement. Bobby had composed the pop hits 'A Taste of Honey' and 'He Ain't Heavy He's My Brother.' We made 'Let It Be' down in Memphis at American Sound Studio with Elvis Presley's rhythm section. Talk about intertwined."

But not all jazz artists in the 1960s embraced pop-rock hits. Miles Davis, Eric Dolphy, Charles Mingus, John Coltrane, Ornette Coleman, and many others continued to record albums that reflected their personal visions of jazz. From the listeners' standpoint, familiarity with artists like Miles Davis and John Coltrane could help them appreciate their experimentation and development. But for record buyers who weren't familiar with them and jazz, the music they heard was increasingly difficult to understand. In the pop-rock era, for musicians who had set out to become jazz artists, work was harder to find, especially in Chicago, where a declining number of recording and club opportunities existed.

With the antiwar and civil rights movements gaining momentum and grassroots community-organizing efforts taking hold in major cities, a group of Chicago jazz musicians decided to form a nonprofit organization to nurture their own music. The group's purpose—in addition to its creative mission—was to make a clean break from the traditional commercial path that most musicians had traveled on and explore a new model of artistic development and economic self-sufficiency. For them, pop, R&B, and even existing jazz styles up until this point needed to be eschewed.

9   Alienation and the Avant-Garde

When the saxophonist Joseph Jarman was discharged from the army in 1959, he found he wasn't able to talk for a year. As a member of the 11th Airborne Division, he had been dropped by parachute at night on a mission in Vietnam, along with twenty other soldiers in his unit. Their secret mission—the United States did not officially have troops in the country at the time—was to raid and destroy a strategic, well-fortified North Vietnamese military outpost. But as the soldiers drifted down through the sky at 2:30 A.M. on the moonless night, something went terribly wrong. Fourteen of the soldiers in the unit landed unexpectedly in a wide river. Weighed down with heavy gear, they drowned. Only Jarman and five other soldiers touched down safely on shore.

"We moved quietly toward our objective, a house where the North Vietnamese were supposed to be," Jarman said. "We kicked in the door with our guns blazing. But there weren't any soldiers in there, just women and children. We had shot them all down by mistake. It was horrible. I went into shock. After we were pulled out by helicopter and returned to base, I couldn't talk and had to go to two or three Army hospitals for treatment."[1]

When Jarman returned to Chicago at the dawn of the sixties, he resumed his music career. He had learned to play the saxophone in high school and continued after joining the army. In the years following his discharge, Jarman came in contact with other Chicago musicians who were increasingly frustrated by mainstream jazz and pop, and horrified by print and TV news images of presidential assassination, war in Southeast Asia, and escalating racial violence in the South. "Music was therapy of sorts for me and for the other musicians I knew," Jarman said.

When Jarman met the pianist Muhal Richard Abrams in 1962, Abrams invited him to a studio in the basement of his house. There, Abrams had organized a group called the Experimental Band. "Muhal's music was unlike anything else I had heard," Jarman said. "Muhal's playing was strong and very experimental. It was much freer and more expressive than the music I had heard on jukeboxes or the radio." For Jarman, Abrams's music—original, free of formal structure, and highly expressive—was an awakening. Little by little, he let go of the jazz with which he had been familiar and began to develop his own style. He also began to talk again.

By 1963 growing numbers of black jazz musicians in Chicago had stopped emulating the jazz stars they had listened to growing up. This shift was motivated partly by necessity. As the number of jazz clubs in Chicago declined, owners remained in business by booking jazz artists who played familiar styles such as bebop and hard bop. Or they booked R&B and soul acts. But the black jazz musicians in Chicago who resisted those styles sought a new approach. Since 1959 established jazz artists such as John Coltrane, Miles Davis, and Charles Mingus had achieved increased visibility and success by playing and recording their own compositions. Equally influential were the free-jazz pioneers of the late 1950s and early 1960s, such as Sun Ra, Cecil Taylor, and Ornette Coleman.

Lacking interest in mainstream success, young black jazz musicians in Chicago became increasingly estranged from the mainstream jazz culture. Increasingly, they embraced originality, detached themselves from traditional approaches to jazz, and began to organize around common artistic approaches and beliefs. In May 1965 they formed the Association for the Advancement of Creative Musicians (AACM). The goal of the founders— the pianists Muhal Richard Abrams and Jodie Christian, the drummer Steve McCall, and the composer Phil Cohran—was to start a nonprofit organization that would help fund their creative ambitions. The organization was a cooperative that collected dues from members and used the proceeds to encourage, support, and stage their new, original music.

This movement of Chicago's avant-garde jazz artists in the mid-1960s had roots in the expressions of earlier black jazz musicians who sought recognition as artists rather than entertainers. Among the most outspoken was Miles Davis, who grew increasingly bitter following a police beating and arrest outside Birdland in August 1959. Davis disdained audience members who conversed in clubs during his performances and disparaged overfriendly fans who sought to engage him after sets. "You ever see anybody go up bugging the classical musicians when they are on the job and trying to work?" Miles Davis asked Alex Haley, when Haley interviewed him for the September 1962 issue of *Playboy*.[2] When Davis, was asked if he felt that media complaints about his reaction were motivated by race, he responded affirmatively. "I know a damn well a lot of it is race. White people have certain things they expect from Negro musicians—just like they've got labels for the whole Negro race. It goes back to the slavery days. That was when Uncle Tommy got started because white people demanded it. Every little black child grew up seeing that getting along with white people meant grinning and acting clowns. It helped white people to feel easy about what they had done and were doing to Negroes and that's carried right on over to now. You bring it down to musicians, they want you to not only play your instrument, but to entertain them too with grinning and dancing."[3]

By 1964 a growing number of black jazz musicians felt further alienated by a culture that celebrated conformity, television, and the youth market. It was easy to see how, from their perspective, the prolonged civil rights struggle had inadvertently restrained black cultural achievement and acceptance while allowing white musicians—some from other countries—to benefit hugely from music that had originated in black communities. Increasingly, black jazz musicians found themselves in sync with Davis's view that jazz was an exceptional black performance art that demanded the same audience attention and respect afforded to white classical music. The movement by Chicago's AACM artists toward abstract expression and originality, and away from the restrictions of earlier jazz styles, united a group of the city's struggling musicians, for whom the trappings of past styles no longer had commercial or emotional currency. Diminished bookings in the clubs and the dearth of recording possibilities compelled jazz musicians to rethink the use of their creative energies. With the advent of pop-rock in the early 1960s and the music's perceived superficiality, black jazz musicians, particularly in Chicago, began to view club owners and record executives as agents of the forces that were marginalizing black music.

Even though Chicago's AACM was not formed directly to protest discrimination or war and did not adopt protest as its ultimate mission or purpose, the organization and the art movement it engendered were nonetheless created in reaction to the time. Music by AACM artists wasn't driven by social agendas, nor were their recordings "statement" works like those released by artists on Impulse and other record labels in the 1960s. Instead, the AACM was inspired by the protest movement, but once the organization was established, art became its driving force, not the sociopolitical issues of the day.

It's no coincidence that the AACM emerged just as social upheavals were taking place nationwide. Sit-ins at southern luncheonettes began in early 1960. In the spring of 1961 Chicago's Congress of Racial Equality (CORE) organized the first Freedom Rides to highlight entrenched segregation at southern bus terminals. In 1962 James Meredith struggled to overcome harassment and attend the University of Mississippi. In March 1963 Martin Luther King Jr. led a march on Washington and delivered his "I Have a Dream" speech. In September 1963 a church bombing in Birmingham, Alabama, killed four black girls. In June 1964 three civil rights workers were murdered in Mississippi by the Ku Klux Klan, an event that ultimately led to the passage of the Civil Rights Act of 1965.

AACM musicians were protesting as well, but against the restrictive nature of the jazz establishment. Such art protests were not without precedent. In the summer of 1960, Charles Mingus organized a Rebel Jazz Festival in Newport, Rhode Island, to protest George Wein's more mainstream Newport Jazz Festival. As Nat Hentoff wrote in *The Jazz Life:* "Another cumulative grievance among musicians—and a basic reason for the rebellion at Cliff Walk [in Newport]—was the NJF's cavalier financial attitude toward jazzmen who lacked mass name appeal but who were recognized by their colleagues as among the most important of current contributors to the language. A Louis Armstrong or a Benny Goodman had the box-office appeal and a sufficiently tough booking office to get top fees from the NJF, but the less widely renowned jazzmen were often pressured into coming to Newport for smaller sums than they deserved, particularly since the announced goal of the weekend was to advance jazz as an 'art form.'"[4] Protest was also used to make a point with fellow black musicians. In 1961 Max Roach walked out on stage in New York with a picket sign as Miles Davis performed, taking him to task for playing a benefit for the Africa Relief Foundation, which Roach said perpetuated African colonialism.[5]

Jazz, by the early 1960s, was no longer music that solely exhibited the dexterity and creative gifts of musicians: it also expressed the individual rights and philosophy of the artists who played it. "The main thing that affected me during this period was the change going on in this country with the civil rights movement and the Vietnam War," Sonny Rollins told the writer Eric Nisenson. "This is the main reason for what happened with music during this time: things just reached a point where people wanted to say something about it. . . . People were trying to escape from the restriction of society, all this racism and these kinds of things, so that in doing that, they felt that they should break down these song forms. It was just a way to show something new, and to get away from some things that were obviously not positive, for a lot of people. There were some attempts to break down a lot of these conventions."[6]

Free jazz—starting with Ornette Coleman's *Something Else!!!* (1958) and *Tomorrow Is the Question!* (1959) and moving on to *The Shape of*

Jazz to Come (1959) and *This Is Our Music* (1960)—shred the template for mass-market appeal by dropping traditional melody, harmony, and form, leaving the listener without the traditional means by which to track the articulation of the musician. Instead, free jazz forced the listener to accept the music and musicians on their terms rather than on terms that made the listener comfortable. The listener had to accept the entire work as a personal expression rather than as a creative interpretation. But protest was a component of the music as well: "I grew up in a white society with white rules and a white philosophy, but I grew up with a black conscience," Ornette Coleman told the drummer Art Taylor in Paris in October 1969. "My consciousness of myself as a black man makes me realize that unless I can be integrated into white society and its values, I can't achieve the wealth they have created. They have created a society where any unknown white person can put something on the market and become successful. I don't see why a black person can't do that. They have to control what you do first, then give it to you like welfare."[7]

Although Coleman himself was not part of the AACM movement, the nonprofit was influenced by his approach to music. In Chicago the AACM not only succeeded in creating music that was free of earlier jazz forms but also united like-minded musicians who had no interest in commercial values instituted by record companies, traditional concert promoters and radio disc jockeys. The result was a radically new and highly expressive jazz style that was no longer tied to the dictates and standards of commercial recording. In the process, the AACM detached itself from the mainstream, for better or worse.

LOSING THE BLUES IN CHICAGO

Why did the AACM emerge in Chicago and not other major cities? Part of the reason was the city's long tradition of making music that carried a powerful emotional punch—from the frantic energy of hot jazz and the gritty naturalness of the blues to heartfelt swing and socially conscious folk. In the early 1960s, Chicago may not have been the center of film and media, the way Los Angeles and New York were, but the city's musicians shared a common bond: They cared deeply about the emotional quality of their music and were fully aware that it could be an agent for change. For the Chicago musician, there was almost a religious sense of pride in being able to deliver a performance so honest and pure that it could transform how audiences felt about themselves and each other. The music's sheer primal value not only could soothe the stress of modernity but could also compel audiences to think differently about racism, poverty and injustice, love and sex, and life in general. In Chicago, music demanded artistic integrity and a boundless passion for humanity.

"One reason why the [AACM] movement didn't happen in Memphis or Indianapolis or Detroit or Pittsburgh is that Chicago was the destination of the migrant black tenant farmer," said Howard Mandel, a Chicago native who attended AACM concerts and the author of *Miles, Ornette, Cecil: Jazz Beyond Jazz.* "People ended up there. They were strivers and wanted to change their lives, and they gave that feeling to their children. Becoming a musician was protection. It was as if to say, 'I'm an artist,' which in that community was as respected as sports or politics."[8]

In the years after World War II, Chicago attracted tens of thousands of black migrants from the South, and the city quickly became racially diverse. From 1950 to 1965, Chicago's black population doubled in size, making up 28 percent of the city's inhabitants.[9] Despite Chicago's surging population growth, however, the number of jazz clubs in the city dwindled in the early 1960s. By mid-decade only a handful of jazz venues remained. The decline resulted from changing music tastes, a rise in the popularity of records and radio-listening at home, and a nightclub tax structure that was based on the number of musicians performing on the bandstand. In addition, jazz clubs did little to improve real estate values, which the city hoped would rise and encourage gentrification of the largely black South Side.[10]

Even with its long history of subtle discrimination policies, Chicago in the 1950s didn't have a substantial civil rights movement, largely because of relatively low unemployment. But like many cities that experienced sudden inflows of blacks from the South, Chicago had restrictive real estate practices that contained the black community. Though the Congress of Racial Equality had been founded in Chicago in 1941 to battle the city's segregationist policies, economic progress in the 1950s enabled some black advancement, and the prosperity that followed suppressed extensive civil-rights protest and activism.[11]

But in the early 1960s the increasing black population led whites to flee the city for the suburbs—a flight that drained inner-city jobs, increased poverty, and exacerbated racial inequity. The economic squeeze led to increased outrage, particularly in the wake of the southern civil rights movement. Chicago blacks, many of whom had been born in the South, closely followed the unfolding events of black protest and subsequent violence. During the Montgomery, Alabama, bus boycott at the end of 1955, blacks in Chicago held supportive rallies and collected money to send to

Alabama. In 1960, inspired by the southern student lunch-counter sit-ins, a resurgent Chicago chapter of CORE and the NAACP's Youth Council picketed local Woolworth stores.[12]

No issue was more polarizing in Chicago, however, than the overcrowding of the city's public schools, which were populated largely by black students. To cope with the population surge in the mid-1950s, the school system's superintendent initiated double-shifts, so that two sets of students could attend school each day—one early in the morning and the other later in the day. The double-shift system affected nearly all the city's black students.[13] By the late 1950s blacks began advocating for a change in the schools to ease the overcrowding. But they were largely ignored by an educational system that saw no alternative to the solution it had imposed.

Before long, blacks who lived on Chicago's South Side reached their limit. In the summer of 1961, the city's NAACP chapter and the leading black newspaper, the *Chicago Defender*, called for black parents to register their children in less crowded all-white schools. When school officials refused to grant the transfers, black parents who felt that the double-shift system was unsettling and unfair filed a class-action suit. In January 1962 the city's first civil rights sit-in occurred. One mother involved in the protest told James R. Ralph Jr., the author of *Northern Protest: Martin Luther King, Jr., Chicago and the Civil Rights Movement*, "We weren't looking for any notoriety or anything like that. We just wanted our school situation straightened out. We didn't like the fact that they were going to school on double shift. We were just protesting the fact that they [school officials] had ignored us."[14] The problem dragged on, and in October 1963 the Coordinating Council of Community Organizations called for a mass boycott. Some 225,000 students stayed home from schools attended predominantly by blacks. Instead, Freedom Schools were set up in churches and neighborhood clubs so that students could continue their scholastic activities. By late 1963 the double-shift system was ended.[15]

The success achieved in the public schools in 1963 relieved the overcrowding but left many newly formed community organizations without a mission. In 1964 CORE in Chicago and Chicago Area Friends of the Student Nonviolent Coordinating Committee (SNCC) were foundering. Protests that had begun over unfair employment practices, housing discrimination, inadequate welfare programs, and unresponsive political leadership were fizzling out as well. The city's size made it difficult to unify affected residents on key issues and mobilize them effectively to push for social change. To a large extent, the voice that carried the most weight in the early 1960s in advocating power and self-determination was that of

Malcolm X. The civil rights leader had strong ties to Chicago, having first heard Elijah Muhammad speak there in 1952 when Malcolm X belonged to the Nation of Islam.

Two themes recurred in the speeches of Malcolm X—black self-sufficiency and separation from the white power structure. Malcolm X was essentially a cultural whip whose goal was to organize and unify communities so that a new, stronger culture would emerge. To create community solidarity, Malcolm X sought to establish a national conscious-ness that would render ineffective what he referred to as "the old Negro order." He said, "This type of so-called Negro, by being intoxicated over the white man, he never sees beyond the white man. He never sees beyond America. He never looks at himself or where he fits into things on the world stage. . . . And it puts him in the role of a beggar."[16]

When Malcolm X was assassinated in New York in February 1965, his death stunned black communities. In Chicago in April 1965, James Bevel, one of the Reverend Martin Luther King Jr.'s top associates, came to the city for a weekend of speeches and fund-raising. During one of his speeches, Bevel said that "the nonviolent movement in a few days, in a few weeks, in a few years will call on Chicago to address itself on the racist attitude that is denying Negroes the right to live in adequate housing. . . . We're going to have a movement in Chicago. We plan to close [Chicago] down."[17]

In less than five months, King and Andrew Young, a leader in King's Southern Christian Leadership Conference (SCLC), announced that they had selected Chicago as the target of SCLC's first northern campaign. Since 1962, SCLC had chosen a different southern city each year for a range of nonviolent demonstrations to shed light on racial injustice. The most successful of these efforts, in Birmingham, Alabama, in 1963, and Selma, Alabama, in 1965, had created sufficient outrage that state laws were passed to change the status quo.[18] Chicago was now in the crosshairs of the SCLC. What's more, a new spirit of community organizing was sweeping the city along with a desire to take up where Malcolm X had left off with regard to self-determination, creating an environment that was distinctly black and honoring black culture and causes.

ORGANIZING THE AACM

For young black Chicago jazz musicians of the mid-1960s, opportunities to record and play in clubs were drying up. To remain jazz musicians in this environment, artists had to reimagine the future and redefine the terms of their own creative self-satisfaction. The pianist Muhal Richard Abrams had recognized for some time that relying on white-owned recording companies and clubs would result in neither creative fulfillment nor a sufficient personal income. Chicago simply wasn't as diverse a recording town as New York or Los Angeles. And by 1965 clubs were booking R&B, soul, and rock bands to draw a younger market. Even bebop and hard bop—the jazz of Chicago's youth—had run their course and sounded dated.

But the decision to found a musician's organization to stage, promote, and support jazz presented Abrams with a range of challenges: jazz musicians weren't especially known for their adherence to structure or deadlines: the true nature of a creative artist compels him or her to rail against structure and resist being part of a collective group; and the self-confident musician, like all competitive individualists, will naturally want to take charge and stand out rather than accept a limited participatory role. Attempts by musicians in several other cities to form cooperatives that would help artists control their own works would be short-lived. Individual musicians like Randy Weston had attempted to do this on their own in the early 1960s in coordination with attorneys and a few other musicians. But those attempts had always been difficult, costly, and often lacked broad support among major band leaders. In 1964, two collectives were formed—the Underground Musicians' Association (UGMA) in Los Angeles and the Jazz Composer's Guild (JCG) in New York. But neither group was able to gain much traction. Both markets were status driven, and the better musicians preferred to gravitate toward one another for work rather than to foster the art of the collective. Meetings of the collectives would dissolve into clubhouse conversations or group therapy sessions as members viewed them as opportunities to complain about a wide range of work-related issues.[19]

Musicians in Chicago, however, had a different vision of a collective. The musicians who founded the AACM viewed it as an opportunity to champion and support a new form of original jazz rather than to find gigs by networking or protest conditions. When Muhal Richard Abrams, Phil Cohran, Steve McCall, and Jodie Christian met in early 1965 to discuss forming a nonprofit collective, their goal initially was an organization that would help black jazz musicians who were struggling. Just months after Malcolm X's assassination, the group's thinking was very much in line with the late civil rights leader's deep belief in self-determination and do-it-yourself achievement. As George Lewis pointed out in his book

A Power Stronger Than Itself: The AACM and American Experimental Music, the writer Jacques Attali identified remarks by Malcolm X as foreshadowing the kind of organization that was fervently desired by these artists: "The white musician can jam if he's got some sheet music in front of him," Malcolm X had said shortly before his death. "He can jam on something he's heard jammed before. But that black musician, he picks up his horn and starts blowing some sounds that he never thought of before. He improvises, he creates, it comes from within. It's . . . within himself. And this is what you and I want. You and I want to create an organization that will give us so much power we can sit and do as we please." Lewis also noted that Attali, writing in his book *Noise: The Political Economy of Music,* saw in these words how Malcolm X "valorizes improvisation as a way to create conditions for change" and sketches "the mindset that was emerging in important segments of the black community at mid-decade."[20]

In Chicago early in 1965, many black jazz musicians sensed that the recording and radio industries had tired of jazz and had moved on to seek larger profits other forms of music. There was also concern that white rock musicians from Britain—who had leveraged American blues and R&B—were achieving enormous popularity and success at the expense of black musicians. As the co-founder of the AACM Phil Cohran told Lewis, "There was a general feeling that we had been robbed of our culture."[21]

In April 1965, Abrams, Christian, Cohran, and McCall sent out postcards to Chicago's black jazz musicians, inviting them to a May 8 meeting at Cohran's home. The musicians who attended these early meetings never referred to what they were doing as avant-garde or free jazz. They defined their new approach as anything but the style of jazz that already existed. "With Muhal, the music you played had to be creative," said the saxophonist Joseph Jarman, one of the first AACM members, who would later join the Art Ensemble of Chicago. "He wouldn't accept what you had written if it sounded like Miles Davis or Ornette Coleman. If you wrote music like they did, he would make you feel guilty by saying the music was as though they had written it, not you. So you had to push yourself to write music that didn't sound like the things you had already heard, no matter how far out the music became. That was a standing rule. Muhal said we had to liberate ourselves and come up with our own perspectives."[22]

At first, the musicians who met at Cohran's home were stuck on a definition of "original music." The saxophonist Gene Easton, who attended the meetings, told Lewis: "Original, in one sense, means something you write in the particular system that we're locked up with now in this society. We express ourselves in this system because it's what we learned. As we learn more of other systems of music around the world, we're getting closer to the music that our ancestors played and which we are denied the right to really stretch out in. I feel that the authors of this business structure here had in mind sound-conscious musicians, if necessary finding a complete new system that expresses *us*. We're locked up in a system, and if you don't express in the system that is known, you're ostracized. And there are many, far too many good musicians put in that position because they don't, uh, [conform]."[23]

As the first meeting came to a close, the participants agreed that artists who belonged to the group would have to present their own original music. At the second meeting, on May 15, the attendees agreed that members would not work for club owners but instead would only hold concerts. They also agreed that they would be a nonprofit and that they would elect officers, who would iron out in future meetings exactly what a nonprofit had to do to comply with state laws.

At the next meeting, on May 27, the group struggled with the new organization's name until the pianist Ken Chaney mentioned that on the original postcard invitations that went out, Abrams had said it was a meeting for "the advancement of creative music." So the group was named the Association for the Advancement of Creative Musicians. At a meeting on May 29, the members voted and agreed to adopt their organization's name. But another issue emerged. Abrams suggested that membership be confined to a certain group of musicians: "We're going to have to make a consideration as to whether we're going to have an interracial organization, or have it as it stands now in reference to membership."[24]

The white pianist Bob Dogan wanted clarification: "You mean that if someone is a certain race then they can't come into the group?" Abrams replied, "I mean that we are going to have to decide whether we will have an interracial group or not. Being frank about it, when we started we didn't intend to have an interracial group. Not as opposed to another race, but we made it on the premise that each has his own, up to a certain height. Then the collaboration and contact with the other races or body takes place." To which Dogan responded: "Yeah, but that would throw some low blows to a lot of cats that might really be interested."[25]

At the end of the meeting, Abrams said, "There are good musicians on the North Side, too, I mean white musicians. It's not their fault the way these people manipulate things. The musicians don't do it. It's the people that control the thing. . . . Our ticket is to get ourselves together as a body. They got the thing set up in a certain way, but they can't control us because we have the music and this is what they're after. Now, if that's not a good reason for organizing, I don't know what is. Don't think in terms of 'Aw man, I ain't prejudiced.' That's not the point. We're talking about getting an alliance. We're not fighting a racial fight. We're promoting ourselves and helping ourselves up to a point where we can participate in the universal aspect of things, which includes all people."[26]

The AACM formulated and approved nine goals or "purposes":

1. To cultivate young musicians and to create music of a high artistic level for the general public through the presentation of programs designed to magnify the importance of creative music.

2. To create an atmosphere conducive to artistic endeavors for the artistically inclined by maintaining a workshop for the express purpose of bringing talented musicians together.

3. To conduct a free training program for young aspirant musicians.

4. To contribute financially to the programs of the Abraham Lincoln Center and other charitable organizations.

5. To provide a source of employment for worthy creative musicians.

6. To set an example of high moral standards for musicians and to uplift the public image of creative musicians.

7. To increase mutual respect between creative artists and musical tradesmen (booking agents, managers, promoters and instrument manufacturers, etc.).

8. To uphold the tradition of cultured musicians handed down from the past.

9. To stimulate spiritual growth in creative artists through recitals, concerts, etc., through participation in programs.[27]

On August 5, 1965, the Association for the Advancement of Creative Musicians received its charter from Illinois, establishing the organization as nonprofit and tax-exempt. Its mission was to stage original contemporary music in concert settings, compelling audiences to listen to and experience the music rather than treat it as background for their own conversations.

"Muhal Richard Abrams was a brilliant organizer," said Mandel. "From what I saw, which was later validated by George Lewis's book *A Power Stronger Than Itself: The AACM and American Experimental Music*, he was behind everything back then. He was self-educated and not particularly well traveled, but he had a strong curiosity and penetrating intellect, which helped the AACM get its bearings in the early years. Later, friction did arise over the jockeying between the musicians in the Art Ensemble of Chicago [AEC] and those who weren't a part of their immediate circle. Lester Bowie of the AEC, who was AACM president for a while, seemed less interested in bringing newer groups along than in supporting those musicians who already had acquired some visibility and career momentum."[28]

ACHIEVING CREATIVE FREEDOM

By insisting that music performed by members be wholly original, the AACM initiated a jazz style that sounded to the untrained ear like free jazz combined with global elements now known as world music. "The sensibility that led to the AACM's formation wasn't a direct result of civil rights protest or black power," said the jazz critic Larry Kart, who grew up in Chicago and regularly attended AACM concerts in the 1960s. "Its creation was certainly in harmony with the civil rights movement and perhaps even at the forefront of it. But the reality is that the AACM movement was driven by a desire to be free in every conceivable sense. What motivated these musicians wasn't rebellion against white culture. The AACM was a way for them to appropriate all forms of music through an original expression. Their view was, 'Here are these tropes or language—we can play with them to create artistic freedom, which was always the goal."[29]

But it's impossible to evaluate the AACM's formation without taking into consideration the charged times and the climate in which the organization was formed. "The AACM in some ways was the ultimate protest," Kart said. "The AACM believed that the most effective form of protest was to change the system by expressing themselves artistically. But music wasn't a medium of protest for these guys. They believed that if protest is all they could do with their music, then they'd be slaves to the same system that failed them. What they wanted to do was make music that they found interesting—free from boundaries imposed by others. That was a pretty tall order." Most listeners—both black and white—struggled to understand and appreciate the AACM's artistic message. Much of the original music lacked the buildup-and-release song structure of earlier jazz styles. Nor did it have a steady beat, repetitive melodies, or anything consistent in the traditional sense. But like the action painters of the early 1950s and some of the New York poets of the late 1950s, AACM musicians made music that was largely about sound textures and emotional force.

"The AACM arose during the middle of the civil rights era, and I was very interested in the cause," Mandel recalled.[30] "I liked the musicians who belonged to the AACM because they weren't just power-blowing high-energy free jazz. Their music was more structured and compositional. There were many more formal things taken into account than what we heard on records by many of New York's avant-garde musicians. AACM musicians were playing much more absorbing compositional ideas. The music was thoroughly original, yet the artists were obviously jazz musicians. I'd go to places like the Jazz Showcase to hear more mainstream jazz saxophonists like Jimmy Forrest, Eddie 'Lockjaw' Davis, Johnny Griffin, and Dexter Gordon. Their playing was great, but it was formulaic—the same swing-to-bop bluesy chord changes at top speed over and over. AACM saxophonist Fred Anderson was certainly capable of playing the same thing over and over, but what he played was modal, harmonically different, just as intense, and more exciting to me.

"Most AACM musicians also were not overtly political. If you look at the titles of compositions by AACM musicians versus originals by artists on the Impulse or Blue Note labels at the time, you'd see they were not making the same kinds of political references or statements. For the most part, AACM musicians were not associated with the rhetoric of black nationalism or separatism and were not confrontational, except aesthetically. Certainly, there were times when I was the only white kid at a performance at the Pumpkin Room or Los Brisas. But no one ever looked at me and said, 'What are you doing here?' They said, 'Cool! We hope you like it.' These guys wanted an audience."

The first AACM event was held on August 16, 1965, and featured the Joseph Jarman Quintet.[31] "As a young musician in Chicago, you couldn't help but be influenced by jazz," Jarman said.[32] "This was especially true [as students] in the crowded high schools. Everyone was pushed together, and we were constantly interacting. At Dunbar High School in the fifties, during our breaks at lunch, a friend and I used to go to a restaurant nearby where they had music playing over the speakers. We'd listen to hard bop as we ate a hotdog or a hamburger. We loved the music and the blues. It was part of us. But when I returned to Chicago after being discharged from the army, I loved the new energy of what Muhal Richard Abrams was doing and the chance to be creative and to play.

"The AACM wasn't established to be a protest movement. It was an art movement. But we also weren't living in a vacuum. We knew about the racism down South, the terrible things going on Vietnam, and the racial divide in Chicago. I don't know how to put this. Music for us was a place far away emotionally, but we were making a statement at the same time. Sometimes the energy of pulling away creates energy going the other way. That's what was happening. Our music wasn't a slap in anyone's face, or a rebellion against traditional jazz and the blues. We wanted to be free of convention and what had come before us. This was about being completely liberated artistically and about playing jazz as we pleased, without having to worry about the listening public at large.

"Ours was mind music, not music for the feet," Jarman continued. "Most of jazz had been about dancing or sitting at a table tapping your feet. It was music to entertain listeners physically. If they also chose to think about what they were hearing, great, but it wasn't necessary. The AACM's music required that listeners think. You couldn't appreciate what we were playing unless you let yourself go and thought about what we were saying and what you were thinking. We didn't expect to reach large numbers of people, just those who could suspend traditional ways of listening to music and could hear our message. The message wasn't about protest but about global unity, about world thinking. This is still true today. Most people expect jazz to be relatively basic—a beat, a melody, a solo or two, and then that's it. We were free from all that. All that mattered for us is how musicians channeled their minds and expressed themselves spiritually."

But the avant-garde movement in Chicago was a secessionist movement of sorts, a collective of artists withdrawing from the mainstream to be original. In the eyes of AACM musicians, the mainstream was hopelessly corrupted and jazz was compromised as a result. "The AACM was an awakening for me," Jarman said. "We were rejecting the hostility and anger you saw in the news all the time. All of those images were a revelation and revolting at the same time. Muhal [Richard Abrams] allowed us to play our music, to go on and on and on with what we were trying to say. Through this, we developed new ways of expressing ourselves and expressing jazz."

Yet, at the same time, the music served as therapy, a way to remain optimistic—not about the future survival of jazz but about jazz as an aesthetic movement free from jazz employers and their conditions for payment. "There were places in Chicago where AACM musicians could play music," Jarman said. "A lot of the master jazz musicians saw us at those places and asked to play with us, so we knew we were on to something. One night John Coltrane invited me, Roscoe Mitchell, and Lester Bowie to play with him on Chicago's North Side. He knew we were into some stuff. It was extraordinarily exciting.

"What I learned from Coltrane is to keep moving forward and to make what you're playing strong. Again, this wasn't a protest movement or a civil rights thing. It was an artistic, intellectual revolution. We were aware of current events, and we all wrote stories and songs inspired by what was happening. But the music was about expression and freeing ourselves from those negative experiences, not using them to make a point. The AACM's music was about the wonderfulness of music and the uniqueness of all the universe."

The AACM seemed to have little or no desire to convince mainstream record companies to take notice. "When I first heard these musicians in January 1966, the AACM was less than a year old," said John Litweiler, a Chicago native and author of *The Freedom Principle: Jazz After 1958*. "The organization was new and very do-it-yourself. The AACM musicians I met supported the civil rights movement and played some benefit concerts. They felt strongly about civil rights. The others did, too. All of the musicians were aware of the civil rights movement and found the black consciousness in speeches by Malcolm X and Reverend Martin Luther King Jr. inspiring. But their main impetus was to create something new and perform it for audiences. And from the beginning, they found they were playing for large, appreciative audiences."[33]

What then is the AACM's lasting impact on jazz? "The AACM got and is still getting as much mileage as it could or should have," said the jazz critic Larry Kart. "All of the AACM's music that really mattered has been made and heard. And it has meaning to those people for whom it would have meaning. In reality, given the free nature of the kinds of music that the various musicians wanted to make and did make, how popular can any of that music really be in our world? Their music wasn't intended to please broadly or be absorbed without some strain.

"But all in all, the AACM has done pretty well for itself in terms of the quality of the music its musicians produced. You had a bunch of talented musicians who wanted to follow a new set of ideals without restriction. The result was music that was completely lucid. There's no groping there. The AACM's protest movement was against established jazz styles, and the result was a completely new form that truly liberated the musicians who played it."[34]

But for jazz musicians in New York and Southern California, who earned a living by making club appearances and record dates, acoustic jazz was on the ropes. By 1967 jazz played on saxophones, trumpets, trombones, upright bases, and even pianos was losing ground to the appeal of rock and soul-funk music and the widespread use of electronic instruments.

Evidence of this shift was mounting in the form of new outdoor music fes-tivals and concerts that attracted tens of thousands of fans. Concert series like the Newport Jazz Festival had been held since the 1950s, but the jazz crowds that arrived with picnic baskets to see the performances of Duke Ellington, Gerry Mulligan, and Dinah Washington were never that large.

For young rock concertgoers, part of the appeal was the music and a chance to be free among thousands of other young people doing as they pleased. But what made the experience particularly exhilarating was expo-sure to new technology. Rock in 1967 began to break free of the 45-rpm format and was beginning to assume jazz's long-solo format in concerts and its freedom of expression on albums. But electronic instruments, dramatic lighting techniques, and louder volume were the elements that attracted and energized the crowds attending outdoor and arena concerts. Jazz, for the first time in its history, had some catching up to do.

10 Lights, Volume, and Fusion

In February 1969 Bill Hanley received a phone call from Stan Goldstein that would eventually change the direction of jazz. At the time, Hanley ran Hanley Sound, a company in Medford, Massachusetts, that designed sound systems for jazz and pop concerts. His company had already created systems for more than forty events, including the Newport Jazz Festival in the late fifties and sixties, President Lyndon Johnson's inauguration in 1965, and the Miami Pop Festival in 1968. Goldstein, in 1969, was a recording engineer who, with Michael Lang, had organized the Miami Pop Festival the preceding year. After some small talk, Goldstein asked Hanley how he might go about designing a sound system for a large-scale outdoor concert that he and Lang were planning for later that summer. "I didn't tell Stan a thing," Hanley recalled. "I felt that if I did, he would try to design the system himself."[1]

In the weeks that followed his phone conversation with Goldstein, Hanley continued to hear talk among colleagues about Lang's pending concert and how big it was going to be. "The more I heard, the more I wanted to do the job," Hanley said. "That spring I drove down from Medford to Michael Lang's office in New York's Greenwich Village. We spoke, and I told him that I wanted to design the sound system. Michael said he wanted me to do it, too, since all the rock acts were already familiar with me."

Lang hired Hanley, and the two agreed to meet that spring at the home of Max Yasgur, a dairy farmer. "When Michael arrived, he spoke with Max and we agreed to drive out and look at Max's properties, to pick the one that was most suitable for the concert," Hanley said. When the three men drove off in Lang's car, Yasgur pointed out his different fields. "They were all too flat and not really ideal from a sound standpoint," Hanley said.

"But as we approached Hurd Road, I spotted a long sweeping slope of land that made more sense. I asked Michael's driver to pull over. Michael, Max, and I got out, and we split up to walk the property. First I examined the hill. From a sound guy's standpoint, there was a straight line of sight from anywhere up on that hill to where the stage would be below. This meant that no matter where someone sat, they'd be able to see and hear the acts without anyone blocking them. I also liked the shape of the hill. It was like a bowl—rising on the left, right and center. It was a natural arena."

Lang and Hanley had found their thirty-seven acres for the Woodstock Music and Art Festival. They also leased several hundred additional acres from Yasgur and neighboring landowners for the festival grounds. But only thirty days remained before the start of the festival, and Hanley had to design and build a sound system for the event. He raced back to Medford to begin the task. He decided he would create two seventy-foot towers made of scaffolding, with speakers mounted on each frame. "The towers needed to be tall enough so the music could reach the highest spots on that hill," Hanley said. "I wanted the sound to reach into the little pockets in the back of the slope."

The speaker system would be bigger than anything Hanley had ever designed for the Newport Jazz Festival or his earlier pop and rock concerts. "Each tower I erected for Woodstock had an upper and lower speaker system," Hanley said. "The top section featured full-range speakers focused on the back of the property—which was the highest point on the hill. The bottom speaker sections had to be designed to reach everyone else who was seated on the ground level. I knew that gaining access to electrical power wasn't going to be a big problem, so I wasn't worried about that. They were going to bring in three-phase power from the town's utility, which would give us enough available power to run lights and sound."

The next step was to erect twelve-foot high walls around the stage and towers. The purpose was two-fold—to discourage crowds from surging forward, since crowds weren't likely to advance if they couldn't see, and to protect the performers. Audiences for hard rock at the time were different from those who turned out for jazz, folk, or pop. Uninhibited performances by rock artists tended to energize crowds, causing them to want to move closer to the stage to show their support and enthusiasm. But at an event of Woodstock's size, such a routine crowd surge could lead to disaster. "I had watched crowd-control problems unfold at the Newport Folk Festival in 1965 when Bob Dylan decided to play a set on an electric guitar," Hanley said. "I had become a student of this type of behavior. My solution at Woodstock not only protected the crowds and performers but also allowed for a trench between the stage and the wall to allow the film guys to run their camera dolly back and forth."

But as growing numbers of people arrived at Woodstock with sleeping bags, tents and blankets, Hanley realized that his speaker system—designed for an audience of a hundred thousand—would have to reach more than four times that number. In simple terms, he would need to crank up the volume without distorting the music. "When I saw how many people were sitting up on that hill behind my original line of reach, I had to change things around," Hanley said. "On the first day, I went under the stage to the amplifiers and changed the compressors. These controlled how much information was being sent to the amplifiers. My change brought up the lower levels of music but also made sure that the higher levels didn't distort. This resulted in less dynamic range, preventing the bass from becoming rubbery and the high end from crackling with distortion. The music could be heard loud and clear across the entire property."

The increased volume had an interesting psychological effect on the people who were there. "Even if you were far from the stage and could just make out the acts down the hill, you still could hear everything clearly," Hanley said. "It was an audio illusion. You were looking at something small and very far away—but you could hear everything as clearly as though you were sitting close to it. There's a certain excitement in that. No matter where you were, you had a great seat from a sound standpoint. And because of the hill you had a great view." After Woodstock, feeling rock—in many cases to excess—became as important as hearing it at concerts. "Volume without distortion raised the stakes and made rock more spectacular," Hanley said. "From a sound perspective, I had never before designed anything as large as I had for Woodstock—or as powerful."

Given that nearly a half-million people were drawn to a series of fields in August 1969, rock proved there that it could attract enormous crowds. But at Woodstock, rock itself was transformed into a showcase for electric instruments and a celebration of music that lasted longer than a 45-rpm record. With the rise of the rock album—complete with a color cover, photos, liner notes, and a list of band members—fans felt a strong emotional connection to the artists and to music's new longer format. What's more, Woodstock and the music performed there seemed to bypass traditional industry formulas. Whether stoned or straight, Woodstock performers came across as passionate performers, committed to the music. Acts didn't need fan clubs, Saturday-morning cartoon shows featuring their animated likenesses, or dolls and board games. With the rise of the rock concept album in 1967, the music changed dramatically from its pop-rock incarnation. For the hundreds of thousands of young people who camped out at Woodstock in August 1969, longer songs and solos were musical extensions of their own rebellions and anxieties.

But the extended songs and solos, with their greater reliance on instrumental expression, inadvertently triggered another significant change. They shifted the demographics of rock. After years spent wooing female record buyers with gentle love songs, rock by 1969 was growing more brutish and attracting more male consumers. Rather than offer a collection of singles of varying quality, albums after 1967 featured long original pieces with a focus on instrumental solos. When there were lyrics, the words often relied on psychedelic imagery or the blues rather than on dating, stolen love, and breaking up—themes that had appealed largely to teenage girls. This shift had the greatest impact on men, boosting their attendance at concerts. While protest and rebellion were on the minds of many young concertgoers in 1969, women could have crushes on the male musicians while men imagined themselves up onstage, playing guitar, bass, or drums with the band. By 1969, rock offered fantasies for everyone.

After Woodstock, as rock itself changed, so did its presentation to its audience. It was now firmly about electricity and power, manifested in volume—a loud, clear sound that could fill indoor venues with large audiences that wanted a taste of the collective music-listening experience. After Woodstock, a rock concert had to be not only heard but also felt. Volume and sonic clarity were now essential, especially after touring rock bands in the late 1960s began performing in indoor sports arenas. Jazz musicians took notice of the changes. To compete and attract large crowds, a growing number of them in the late 1960s and early 1970s took up electronic instruments, performed at a louder volume, embraced the psychedelic movement, developed concept albums, and dabbled in the Eastern religions and New Age spiritualism popular among West Coast rock bands, particularly in the San Francisco area. Young jazz audiences were changing as well.

ROCK'S WAR, JAZZ'S GAIN

By the end of 1966, rock was at war with itself. The war had started a year earlier with the vocal outrage by audience members at the Newport Folk Festival over Bob Dylan's decision to play the electric guitar. Older folk traditionalists—musicians and fans—were incensed by the use of electric instruments by younger folk musicians, fearful that amps and egotism would corrupt the music's selfless political message and undercut older legends' position as folk icons. A growing number of San Francisco and Los Angeles electric folk-rock groups—the Byrds, the Grateful Dead, Jefferson Airplane, Big Brother and the Holding Company, and Canned Heat—leery of judgmental folk purists in New York's Greenwich Village—decided to skip New York and take up residence in rural Laurel Canyon, on the outskirts of Los Angeles, and in Mill Valley, north of San Francisco.

In 1966 the West Coast's electric folk-rock movement began to expand, creating music meant to reflect or ease anxieties over future shock. News headlines indicated that something in the culture was broken and that unless musicians articulated the problem and a generation spoke up, the slide would only continue. For these musicians, the world was becoming frighteningly obsessed with science and technology and neglecting individuality and humanity. Consider the major news stories of the year: Surgeons completed the first successful heart transplant, an H-bomb was lost in the Pacific, Surveyor I landed on the moon, the civil rights leader James Meredith was shot, America expanded its bombing campaign of North Vietnam, the serial killer Richard Speck was arrested, draft cards were burned, Charles Whitman went on a shooting spree in Texas, killing fifteen people and wounding thirty-one, polls showed that most Americans doubted the truthfulness of the Warren Report's investigation of President Kennedy's assassination, and the 1966 elections resulted in big gains for Republicans. In California, Ronald Reagan was elected governor and instantly became a lightning rod for the West Coast youth culture's grievances on college campuses.[2]

But perhaps the social trend of 1966 with the biggest impact on the music was the growing black market for lysergic acid diethylamide (LSD). Two years earlier, the lab-made hallucinogenic drug had been popularized by three Harvard psychologists—Timothy Leary, Richard Alpert, and Ralph Metzner—in their book *The Psychedelic Experience.* LSD, easy to produce synthetically and increasingly popular on college campuses, was promoted by medical "experts," who claimed it released artistic impulses. Leary in 1964 spoke of LSD as a tool that electrified all the senses, "a sacred biochemical which can carry men though all the levels of consciousness . . . through which men can be their own Buddha, own Christ, or own Confucius."[3] Leary warned, however, that use of the drug required careful preparation and the presence of a "guide"—someone familiar with LSD and aware of the terrors and ecstasies it might cause. The experience, Leary said, could be "electric with ecstasy" or terrifying, though he promised that the terror did not result in damage. But in April 1965 the Food and Drug Administration addressed college administrators in a letter warning of LSD's dangers. Estimates of LSD use at the time varied from less than 1 percent to a third of all college students. States, unwilling to wait for the federal government to crack down on LSD's use, took action.[4]

In late 1965 Switzerland's Sandoz Laboratories, at the request of the U.S. government, stopped shipping LSD to the United States for research and psychiatric use. But by April 1966 the use of homemade LSD had become so widespread that *Time* magazine warned about its dangers. Finally, in 1966, California enacted a law prohibiting the illicit manufacture, distribution, and possession of LSD, and on October 6, 1966, LSD was made illegal in the United States and was controlled so strictly that possession and recreational use were criminalized and all legal scientific research programs on the drug in the country were shut down.[5]

Many of the renegade chemists or "cooks" who manufactured LSD were based in Northern California; they were able to continue producing it for a large and growing college and post-college market.[6] As folk-rock musicians took up residence in California, the audience for their music grew, thanks initially to the state's massive concentration of college-age students. These musicians and college-age audiences also began experimenting with LSD. By early 1967, California folk-rock musicians had recorded songs that re-created trip experiences. "LSD was new then," said Grace Slick, the lead singer of Jefferson Airplane. "It opened up our heads and gave us new insight into the fact that reality isn't just one thing. That excited us. But it was also terrifying if your head wasn't in the right place. So in hindsight, our advocating for LSD was kind of dangerous. As a group, Jefferson Airplane didn't take acid and record. But we were taking the listener on a musical interpretation of a trip, depending on who in the group wrote the song. Those who did take LSD found that you can go pretty much wherever you wanted to go—musically and artistically."[7]

The new folk-rock groups that settled in California often resisted the mandates of traditional record-industry executives who relied on marketing gimmicks to garner TV and radio publicity for pop-rock groups. The folk-rock groups tended to view mainstream pop-rock acts as artistic sellouts who embraced synthetic, formulaic models. What's more, musicians knew well that most pop-rock acts weren't recording the instruments on their own singles and albums. Many acts were merely fronts for studio musicians in Los Angeles, Detroit, and New York, who did much of the actual recording.

"When the demand for rock exploded at the very start of the sixties, record companies had to churn out tons of music fast with a big beat and tight sound," said Hal Blaine, a studio drummer in Los Angeles who recorded on hundreds of pop-rock singles, including thirty-nine no. 1 hits in the 1960s and 1970s. "To hold down studio costs, producers had no choice but to bring in professional musicians who could nail songs the first time through. That meant us. This is why so many of the pop-rock groups didn't sound great in concert. They weren't proficient enough to sound like their own records. Then again, teens tend to hear with their eyes at concerts. Subconsciously, audiences were willing to cut bands slack onstage, but not when they bought their records. To be a hit, a single had to have a certain snap."[8]

By the end of 1966, a new form of folk-rock surfaced on the West Coast that emphasized vocal harmony and electronic instruments. Among those new instruments was an amplified twelve-string Rickenbacker guitar that was favored by Roger McGuinn of the Byrds. "It wasn't part of my arsenal back in the folk days 'cause it hadn't been invented yet," McGuinn told the writer Harvey Kubernik. "F. C. Hall came up with the idea [for the guitar] in the early '60s, and I asked him why he did it. He said, 'For folk music.' He didn't realize that no self-respecting folk singer would be caught dead with an electric guitar at the time. And so he made this folk electric guitar, which was perfect for what I was doing."[9]

As the rock record industry expanded in Los Angeles and San Francisco to take advantage of the folk-rock talent, bands like the Doors, 13th Floor Elevators, Great Society, and the Grateful Dead began recording and performing longer songs with extended solos. Some of these artists were influenced by John Coltrane, Ornette Coleman, Miles Davis, and other jazz artists who were already playing lengthy tracks in a freer style. Though many of these folk-rock groups released singles, they largely rejected the restrictions of the 45-rpm, preferring instead to explore music by making greater use of instrumentals on albums.

Following the release of the Beatles' *Sgt. Pepper's Lonely Hearts Club Band* in 1967, West Coast rock began to dominate album sales, and jazz was an unintended beneficiary. Once album-oriented rock had established itself with the use of extended original compositions, jazz no longer was compelled to cover three-minute pop-rock hits. Instead, jazz became a collaborator in the psychedelic, long-form folk-rock culture, which by 1967 prized extended instrumentals over vocals. To survive in this new era and appeal to young album buyers and concertgoers, particularly on college campuses, jazz artists began to incorporate elements of San Francisco rock.

Jazz musicians like the guitarist Larry Coryell and the vibraphonist Gary Burton were experimenting, separately, with jazz-rock hybrids as early as 1966. Late that year, Coryell's group, Free Spirits, recorded *Out of Sight and Sound*, on which jazz themes took a back seat to a pounding beat and electric rock guitar and bass. When interviewed by his wife for her 1978 book *Jazz-Rock Fusion*, Coryell reflected:

JULIE: Did moving to New York affect your music?

LARRY: New York represented two things: the old jazz tradition, because all the great players were there, and something new, because Bob Dylan and the Beatles were just happening then, and I felt that New York was kind of going to have something to offer in the way of non-jazz music as well. I always admired rock and roll, and I love to play blues—especially string bending. Jazz was always the first priority. I never confused the musicality and the integrity of jazz with the spirit and different rhythmic infusions of rock.

J: Infusions, you say?

L: Yeah, because at that time, jazz was dotted eighth note and sixteenth note type of time—almost like a perverted straight eight. And I felt that one of the groovy things about rock was that it was more related to Latin music and had another kind of syncopated sophistication that jazz had kind of squeezed out of the dotted eighth and sixteenth thing. I felt it was only a matter of time before somebody who liked Elvin Jones could also like George Harrison.

J: Was Jimi Hendrix a main influence on you?

L: Jimi was a main influence on everybody. The reason a lot of people compare me to him is because we both admired a lot of the same blues, and we were also the same age. He was really the best electric guitar player I ever saw.

J: The Free Spirits was one of the earliest fusion bands to record (1966). Tell me about its inception.

L: The Free Spirits came about as a result of five tripped-out cats—Columbus "Chip" Baker, Jim Pepper, Chris Hill, Bobby Moses and myself—from all parts of the world who moved into the same block of the same neighborhood. We felt that we would be years ahead of our time if we made the music we wanted to.

J: Which was what?

L: What later became known as jazz-rock.[10]

In truth, Coryell's efforts with Free Spirits in 1966 didn't really contain enough jazz to be considered jazz-rock fusion. Gary Burton's *Time Machine*, from the same year, suffered from a similar problem—it clung too closely to jazz to be called rock or even a hybrid. Not until Burton and Coryell united, in early 1967, did jazz-rock fusion start to crystallize.

RISE OF JAZZ-ROCK FUSION

The beginning of jazz-rock fusion dates roughly to the spring of 1967, and the vibraphonist Gary Burton's experiments with the guitarist Larry Coryell, documented on Burton's album *Duster*. Jazz hybrids have been around since the earliest days of the music, and jazz itself was a fusion of forms—a mashing of ragtime, syncopated New Orleans parade music, and the blues. As radio and phonograph records became popular in the 1920s, jazz borrowed and merged with popular music to give itself an air of sophistication and mass appeal. Popular music, in turn, reached out to jazz to create greater excitement and earthiness. George Gershwin's *Rhapsody in Blue* in 1924 is one of the early jazz-classical hybrids. Duke Ellington's orchestra in the 1920s can be considered a fusion band, adapting classical motifs as well as the blues. With the arrival of the rumba in the late 1920s, Xavier Cugat blended Latin and jazz.

In the decades that followed, jazz musicians continued to incorporate different music forms in an attempt to remain relevant, create a new sound, and earn a living. At the same time, other genres adapted jazz. Country acts of the late 1940s like Bob Wills and His Texas Playboys, Spade Cooley, and Merle Travis adapted jazz motifs to attract dancers, resulting in Western Swing. In the fifties and early sixties jazz and Latin forms bounced back and forth to create entirely new genres. This was certainly true of R&B and jazz in the late 1940s and early 1950s, and the bossa nova and jazz in the early 1960s.

By the 1960s a younger generation of jazz musicians wanted to embrace the power of rock and soul. These musicians weren't bitter about the arrival of rock, but they wanted to create a larger following for their own music. Perhaps no rock group had a bigger influence on young white jazz artists in the mid-1960s than the Beatles. "I had just left Stan Getz and started my own band," Gary Burton said. "I knew I needed to get a record done to promote my new quartet. I had met Larry Coryell at a jam session in New York and invited him to join the group. Bassist Eddie Gomez and drummer Joe Hunt were in the group as well. We worked in Boston and at Café Au Go Go in New York. Then I started looking around for new material.[11]

"From the start, I wanted to merge country, rock, and classical into our jazz quartet. Steve Swallow joined the group, but the drum chair was unsettled for a while. I wanted Roy Haynes, but he was still with Stan Getz, and he wanted to wait until I had become more established. He wasn't sure the job I offered him would last. But Roy came over soon after, and we went into the RCA studio in April 1967."

Burton's concept was to integrate rock with jazz and attract younger listeners. "Audiences for Stan were twice my age," Burton recalled. "I had this sense that straight-up jazz was not a good long-term setup, careerwise. I wanted to connect with listeners my own age, and I was digging the new rock music that had arrived. It seemed natural to incorporate them into my band. I was a huge Beatles fan. I was fascinated by what they were doing musically. When I left Stan to start my own thing, I knew I had to find a new niche. I looked at what Stan had done by combining Brazilian music with jazz, and asked myself, 'What do I relate to emotionally?' The answer was rock and country. My creative partner in this was Steve Swallow. He got the drift right away and helped me write tunes and make choices."

Did Burton realize that he had invented a new form of jazz in 1967? "Not at the time," he said. "I didn't see *Duster* as a groundbreaking thing. It was just another record. For the first year or so, my quartet was like the Lone Ranger, playing this new music that we called jazz-rock. We were really the only ones doing this at that point. Others were beginning to, like Gabor Szabo. Not until later in the 1960s did Miles Davis advance the concept, and in the early 1970s there was John McLaughlin with the Mahavishnu Orchestra and Chick Corea and Stanley Clarke with Return to Forever."

But Burton at first wasn't a hard-rock fan. "With *Duster*, my philosophy was simply to get out of the box that jazz was trapped inside of. My rock listening in '66 and early '67 wasn't much beyond the Beatles and Dylan. Until, that is, I got the band going and we traveled to San Francisco in '67 and played the Fillmore Auditorium opposite the Cream. I was impressed with the Cream's musicianship and realized that rock was more than just looking good onstage. I had grown up in an age when rock musicians were considered musical idiots by those who were well trained. Yet with the Cream, here were guys who were superb musicians. All of the guys from Cream knew how to play jazz and the blues. They were more mature than musicians in other bands, who were always so stoned out and living in a different world. The same was true of Mike Bloomfield, who had played with the Paul Butterfield Blues Band and Bob Dylan. He was a first-rate musician."

The Gary Burton Quartet spent extended periods in San Francisco, at one point playing for a month at the Trident in Sausalito. "This was the height of the psychedelic scene out there, which was a big influence on our music," he said. "Then producer Bill Graham discovered us. I had known Bill from the early sixties, when he had booked the George Shearing Quintet, when I was a member of the group. Bill told me he wanted to include more jazz at the Fillmore Auditorium in San Francisco. He said his biggest challenge was that most jazz groups were too stylistically removed to be compatible with the rock scene. He said my group was perfect."

Burton's quartet ended up spending eight weeks at a shot playing around San Francisco. "We'd go out to Mill Valley in Marin County north of San Francisco with [rock guitarist] Mike Bloomfield," Burton said. "Many rock acts of the time had homes up there. At parties, we'd hear talk about Jefferson Airplane. We were both on the RCA label at the time. I liked the band personally, but I wasn't a huge fan of their music. By the time my group recorded our second album, *Lofty Fake Anagram*, we had become practically a part of the San Francisco and Mill Valley scenes, and our form of jazz-rock fusion reflected it."

Drugs in San Francisco had become so prevalent by 1968 and 1969 that Burton recalled performances at the Fillmore as surreal for musicians. "You'd be onstage playing to a couple of thousand stoned-out young people milling around in front of you while a light show swirled on a screen behind you, and no one paid much attention to the band. The first time we played the Fillmore Auditorium, we had an acoustic bass and we didn't have gigantic amps. As we played, I noticed about a hundred people standing in front of the stage watching us. Everyone else was walking around like zombies. I thought we were dying up there, that we had turned off everyone or we hadn't been able to connect. When we came off the stage, I saw Bill Graham and apologized for not exciting the audience. Bill said, 'Gary, are you kidding? That's the biggest reaction to a jazz band we've had. They actually stood there and listened!'"

Although Miles Davis included electric instruments for the first time when he recorded *Miles in the Sky*, in January and May 1968, he didn't fully integrate electronic instrumentation and the soul-funk-rock influences of James Brown, Jimi Hendrix, and Sly Stone until *Filles de Kilimanjaro* in June and September 1968. On *In a Silent Way*, recorded in February 1969, Davis provided a more fully developed jazz-rock fusion model, adding an electric rock guitar for the first time.

"The sound of jazz began to shift during the time I was in Miles Davis's band starting in 1968," Chick Corea said. "Before joining Miles, I had been pretty much a purist in my tastes. I loved Miles and John Coltrane, and all the musicians who surrounded them. But I didn't look much further into rock or pop. I listened to a little bit of classical music, but that was it for me. When Miles began to experiment, I became aware of rock bands, the energy and the different type of communication they had with audiences during shows. I'd see young people at rock concerts standing up to listen rather than sitting politely. It was a different vibe and more my generation. It got me interested in communicating that way. People were standing because they were emotionally caught up in what they were hearing.

"Though Miles didn't give up his form of jazz, he did want to communicate with that new crowd—a younger, more emotionally expressive audience. So the sound and rhythm of his music changed. Volume, lights and stage drama were a big part of rock's appeal and the audience's vibe. If you performed at New York's Palladium or Fillmore in the late sixties, they were rock venues, so audiences there knew that the vibe was going to be different. They expected it. Concerts had to be noisier and more explosive because it was a younger scene than at jazz clubs. Jazz musicians almost had to respond with more intensive and experimental forms of music if they wanted access to these audiences."[12]

With the growing popularity of jazz-pop horn bands like Blood Sweat & Tears and Chicago in 1968 as well as the funk-rock group Sly and the Family Stone and the soul-funk artist James Brown, Davis, in 1969, again rebuilt his vision of jazz-rock fusion, documented by his recordings *In a Silent Way* and *Bitches Brew,* which pulled fusion firmly back into jazz's improvisational space while retaining rock's passion for electronics and free-form improvisation. The move by Davis was ironic, in that he had built his career on space and a lighter, more breathy playing style. "I know what the power of silence is," Miles Davis told Julie Coryell in her 1978 book. "When I used to play in clubs, everybody was loud; there was a lot of noise. So I would take my mute off the microphone, and I would play something so soft that you could hardly hear it . . . and you talk about listening."[13]

By 1969 jazz-rock fusion had gelled and intensified, relying more extensively on the electronic textures and circular modal forms that allowed for long open-ended solos. The drummer Tony Williams formed his Lifetime trio, with the organist Larry Young and the electric guitarist John McLaughlin, whom Williams coaxed to leave London to join the group. The move by McLaughlin was critical to the development of jazz-rock fusion, because he brought to the jazz guitar an entirely new, more metallic sound. There was plenty of free improvisation but also a steely wailing that was increasingly popular among lead guitarists in British hard-rock bands at the time.

"In 1969, bassist Dave Holland and I were sharing an apartment in London," McLaughlin said. "Dave was playing in one house band at Ronnie Scott's club, and I was in another. Plus, Dave was playing in a group I'd put together with saxophonist John Surman and drummer Tony Oxley. During the summer of 1969, pianist Bill Evans was playing at

Ronnie Scott's. Playing drums with him was drummer Jack DeJohnette. Jack loved to jam during the day, and Dave and I jammed with him during that time at Ronnie's. I was unaware that Jack had recorded one of our jams and had played the tape back in New York to Tony Williams, who told Jack that he was looking for a guitar player. Tony called me, and the rest is history. Of course, every European jazz musician considers New York paradise, so I didn't hesitate when Tony called."[14]

The Tony Williams Lifetime—with McLaughlin on guitar, Larry Young on organ, and Williams on drums—dramatically altered the direction of jazz, creating a challenging fusion model. The group had a distinct sound, with an emphasis on extended solos that embraced electronic instruments, volume, and layered sonic textures. The Tony Williams Lifetime recorded its first album, *Emergency!*, in May 1969—three months before McLaughlin began recording *Bitches Brew* with Miles Davis. "In a way, the shift to electric jazz was inevitable," McLaughlin said. "The '60s were phenomenal in terms of musical evolution and innovation. With the new concepts Miles was advocating, the fantastic work Coltrane was doing in the realm of integrating the spiritual dimension in jazz, the huge blues wave that had hit the U.K. a few years previously, and groups like the Beatles, who were incorporating their psychedelic experiences into a new kind of music, we were all being influenced by many aspects of music. By the time I arrived in New York, Miles was ready to begin the biggest jazz-rock fusion project of all time—*Bitches Brew*."

Davis recorded *Bitches Brew* in August 1969, though he had performed part of the material for the studio album at the Newport Jazz Festival in July. The album is widely considered one of the first to create a full-blown architecture for jazz-rock fusion. But even in Davis's hands, the music was largely jazz aimed at fans of jazz or highly sophisticated instrumental rock. *Bitches Brew* had plenty of electronics and lengthy solos, but it lacked rock's more predictable beat and excitement—or at least what younger rock audiences of the time found exciting. By 1970 the electric guitar, with its high-pitched shrieks and blues notes, had replaced the trumpet and saxophone as the lead instrument of choice for rock fans. The electric guitar could be cranked up, and it allowed the player's facial expressions to be seen, creating an emotional connection with male and female audience members. Because the trumpet and saxophone were played with the mouth, it was all but impossible for instrumentalists to detach them while performing to let audiences see the emotional expression of their own efforts, which guitarists could do with great effect. Yet trumpeters like Miles Davis and Freddie Hubbard remained major jazz innovators during the rock era.

In January 1970 the trumpeter Freddie Hubbard recorded *Red Clay*, in some ways his electric fusion response to *Bitches Brew*—with the saxophonist Joe Henderson, the pianist Herbie Hancock, the bassist Ron Carter, and the drummer Lenny White. In that same year, Weather Report was formed, recording its first album in February and March 1971. John McLaughlin founded the Mahavishnu Orchestra in 1970, introducing the violin and Indian spiritualism into the fusion mix. And in late 1971 Chick Corea formed Return to Forever, and the group recorded its first album—a jazz-Latin hybrid—in February 1972.

But perhaps Mahavishnu represented the most significant spiritual shift in the jazz-rock idiom, and young jazz and rock audiences responded instantly. Fans responded to the orchestra's sheer electric power and the mystical, psychedelic feel in McLaughlin's torrid extended compositions and playing. Many jazz traditionalists, however, found the music difficult to listen to, particularly because of its volume and distinct lack of formal melodies. "Mahavishnu was the first band to come out with a kind of spiritual vibe that was so much in the air by the end of the 1960s and early '70s," McLaughlin said. "Plus, we were really loud and playing a new kind of music that demanded great musicianship. One of the more powerful aspects of Mahavishnu was the combination of drummer Billy Cobham and me. It was about the electric guitar and drums—especially when just the two of us played. That was a real killer from time to time, I don't think anyone had seen that kind of performance before Billy and I did it. There was a new kind of communication between us with the volume, the virtuosity, the fun and deep feelings all in there."

Other bands, like Chick Corea's Return to Forever, picked up on the electronic layers and mystical, psychedelic imagery starting in 1973, with musician changes and a new album—*Hymn of the Seventh Galaxy*. The album was particularly attractive to young jazz record buyers who were investing in affordable higher-end component stereo systems. In the early seventies jazz-fusion developed into a form that was also heavily influenced by soul and funk. "It happened one day," Herbie Hancock wrote in the liner notes to a CD reissue of his *Head Hunters* album, recorded in 1973. "I was chanting. I knew I didn't want to play the [jazz] I had been playing but I didn't know what music I wanted to play. . . . The more I chanted, the more my mind opened up, relaxed and began to wander. I started thinking about Sly Stone and how much I loved his music and how funky *Thank You for Letting Me Be Myself* [sic] is. I was hearing the song over and over and over again. Then I had this mental image of me playing in Sly's band, playing something funky like that. Then the next image that came to me was about my own band playing in Sly Stone's musical direction. My unconscious reaction was, 'No, I don't want to do that.'

"What I saw in this reaction was seeing in myself the same things I hated about many other jazz musicians that put jazz on a pedestal, and at the same time putting funk and rock on a secondary level. I don't like that about anything. There's room for everything. But I noticed my gut reaction was the same kind of hierarchical look of putting jazz on a pedestal. I said to myself, 'Whoa! What are you doing?' I knew I had to take the idea seriously. Would I like to have a funky band that played the kind of music Sly or someone like that was playing? My response was, 'Actually, yes.' "[15]

CONCERTS GET LOUDER

In 1969 rock bands began to move out of creaky 2,500-seat ballrooms and auditoriums and into larger newly built sports arenas and their adjacent theaters in major cities. Arenas such as Inglewood, California's Forum (1967), New York's Madison Square Garden and Felt Forum (1968), and San Diego's Sports Arena (1970) needed events to fill seats on nights when professional sports teams were out of town. Such indoor arenas offered size, sound and lighting systems, security, and crowd control. Changes taking place on the radio, moreover, were helping to stimulate interest in hard rock. In the early 1960s the Federal Communications Commission had permitted a new FM radio band but prohibited companies from simulcasting the programming on their AM and FM stations. But by the late sixties and early seventies, radio stations had figured out how to avoid this problem by letting the newer FM stations devote their airtime to rock albums.[16]

The availability of concert space in major markets, combined with FM radio stations devoted to playing the long tracks of rock albums, made arena rock more appealing to bands and rock fans. Bands such as Three Dog Night, Cream, the Rolling Stones, Jimi Hendrix, and Led Zeppelin began playing these indoor arenas in 1969, attracting crowds and building a mystique with sexually provocative stagecraft. Large audiences assembled in the round for a rock concert were energized by being in a dark, climate-controlled space, free of parental supervision, and sharing an electrifying experience with like-minded members of their generation.[17]

Arena concerts depended on the high-wire performances of rock artists, but they also relied increasingly on the dynamism and spectacle made possible by lighting and volume. "To properly light any act back then, you had to know song lyrics and melodies cold," said Edward "Chip"

Monck, who ran the lighting during the 1969 and 1972 Rolling Stones' arena tours.[18] "This knowledge let you figure out exactly when to change the colors or set the spots for maximum dramatic effect. The goal for me always was to wash the performers in a wave of rich color. Then when the band reaches a great lyric line, I'd pull out a face with a spotlight, to emphasize the band. You'd basically have one bar to figure out the song, so I had to be on my toes.

"We were better able to maximize lighting for dramatic effect in arenas, where we had a controlled environment. The turning point had been Woodstock, when I used twelve spotlights. This was three times the scale of the Monterey Pop Festival, when I ran the lighting as well. Arenas allowed me to turn rock performances into high theater. For example, when the Rolling Stones performed "Midnight Rambler" on their 1972 tour, Mick Jagger took a wide belt and slapped the stage in synch with the beat. On the first belt slap when he dropped to his knees, I had all eight arc follow spots go red. Nothing else. The first time I did that I could hear an audible 'Ahhh . . .' from the crowd. That's when I knew I had locked it."

Whereas lighting enhanced the visual experience, larger speakers, greater volume, and sonic clarity stimulated the emotional experience. "Anyone who wanted to play an arena and fill seats had to think in terms of sound and lights after the Rolling Stones' tour of 1969 and Woodstock," said the sound-system expert Bill Hanley. "Young audiences started to expect it. Soon you no longer could use the systems that these arenas had in place. You had to enhance them with stacks of speakers onstage to pump out the music and engage listeners and bring them together in a shared experience."[19]

Jazz during this period—from 1967 to 1972—was directly affected by the rising popularity of rock and soul and the revolution in concert sound and lighting systems—the technologies that united and stimulated audiences. As jazz attempted to keep pace with rock and soul to attract audiences and fill seats in larger theaters, concert halls, and festival venues, more jazz musicians began to experiment with a range of electric instruments. After Woodstock, it was no longer enough simply to see a concert. The music now had to be experienced in large gatherings and had to leap out into the audience from the speakers and stun everyone, no matter where they were sitting.

In the early and mid-1960s, acoustic jazz instruments struggled to project their sound in concert halls. The lack of volume was particularly frustrating for leading jazz musicians who had watched rock groups grow in popularity simply by turning up the volume on their instruments.

But commercial and competitive interests also played a role in jazz's shift toward rock. "Nineteen sixty-nine was the year rock and funk were selling like hotcakes, and all this was put on display at Woodstock," Miles Davis wrote in his autobiography. "There were over 400,000 people at the concert. That many people at a concert makes everybody go crazy, and especially people who make records. The only thing on their minds is, How can we sell records to that many people all the time? If we haven't been doing that, then how can we do it?

"That was the atmosphere all around the record companies. At the same time, people were packing stadiums to hear and see stars in person. And jazz music seemed to be withering on the vine, in record sales and live performances. It was the first time in a long time that I didn't sell-out crowds everywhere I played. In Europe I always had sellouts but in the United States, we played a lot of half-empty clubs in 1969. That told me something. Compared to what my records used to sell, when you put them beside what Bob Dylan or Sly Stone sold, it was no contest. Their sales had gone through the roof. Clive Davis was the president of Columbia Records and he signed Blood, Sweat & Tears in 1968 and a group called Chicago in 1969. He was trying to take Columbia into the future and pull in all those young record buyers. . . . He suggested that the way for me to reach this new audience was to play my music where they went, places like the Fillmore."[20]

Davis had little choice. Jazz's reach was being limited to some extent by jazz musicians' adherence to static performances and instruments that were inaudible in larger venues. "I think if I regret anything in the mid-sixties with Miles Davis, it was that my bass was not amplified sufficiently," Ron Carter said. "If my bass had been amplified, I could have had more of an impact, because I would have been more audible. We were playing in these big two-thousand-seat halls with just an M-Audio mike and no monitors. I had no real chance to affect the band as much as I could have because we were not sonically equal. I wish it had been the same way live. But again, I don't feel bent out of shape because the technology wasn't available to me. I can live with that. The fact is that the guys in the Miles Davis groups could hear me enough that I could have an impact. I just wished it had been a much broader reach of sound from the bass to the audiences to twenty-five or fifty-five rows back from where we were standing."[21]

Carter finally had a chance to use the amplification he yearned for in 1968, when he recorded on electric bass on Miles Davis's *Filles De Kilimanjaro*. The pianist Chick Corea also played on that album, discovering that the electric piano and other electrified keyboard instruments came with new percussive and sonic textures, allowing him to be heard distinctly rather than just as a muted member of the rhythm section. "When I was in Miles's band, I became aware that jazz was changing and that this thing called fusion and jazz-rock was emerging," Corea said. "When I recorded on Miles Davis's *Filles de Kilimanjaro* in September 1968, I used the electric piano and Dave Holland was on electric bass. So there was a taste of that then. We also used electric piano and electric bass on *In a Silent Way* in February 1969. But the group that did a lot to change the sound of jazz was Tony Williams's Lifetime trio.

"I saw them perform down at the Vanguard, and they blew me away. It's the first time the rock sound was fully integrated into jazz. Remember, in that group there were no horns, just Tony's driving drums, John's rock guitar, and Larry's organ. In fact, the first time I saw Lifetime I had to put plugs in my ears. It was the loudest thing I had ever heard, but I loved it. What they were doing was kind of early for jazz-rock fusion. Tony's *Emergency* [in May 1969] with Lifetime was ahead of Miles at the time. But even though we didn't record *Bitches Brew* until three months later, Miles was still setting the pace, even for Tony. In the face of all the critics and the jazz purists, Miles was changing the form of his music by adapting and integrating changes he heard and saw."[22]

By 1971, the year of Louis Armstrong's death, the jazz trumpet was all but dead as a lead jazz-rock instrument. Though Miles Davis and Freddie Hubbard were largely the exceptions, the instrument no longer resonated with jazz-rock audiences. The jazz trumpeter Randy Brecker, who with his late brother Michael formed the Brecker Brothers, a jazz-funk fusion band, in 1975, recalled: "When I first came to New York in 1967, I joined the original Blood Sweat & Tears. By then, jazz was already on the wane and you had to pay attention to pop and rock if you wanted to be a part of a larger picture. Besides, a golden era of jazz and jazz recordings especially, had already passed four or five years earlier. The goal with BS&T was to form a brass laden-rock band, and Al Kooper was its leader and main conceptualist. We played opposite Cream, and Elton John opened for us on his first U.S. tour. We also did dates with Steve Winwood and Traffic. Stevie in particular was an exceptional musician."[23]

Brecker said he left Blood Sweat & Tears because Kooper had decided to quit and because Horace Silver had offered Brecker a job playing with his quintet. "BS&T wanted to add a lead singer, David Clayton-Thomas, and some of us thought the move was going to be too pop and take the emphasis away from the instrumentalists," Brecker said. "One night we had a band meeting where Al announced he was leaving. I said, 'If Al's leaving, I don't think you guys can make it without him.' I also wasn't getting to solo much. So I told them that Horace Silver had called me and that I was leaving, and that I needed more room to 'stretch out' creatively.

"Before I left, though, I dragged my friend Lew Soloff into the band, urging him to replace me in the group. He was a strictly a jazz guy, but I had talked him into giving the band a try. Of course, a couple of months after I left, BS&T went into the studio and recorded *Spinning Wheel*. More hits followed. Lew and I still took trumpet lessons together in New Jersey, but instead of taking a bus from NYC, he started picking me up in a limo."

But Horace Silver's quintet was hardly a jazz haven for Brecker. In fact, no jazz band could afford to ignore the electric revolution going on in the music business in the early 1970s, since acoustic instruments were hard to amplify and generally considered dated by younger audiences. "By 1971, I knew the trumpet faced new challenges," Brecker said. "Electricity and amplification gear allowed bands to play really loud, making the electric guitar the center of attention. As a trumpet player, it was hard to compete with an electric guitar. I had used just a microphone for amplification and it only worked up to a point. An electric guitar could be cranked up as loud as hell, and the guitarist could move around on stage. You also could use your tongue or teeth to play the guitar strings. It was all very theatrical. Rock guitarists were for the most part also great actors, and girls went nuts over them. So did boys. For trumpet players and saxophonists, we were no longer the main draw. We were just the 'horn section.'"

But Brecker quickly realized that rock was more sophisticated than he initially had thought, with Jimi Hendrix serving as a big influence. Part of this awakening came out of economic necessity, but it was also a cultural movement. "By 1969, everyone I knew who played jazz was scuffling for work," Brecker said, "but because there was not much of a precedence in jazz-rock, I had a lot of room to experiment in this new genre. My brother Michael and I were also asked to be a part of a new jazz-rock group called Dreams, with Barry Rogers on trombone, Jeff Kent on keyboards, John Abercrombie on guitar, Doug Lubahn on bass, and Billy Cobham on drums. Given the premium on volume, I knew we no longer could compete as an acoustic group. But I was still playing the trumpet, not an electric guitar."

So Brecker drilled a hole in his mouthpiece and added an electric pickup to compete and draw attention. "The pickup allowed me to make electric-guitar-like effects with my horn and we could also amp up the volume to compete. This was before Miles Davis did the same thing. We also added a Hammond Condor—an electronic box that produces different electronic sounds. John Abercrombie always played with a wah-wah pedal. He was a jazz guitarist and thought it would give him a rock sound. At one of the rehearsals, he didn't show up and had left the pedal there. I had a pickup in my mouthpiece ending in a quarter-inch guitar jack, so I plugged into his wah-wah pedal, and the result sounded great. Miles Davis came to see us regularly at New York's Village Gate, where we were the house band. Soon after seeing us in 1970, Miles started using a wah-wah pedal, too.

"We really had something different, because there were no arrangements per se—we jammed up everything and there was a lot of room for group improvisation. It was different every night, and Billy Cobham slowly invented a new style of 'fusion' drumming. We had hoped we could parlay our sound into greater visibility, but it never quite happened. As great as an electrified trumpet sounded, rock audiences identified with the electric guitar. The trumpet was still an old-fashioned instrument in their eyes."

But part of jazz-fusion's reliance on electronic instruments was a desire by musicians to connect with younger audiences and capture the sophisticated rock-fan segment of the market. "Musicians always want to communicate," Chick Corea said. "You want to get something across. You can't just do what interests only you. I was influenced a little bit by rock, but not the rock you might imagine. The first rock group that really got to me was John McLaughlin's Mahavishnu Orchestra. I considered that a rock group when first I heard them in 1973. They had quite a following, and it definitely wasn't a Village Vanguard audience. There were long-haired kids with that vibe who lit matches in support of what was happening on stage. To me that was rock 'n' roll—but on jazz's level of intensity."[24]

At the same time, jazz-rock fusion was having an influence on rock bands such as Yes; Emerson, Lake and Palmer; Jethro Tull; and other bands in which musicians were trained and listened to a wide range of music. "Rock didn't exist in a vacuum and neither did jazz," Corea said. "Good musicians listened to many styles—for enjoyment and to find new ideas. I think we rubbed off on rock as their game improved. Musicians put on other artists' records and either they heard something special or they didn't. They didn't choose what they put on based on what section of the store it was sold. As young jazz musicians then, we didn't see ourselves as jazz or rock. We were part of a group, a club. We were all people who are trying to save the planet, and it's the same way today. Musicians are open, and since the late sixties and early seventies there has always been an exchange program between rock, soul, funk, and jazz, as quietly as it has been kept."

Creatively spent after playing in Miles's fusion band of the late sixties and early seventies, Corea decided to launch a neo-Brazilian fusion band. "My first Return to Forever band in 1972 played and recorded mellow music," he said. "I was coming off of two and a half years of playing with Miles Davis and Wayne Shorter and Jack DeJohnette and Dave Holland, where the music was highly experimental, wild and edgy. It was a blast. But that experience took me into new interests. With my band Circle in 1970, we took the experimental concept even further. In that group— Anthony Braxton, Dave, Barry Altschul, and me—we played whole concerts where the music was improvised from beginning to end. There was no song form—we did away with it. We went into a space where we made up the music as we went along. But after a while, I felt I was missing the connection that I got from audiences when I offered them something more lyrical. I wanted to play things that were lyrical. That's what led me to put Return to Forever together in 1972 for the music I had written."

But after two albums in this genre, Corea decided to shift the group to a much more dynamic and bombastic sound, starting with *Hymn of the Seventh Galaxy* in 1973. "It was a quickly evolving thing with me and Stanley [Clarke]," he said. "When we hooked up with drummer Lenny White, we played a week at the Keystone Korner in San Francisco in 1972. We did that just to try out the trio, and the trio took on a kind of fire. I was playing just a Fender Rhodes, and Stanley played amplified upright bass. But after 1973 our approach changed when Lenny came into the group. Lenny's a different kind of drummer than Airto [Moreira]."

But the full conversion to jazz-rock fusion wasn't complete until the band made yet another San Francisco hire. "We had the idea to find an electric guitarist," Corea said. "When I had heard what John McLaughlin had been doing with the electric guitar, I thought, 'Man, I'd like to write for that sound.' So we went out to find an electric guitarist. The result was hiring Billy Connors. We found him that week we played in San Francisco. One of our intentions was to audition guitarists, but only a couple of them came by to the Keystone Korner while we were there. Billy was the one we liked, so we hired him."

Return to Forever's signature psychedelic jazz-rock fusion sound first emerged at a New York City rehearsal. "Stanley and I were just following what we had begun to do, which was to write," Corea said. "The first piece I wrote for our 'grand sound' was 'Hymn of the Seventh Galaxy,' the opening piece for our new group's first record. The rundown of that song at our first rehearsal made the hair on my arm stand up. It was so exciting, and it worked so great and everyone was so enthusiastic about it. The sound really set a new direction and developed from there. Here's how it happened: On the day of that rehearsal, Lenny wasn't able to make it. Though he did play on the trio I had for a while, he still had some commitments to the group Azteca in San Francisco. So I got my friend [Steve] Gadd to play drums. Steve had been at that San Francisco audition along with Billy Connors. We also put in a percussionist, Mingo Lewis, who we also found in San Francisco. He played conga and bongos.

"The rehearsal was held at a loft I was renting downtown in New York. When we took the chart out, Steve just kind of ate it up. He took a hold of it right away. It took me and Stanley and Billy a little longer to learn the notes. But when we started to get it together, like after a couple of runs, we started to put it into tempo and got rid of the sheet music. That's when the thing took fire. When we got rid of the music, we played the tune from beginning to end with energy, and that just blew me away. It blew everybody away. We knew we had something new. So did audiences. We were playing larger venues then, and audiences picked up on the vibe. There was a synergy going on between what we were creating and how audiences were digging it. That kind of grew."

Young jazz musicians, to survive commercially in the early seventies, had little choice but to embrace rock, soul, and funk. "Jazz concert promoters probably played a role behind the scenes in moving jazz in this direction, since larger venues meant more fans and greater revenue," said the lighting engineer Edward "Chip" Monck. "Traditional jazz could only go so far. As soon as venues got really large, jazz lost its intimacy and was no longer appealing to young fans. To attract larger audiences, jazz-rock fusion had to place a greater emphasis on stagecraft, which wasn't what jazz musicians were about. So jazz-rock fusion became stuck in some ways. It wasn't what jazz fans expected and it wasn't even close to connecting with audiences the way the Rolling Stones and the Who did."[25]

Which exposes perhaps jazz's greatest vulnerability and shortcoming in the jazz-rock fusion era. Rock was as much about sex appeal and preening as it was about the music. Playing faster and with greater intricacy wasn't going to be much help to most jazz-rock fusion artists hoping to gain rock-star visibility. "You really needed a massive personality and enormous charisma to engage large audiences for two hours at a clip," Monck said. "I really can't think of a jazz-rock fusion band that managed to do this well. Rock always was about entertainment, and the better groups had superb musicians and menacing performers. Jazz artists, by nature, are brilliant introverts, and the theatrical part doesn't come easy. Even jazz-rock fusion audiences eventually tired of watching lengthy solos by great saxophonists or keyboard players, especially audience members sitting in the fiftieth row and beyond."

11   Jazz Hangs On

Jazz faced new challenges after 1972 from an expanding range of music forms, and it benefited yet again from opportunities presented by business, technology, and cultural trends. Jazz-rock fusion continued to grow in popularity, becoming a sophisticated alternative to hard rock. But new music forms appeared, altering the direction of jazz. The rise of soul artists with sociopolitical messages—including Gil Scott-Heron, Curtis Mayfield, Marvin Gaye, and Isaac Hayes—compelled jazz artists to integrate soul and soul-protest elements into their music.

Disco's rise in the mid-1970s was also influenced by jazz, thanks to the many jazz arrangers and artists who worked on lucrative dance recording sessions. Latin-jazz developed a more pronounced identity at this time, returning to its Afro-Cuban roots and embracing popular contemporary styles, most notably Puerto Rican salsa. To compete, jazz clubs such as Keystone Korner in San Francisco, the Jazz Workshop in Boston, and the Village Gate in New York all began diversifying their offerings by booking nonjazz and jazz-hybrid acts. "Miles Davis thought he was a pop star but he wasn't," said Art D'Lugoff, who owned and ran the Village Gate from 1958 to 1993. "I loved Miles dearly but he wasn't doing the kind of business that pop acts were doing. At one point Miles felt that Blood, Sweat & Tears should open for him. This was [in the early seventies] when the group had huge hits. Blood, Sweat & Tears drew the larger crowds. We didn't underpay Miles. Blood, Sweat & Tears got $25,000 for a week while Miles got $5,000. But that was based on box office."[1]

Free jazz continued to find an audience in the 1970s, but so did acoustic jazz (with recordings from labels such as Cobblestone, Muse, and Pablo), big-band jazz, and a new form of rock-soul jazz pioneered by CTI Records and its subsidiary labels. But in the decades that followed, jazz and jazz musicians would find their audience shrinking in clubs and at festivals in the United States and competition intensifying from other music styles, including rap, hip-hop, house, punk rock, progressive rock, classic rock, British pop, soul-dance, world music, and European and South American jazz. Classic jazz, however, managed to remain relevant, thanks largely to the introduction and acceptance of the CD format in the 1990s. Though jazz purists complained that early digital music sounded brittle and metallic, and that small-type liner notes were hard to read, the CD enabled record companies to reissue classic jazz recordings that had been out of print on vinyl or languishing in vaults for years. For example, extensive portions of the Blue Note catalog that had been out of print on vinyl reemerged on CD in the 1990s. Japanese record companies also began to meet the demand for better-sounding CDs by selling remastered versions in glossy miniaturized LP covers, enhancing the prestige of classic jazz.

Jazz's revival through the proliferation of the CD in the 1990s was given another boost by technology in the 2000s. In 2001 Apple released its iTunes digital music platform as well as the iPod, both of which offered vast catalogues of music for a low price and unimaginable convenience. But there were drawbacks. While iTunes allowed for the instant download of music to a computer, the format began to undercut the album format, because consumers could now buy individual tracks. This trend away from the album concept is still having a ripple effect on music production, recording, and sales.

The mass availability of the cost-efficient high-speed modem in the early 2000s along with improved security at Internet retail sites further accelerated the appeal of online shopping, which in turn made buying music easier. But online shopping doomed the brick-and-mortar CD store, limiting opportunities for new jazz, which music buyers had grown accustomed to discovering by frequenting stores to see what had just arrived. In jazz's favor, copyright laws in Europe allowed American jazz from the 1950s to enter the public domain there. Companies like Spain's Fresh Sound reintroduced on CD jazz recordings that had been overlooked or forgotten by U.S. record companies. As a result, jazz fans today have greater knowledge of jazz's past and are more familiar with artists of the era.

In the past three decades, Europe has emerged as a jazz force, producing a generation of jazz artists who developed their own singular styles rather than mimicked American jazz artists of the past. The popularity of European and Asian jazz festivals has helped to create an international market for jazz, while the decline in booking opportunities in the United States has suppressed the exposure and development of new jazz movements here.

Acoustic jazz continues to make inroads and has all but replaced jazz-rock fusion as jazz's classic form, thanks largely to institutions such as the Kennedy Center and Jazz at Lincoln Center. The trend to electronic instruments and louder volume also began to recede in the 2000s as audiences aged and interest declined. "[The rock-blues guitarist] Mike Bloomfield and I often argued about this in San Francisco in the late sixties," said the vibraphonist Gary Burton. "Mike said music had to be loud enough to have a physical reaction. I disagreed. I didn't feel as though that was a requirement. I didn't think audiences were requesting that music be loud. I think they came to expect it as more groups found technology to make music painfully loud. By 1972 the rock scene left me behind as a result of the volume. Of course, my instrument—the vibraphone—can't get too loud, anyway. So I was at a disadvantage, even if I thought volume was special."[2]

For the past ninety-five years jazz's survival has been based on the ability of musicians to interpret their times without relinquishing the characteristics that define the art form. These characteristics include the blues, a deep feeling for the poetry of the music, and a burning desire by musicians to stand out through improvisation. From 1942 to 1972—when much of the jazz that's consumed today was created and recorded—musicians were able to forge new styles, thanks to dramatic developments in technology, sociopolitical movements, business and economic trends, and the incursion of popular music styles. Such events continue to occur today. Jazz's challenge going forward will be to attract new musicians who are able to find new ways of expressing the music that not only pay tribute to jazz's past but also interpret contemporary life in a way that resonates with new listeners.

When I completed the manuscript for this book, in January 2012, I played the Original Dixieland Jass Band's recordings of "Dixieland Jass Band One-Step" and "Livery Stable Blues." I wanted to hear again the dramatic moment in time when jazz was first documented on record. As I listened to the music, I couldn't help thinking about the irony—that jazz may have been born in New Orleans, but the music's documentation began at RCA Victor's studio on West 38th Street, in the heart of New York's Garment District.

As the music played, I typed the building's address into Google. Using the street-view images feature in Google Maps, I discovered that the original 1916 building was still standing. Curious, I made a few calls and reached the building's owner, who invited me to visit. Several days later, I rode up through the same freight elevator shaft that the ODJB had used ninety-five years earlier to reach the twelfth floor of 46 West 38th Street. As the freight elevator swept past each landing, I could imagine the five ODJB band members standing in the same space, nervously wondering how their recording session would progress.

When the door opened on the top floor, I stepped out and wandered the small hallway, winding up in front of the glass doors to Jimmy Sales Corporation, a maker of men's designer accessories and the floor's largest tenant, with views facing 38th Street. Jack Azizo, the co-owner of the family business, invited me in. After I told him why I was there—that jazz's very first recordings had been made in his office space—Azizo's eyes widened in disbelief. "Get out. Here? You're kidding."[3] Rocking back in his desk chair, Azizo told me he loved jazz and most other forms of music. I asked him if he had ever heard the Original Dixieland Jass Band. He said he hadn't. I asked if he had a CD player in the office. Azizo said he did. I handed him a CD of the band's recordings, and Azizo slipped the disc into a boom box. We listened in silence. As the syncopated calamity of the music rushed out through the speakers, I assumed that this was probably the first time in ninety-five years that the music had been replayed in the space.

Azizo had the same thought. "Man, can you imagine if these walls could talk?" he said, overcome by the wild energy of the quintet. As "Livery Stable Blues" continued—with the cornet, trombone, and clarinet imitating the sounds of barnyard animals—I suspected the walls were overjoyed to hear once again the music they had first experienced live so many years ago. Looking out the windows onto West 38th Street, I also realized that for jazz to evolve during the next ninety-five years and avoid becoming a relic, musicians would need to develop new jazz styles that take into consideration the contemporary interests of young audiences—without losing the hypnotic power of syncopation or the thrill of improvisation. And as history has proved, much depends on the ability of future generations of musicians to capitalize on events that have little or nothing to do with jazz itself.

Notes

INTRODUCTION

1. Victor Talking Machine Co. newspaper ad, *Hartford Courant*, April 21, 1917.

2. H.O. Brunn, *The Story of the Original Dixieland Jazz Band* (Baton Rouge: Louisiana State University Press, 1960), 70.

3. Ibid., 67.

4. A note by Nick LaRocca, a member of the Original Dixieland Jass Band, to the author H.O. Brunn, in ibid., 67–68.

1. RECORD GIANTS BLINK

1. Budd Johnson, interview by Ira Gitler, in Gitler, *Swing to Bop: An Oral History of the Transition in Jazz in the 1940s* (New York: Oxford University Press, 1985), 122.

2. "Dan Burley, "Back Door Stuff: Straighten Up and Fly Right," *New York Amsterdam News*, April 19, 1944.

3. "Local Shop Features Negro Bands, Artists," *New York Amsterdam News*, October 11, 1941.

4. "1,200 Fans Hear Prof. Berton's Jazz Concert at Savoy: Coleman Hawkins, Plus Many Others, Rock Spot," *New York Amsterdam News*, January 16, 1943.

5. Scott DeVeaux, *The Birth of Bebop: A Social and Musical History* (Berkeley: University of California Press), 314–17.

6. Gunther Schuller, *The Swing Era: The Development of Jazz, 1930–1945* (New York: Oxford University Press, 1989), 20–22.

7. Scott DeVeaux, "Jazz in the Forties: A Conversation with Howard McGhee," *Black Perspective in Music*, Spring 1987, 72.

8. Gitler, *Swing to Bop*, 124.

9. Billy Taylor, phone interview by Marc Myers, November 23, 2009.

10. DeVeaux, *Birth of Bebop*, 293.

11. "Bebop? Man, We Called It Kloop-Mop!" *Metronome*, April 1947, 21.

12. Gitler, *Swing to Bop*, 119.

13. Buddy DeFranco, phone interview by Marc Myers, January 16, 2010.

14. "How the Phonograph Record Has Come Back," *Down Beat*, November 15, 1940, 2.

15. Gary Giddins and Scott DeVeaux, *Jazz* (New York: Norton, 2009), 303.

16. Nat Hentoff and Nat Shapiro, *Hear Me Talkin' to Ya: The Story of Jazz as Told by the Men Who Made It* (New York: Dover, 1966), 344.

17. Alyn Shipton, *Groovin' High: The Life of Dizzy Gillespie* (New York: Oxford University Press, 1999), 64.

18. Ibid., 74.

19. Ibid., 102.

20. Joe Wilder, phone interview by Marc Myers, January 4, 2010.

21. Shipton, *Groovin' High*, 103.

22. Brian Priestley, *Chasin' the Bird: The Life and Legacy of Charlie Parker*, (New York: Oxford University Press, 2005), 19.

23. Giddins and DeVeaux, *Jazz*, 301.

24. Frank Driggs and Chuck Haddix, *Kansas City Jazz: From Ragtime to Bebop—a History* (New York: Oxford University Press, 2005), 4.

25. Gary Giddins, *Celebrating Bird: The Triumph of Charlie Parker* (New York: Beech Tree Books, 1987), 54.

26. Ibid., 56.

27. Lawrence O. Koch, *Yardbird Suite: A Compendium of the Music and Life of Charlie Parker* (New York: Bowling Green State University Popular Press, 1988), 29.

28. Ibid., 30.

29. Alfred Balk, *The Rise of Radio, from Marconi through the Golden Age* (Jefferson, N.C.: McFarland, 2006), 210.

30. Anders S. Lunde, "The American Federation of Musicians and the Recording Ban," *Public Opinion Quarterly*, Spring 1948, 46–47.

31. Balk, *Rise of Radio*, 67.

32. Ibid., 69.

33. Tim Anderson, "Buried under the Fecundity of His Own Creations: Reconsidering the Recording Bans of the American Federation of Musicians," *American Music*, Summer 2004, 234–35.

34. Lennie Niehaus, phone interview by Marc Myers, March 31, 2010.

35. Dieter Ladwig, *Jukebox* (Secaucus, N.J.: Chartwell Books, 1994), 27.

36. Robert D. Leiter, *The Musicians and Petrillo* (New York: Bookman Associates, 1953), 63.

37. Mary Austin, "Petrillo's War," *Journal of Popular Culture*, Summer 1978, 13.

38. Richard W. Ergo, "ASCAP and the Antitrust Laws: The Story of a Reasonable Compromise," *Duke Law Journal*, Spring 1959, 259–60.

39. Ibid., 262.

40. "Radio Regulation and Freedom of the Air," *Harvard Law Review*, May 1941, 1,225.

41. Ergo, *ASCAP and the Antitrust Laws*, 262–63.

42. Balk, *Rise of Radio*, 128.

43. Lunde, "American Federation of Musicians and the Recording Ban," 47.

44. Leiter, *Musicians and Petrillo*, 69–70.

45. Ibid., 70.

46. Vern Countryman, "The Organized Musician II," *University of Chicago Law Review*, Autumn 1948, 250–51.

47. Anderson, "Buried under the Fecundity," 237–38.

48. Ibid., 240.

49. Countryman, "Organized Musician II," 269.

50. Ibid., 270.

51. Anderson, "Buried under the Fecundity," 241.

52. "Decca Firsts Mark Chronology Highlights," *Billboard*, August 28, 1954, 50.

53. Countryman, "Organized Musician II," 270–71.

54. Ibid., 272.

55. Ibid., 273.

56. Ibid., 270–71.

57. Ibid., 273–74.

58. Anderson, "Buried under the Fecundity," 246.

59. Balk, *Rise of Radio*, 258.

2. DJS, PROMOTERS, AND BEBOP

1. Hal McKusick, phone interview by Marc Myers, December 18, 2009.

2. Scott DeVeaux, *The Birth of Bebop: A Social and Musical History* (Berkeley: University of California Press), 336–37.

3. Alyn Shipton, *Groovin' High: The Life of Dizzy Gillespie* (New York: Oxford University Press, 1999), 142–43.

4. Nat Hentoff, phone interview by Marc Myers, September 2, 2010.

5. DeVeaux, *Birth of Bebop*, 159.

6. Ibid., 162.

7. Walter "Gil" Fuller, *What Is Bebop?* Royal Roost jazz club brochure, 1948 (author's copy).

8. DeVeaux, *Birth of Bebop*, 158.

9. Serge Guilbaut, *How New York Stole the Idea of Modern Art: Abstract Expressionism, Freedom, and the Cold War* (Chicago: University of Chicago Press, 1983), 108.

10. "Abstract Jazz," *Down Beat*, July 15, 1945, 7.

11. Ira Gitler, phone interview by Marc Myers, February 13, 2010.

12. Ben Ratliff, "Barry Ulanov, 82, a Scholar of Jazz, Art and Catholicism," *New York Times*, May 7, 2000.

13. "Barnard English Professor Barry Ulanov, Noted Jazz Author and Critic, Is Dead at 82," *Columbia University Record*, May 5, 2000. http://bit.ly/jFusAO.

14. Miles Davis and Quincy Troupe, *Miles: The Autobiography* (New York: Simon and Schuster, 1989), 67.

15. "Biography," Leonard Feather Jazz Collection, IJC International Jazz Collections, University of Idaho library, www.IJC.uidaho.edu.

16. Marjorie Hyams, phone interview by Marc Myers, February 15, 2011.

17. "Influence of the Year," *Metronome*, January 1946, 24.

18. Ibid., 30.

19. Ira Gitler, phone interview by Marc Myers, February 13, 2010.

20. Scott DeVeaux, "The Emergence of the Jazz Concert, 1935–1945," *American Music*, Spring 1989, 17.

21. John Levy, phone interview by Marc Myers, January 2, 2010.

22. "New York Stinks, Claims Coast Promoter," *Down Beat*, August 15, 1945, 2.

23. Tad Hershorn, *Norman Granz: The Man Who Used Jazz for Justice* (Berkeley: University of California Press, 2011), 125–26.

24. Lisa Hammel, "Old Hand at Jazz: Symphony Sid of WEVD Has Special Style," *New York Times*, April 27, 1958.

25. Ibid.

26. "Cats Hipped to the Advertised Quality Products," *Baltimore Afro-American;* August 3, 1940.

27. "Major about Town," *Chicago Defender*, December 7, 1940.

28. "Court Rules Dance Hall May Use Recordings for Music at Dances," *Chicago Defender*, April 5, 1941.

29. Ira Gitler, *Jazz Masters of the Forties,* (New York: Macmillan, 1966), 269.

30. Ibid.

31. Leonard Feather, "Again, Stars Fail to Appear at Jazz Foundation Concert," *Metronome*, July 1945, 33.

32. "Kalcheim on Prowl for WM Ork Aids—Watch Band Pacts," *Billboard*, January 26, 1946, 16.

33. "Shaw Signs Four for Gale," *Billboard*, March 23, 1946, 42.

34. "Band of the Year: Dizzy Gillespie," *Metronome*, January 1948, 17.

35. *Metronome*, November 1946, p. 3.

36. "The Bebop Feud," *Metronome*, April 1946, 44.

37. Dave Dexter, quoted in Barry Ulanov, "Who's Dead, Bebop or Its Detractors?," *Metronome*, June 1947, 50.

38. Charlie Ventura, quoted in Ira Gitler, *Swing to Bop: An Oral History of the Transition in Jazz in the 1940s* (New York: Oxford University Press, 1985), 232.

39. Babs Gonzales, quoted in ibid., 234.

40. Lennie Tristano, "What's Right with the Beboppers," *Metronome*, July 1947, 14.

41. Barry Ulanov, "Moldy Figs vs. Moderns!," *Metronome*, November 1947, 15.

42. Anderson, "Buried under the Fecundity," *American Music*, Summer 2004, 250.

43. "Band of the Year: Dizzy Gillespie," *Metronome*, January 1948, 17.

44. "Disc Jockey of the Year," *Metronome*, January 1948, 29.

45. Leonard Feather, "The Street Is Dead: A Jazz Obituary," *Metronome*, April 1948, 16.

46. "Gets Disk Jockey Spot," *Baltimore Afro-American*, June 26, 1948.

47. "Music—as Written," *Billboard*, April 10, 1948, 38.

48. Monte Kay, quoted in Gitler, *Jazz Masters of the Forties*, 269.

49. "52d Street Ops Eye Roost's Move for Jazz on Main Street," *Billboard*, February 28, 1948, 39.

50. "Customers Outbop the Boppers; Roost Doesn't Have to Toss in Towel," *Billboard*, August 25, 1948, 3.

51. "Roost Institutes Bop Weekends," *Down Beat*, May 5, 1948, 2.

52. "Bop Comes Home to Roost; Monk, Dizzy—Ooh, Vop!" *Billboard*, May 29, 1948, 20.

53. "Jazz on B'Way Brings Bux Back Alive: Watkins Experiment Boffo," *Billboard*, August 7, 1948, 1.

54. Creed Taylor, phone interview by Marc Myers, April 26, 2008.

55. Jon Hendricks, phone interview by Marc Myers, June 25, 2009.

56. Customers Outbop the Boppers," *Billboard*, August 25, 1948, 3.

57. Shipton, *Groovin' High*, 197.

58. Buddy De Franco, phone interview by Marc Myers, January 16, 2010.

59. "Joint Jumps as Sarah Vaughan Hits Broadway," *Chicago Defender*, December 18, 1948.

60. "National Association of Disc Jockeys Doings," *Billboard*, May 15, 1948, 35.

61. Fuller, *What Is Bebop?*, Royal Roost brochure.

62. "*Life* Goes to a Party: Bebop, a New Jazz School Is Led by a Trumpeter Who Is Hot, Cool and Gone," *Life*, October 11, 1948, 138.

63. Ibid.

64. Otto Mack (byline) and Virginia Wicks (reporter and writer for this issue), "The Record Parade," *Atlanta Daily World*, November 1, 1949.

3. G.I. BILL AND COOL

1. Bill Holman, phone interview by Marc Myers, January 5, 2010.

2. Clora Bryant et al., *Central Avenue Sounds: Jazz in Los Angeles* (Berkeley: University of California Press, 1998), 5, 8, and 20.

3. Ken Vail, *Dizzy Gillespie: The Bebop Years, 1937–1952* (Lanham, Md.: Scarecrow Press, 2003), 36.

4. Holman, phone interview.

5. "Industry Pressure Needed to Ease Taxation Load," *Billboard*, February 16, 1946, 46.

6. Suzanne Mettler, *Soldiers to Citizens: The G.I. Bill and the Making of the Greatest Generation* (New York: Oxford University Press, 2005), 16.

7. Geoffrey C. Ward and Ken Burns, *Jazz: A History of America's Music* (New York: Knopf, 2000), 296.

8. Peter J. Levinson, *Tommy Dorsey: Livin' in a Great Big Way* (Cambridge, Mass.: Da Capo Press), 166.

9. Ward and Burns, *Jazz*, 296.

10. Ibid.

11. Levinson, *Tommy Dorsey*, 160.

12. Buddy Collette, quoted in Bryant et al., *Central Avenue Sounds*, 145

13. Benny Powell, phone interview by Marc Myers, May 9, 2008.

14. Teddy Charles, phone interview by Marc Myers, February 4, 2008.

15. Hal McKusick, phone interview by Marc Myers, December 28, 2007.

16. Al Stewart, phone interview by Marc Myers, January 1, 2010.

17. Frank Mathias, *GI Jive: An Army Bandsman in World War II* (Lexington: University Press of Kentucky, 1982), 39.

18. Dick Hyman, phone interview by Marc Myers, January 2, 2010.

19. Mathias, *GI Jive*, 39.

20. Dave Brubeck, phone interview by Marc Myers, January 9, 2010. Quotations of Brubeck in the paragraphs that follow are from the same interview.

21. "GIs Demand Jobs Back," *Metronome*, August 1946, 13.

22. George Wein, phone interview by Marc Myers, January 26, 2010.

23. Mettler, *Soldiers to Citizens*, 55.

24. Ibid., 22.

25. Ibid., 6.

26. "The Servicemen's Readjustment Act (G.I. Bill)," transcript of original, June 22, 1944, www.Nolo.com.

27. Mettler, *Soldiers to Citizens*, 7.

28. Ibid., 29.

29. Suzanne Mettler, phone interview by Marc Myers, June 7, 2010.

30. Mettler, *Soldiers to Citizens*, 67.

31. Janet D. Schenck, *Adventure in Music: A Reminiscence; Manhattan School of Music, 1918–1960* (New York: Manhattan School of Music, 1960), 58, 62, 73.

32. "Training for Professional Musicians in All Branches of Music," *Metronome*, February 1947, 3.

33. Jessie Carney Smith, *Notable Black American Women, Book II* (Detroit: Gale Research, 1996), 351.

34. Ray Santos, phone interview by Marc Myers, February 7, 2010.

35. Juilliard School of Music archives, New York.

36. "Report of the President to the Directors of the Juilliard School of Music," October 1, 1946, Juilliard archives.

37. Dick Katz, phone interview by Marc Myers, July 10, 2009.

38. Wein, phone interview, January 26, 2010.

39. Lennie Tristano, "What's Wrong with the Beboppers?" *Metronome*, June 1947.

40. Miles Davis with Quincy Troupe, *Miles: The Autobiography* (New York: Simon and Schuster, 1989), 74.

41. Walter Simmons, *Voices in the Wilderness: Six American Neo-Romantic Composers* (Lanham, Md.: Scarecrow Press, 2004), 158.

42. Hyman, phone interview, January 2, 2010.

43. Buddy Collette, quoted in Bryant et al., *Central Avenue Sounds*, 147.

44. Britt Woodman, quoted in ibid., 131.

45. Brubeck, phone interview, January 9, 2010.

46. Ibid.

47. Peter J. Levinson, *September in the Rain: The Life of Nelson Riddle* (Lanham, Md.: Taylor Trade Publishing, 2005), 75.

48. Bill Perkins, interview by Les Tompkins, JazzProfessional.com, 1987.

49. George Simon, "Jazz Goes to College," *Metronome*, September 1948, 18.

50. Holman, phone interview, January 5, 2010.

51. Russ Garcia, phone interview by Marc Myers, April 30, 2008.

52. Wein, phone interview, January 26, 2010.

53. Gunther Schuller, phone interview by Marc Myers, January 8, 2010.

54. John Carisi, in the oral history "Recollections of Stefan Wolpe by Former Students and Friends" (interview of Carisi conducted in New York, October 21, 1984), Evergreen State College, Olympia, Wash. http://bit.ly/mixojf.

55. Shorty Rogers, interview by Les Tompkins, JazzProfessional.com, 1983.

56. Buddy Collette, phone interview by Marc Myers, February 15, 2010.

57. Holman, phone interview, January 5, 2010.

4. SPEED WAR, TAPE, AND SOLOS

1. Ira Gitler, phone interview by Marc Myers, February 13, 2010. The quotations of Gitler in the paragraphs that follow are from the same interview.

2. George Avakian, Columbia's director of pop LPs, said in a phone interview by Marc Myers, February 2, 2012, that starting in 1948, Columbia's first hundred 10-inch pop albums featured liner notes on the backs of covers that were written by George Dale, who worked in the company's publicity department. Avakian also wrote the first jazz-album liner notes (a twelve-page booklet) in 1940 for Decca's *Chicago Jazz*, a collection of six 78-rpm records.

3. "Full Columbia LP Story: Columbia's LP Disk Data," *Billboard*, June 26, 1948, 18.

4. "Columbia Starts Plugs for LP Dance Disks," *Billboard*, June 3, 1950, 14.

5. *Command Performance*, RCA Victor documentary, produced by William J. Ganz, on the manufacture of 78-rpm records, 1942.

6. "The Challenge of Change: The Recording Industry," *Billboard*, December 15, 1984, 4.

7. Charles L. Granata, *Sessions with Sinatra: Frank Sinatra and the Art of Recording* (Chicago: A Cappella Books, 1999), 47.

8. Gary Marmorstein, *The Label: The Story of Columbia Records* (New York: Thunder's Mouth Press, 2007), 155 and 154.

9. Edward Wallerstein, "Creating the LP," *High Fidelity*, April 1976, 56–61.

10. Marmorstein, *Label*, 158.

11. Ibid., 160.

12. Wallerstein, "Creating the LP," 56–61.

13. George Avakian, phone interview by Marc Myers, March 3, 2010.

14. Wallerstein, "Creating the LP," 56–61. The account and the quotation in the paragraphs that follow are also from Wallerstein's article.

15. Marmorstein, *Label*, 165.

16. Ibid., 166.

17. Roland Gelatt, *The Fabulous Phonograph: 1877–1977* (New York: Macmillan, 1977), 293.

18. Wallerstein, "Creating the LP," 56–61.

19. Avakian, phone interview, March 3, 2010.

20. Gelatt, *Fabulous Phonograph*, 294.

21. Ibid., 300.

22. "Lowdown on New RCA Disc," *Billboard*, January 8, 1949, 3.

23. Ibid.

24. Gelatt, *Fabulous Phonograph*, 295.

25. "RCA Sets 3-Speed Plans," *Billboard*, December 10, 1949, 14.

26. Jim Dawson and Steve Propes, *45 RPM: The History, Heroes, and Villains of a Pop Music Revolution* (San Francisco: Backbeat Books), 37.

27. Gelatt, *Fabulous Phonograph*, 295–96.

28. Peter Hammer, "John T. Mullin: The Man Who Put Bing Crosby on Tape," *Mix*, October 1, 1999. MixOnline.com.

29. Ibid.

30. Wallerstein, "Creating the LP," 56–61.

31. Avakian, phone interview, March 3, 2010. Subsequent quotations of Avakian in this section of the chapter are from the same interview.

32. Creed Taylor, phone interview by Marc Myers, March 6, 2010.

33. Avakian, phone interview, March 3, 2010. Quotations of Avakian in the paragraphs that follow are from the same interview.

34. Taylor, phone interview.

35. Orrin Keepnews, phone interview by Marc Myers, March 1, 2010. Quotations of Keepnews in the paragraphs that follow are from the same interview.

36. Avakian, phone interview, March 3, 2010. Quotations of Avakian in the paragraphs that follow are from the same interview.

37. Pete Welding, CD liner notes, *Miles Davis: The Complete Birth of the Cool* (Capitol Jazz).

38. Avakian, phone interview, March 3, 2010. Quotations of Avakian in the paragraphs that follow are from the same interview.

39. Taylor, phone interview, March 6, 2010.

40. Avakian, phone interview, March 3, 2010. The quotation of Avakian in the paragraph that follow is from the same interview.

41. Taylor, phone interview.

5. SUBURBIA AND WEST COAST JAZZ

1. Dave Pell, phone interview by Marc Myers, April 27, 2010.

2. Richard W. Haines, *Technicolor Movies: The History of Dye Transfer Printing* (Jefferson, N.C.: McFarland, 2003), 52–53.

3. "3-Speed Phono Sales Zoom," *Billboard*, April 22, 1950, 46.

4. Pell, phone interview.

5. Ted Gioia, *West Coast Jazz: Modern Jazz in California, 1945–1960*, (New York: Oxford University Press, 1992), 362.

6. William Claxton, "Clickin' with Clax: A History of Pacific Jazz Records," in *Jazz West Coast* (Tokyo: Bijutsu Shuppan-Sha, 1992), 7.

7. Gioia, *West Coast Jazz*, 366.

8. William Claxton, foreword to Glyn Callingham, Graham Marsh, and William Claxton, *California Cool: West Coast Jazz of the 50s and 60s; The Album Cover Art* (San Francisco: Chronicle Books, 1992), 5.

9. Kenneth T. Jackson, *Crabgrass Frontier: The Suburbanization of the United States* (New York: Oxford University Press, 1985), 3.

10. Johnny Mandel, phone interview by Marc Myers, April 2, 2010.

11. Tom De Simone et al., *Lavender Los Angeles: Roots of Equality* (Charleston, S.C.: Arcadia Publishing, 2011), 9.

12. "Los Angeles Is the Damndest Place." *Life*, November 22, 1943, 102.

13. See Martin J. Schiesl, "City Planning and the Federal Government in World War II: The Los Angeles Experience," *California History* 59, no. 2 (Summer 1980): 129, 130, and 131, on the history recounted in this paragraph.

14. Jackson, *Crabgrass Frontier*, 239.

15. Allen J. Scott and Edward W. Soja, eds., *The City: Los Angeles and Urban Theory at the End of the Twentieth Century* (Berkeley: University of California Press, 1996), 8.

16. See Schiesl, "City Planning and the Federal Government," 138, for the quotations and data given in this paragraph.

17. Ibid., 132–33.

18. Pell, phone interview, April 27, 2010.

19. Jackson, *Crabgrass Frontier*, 166.

20. Ibid., 167.

21. Oliver Gillham, *The Limitless City: A Primer on the Urban Sprawl* (Washington, D.C.: Island Press, 2002), 262 n. 26.

22. Scott L. Bottles, *Los Angeles and the Automobile: The Making of the Modern City* (Berkeley: University of California Press, 1987), 243–44.

23. Ibid., 20–21.

24. Douglas Henry Daniels, "Los Angeles' Jazz Roots: The Willis H. Young Family," *California History* 82, no. 3 (Fall 2004): 48.

25. Ibid., 50.

26. Clora Bryant et al., *Central Avenue Sounds* (Berkeley: University of California Press), 19.

27. Peter J. Levinson, *September in the Rain: The Life of Nelson Riddle* (Lanham, Md.: Taylor Trade Publishing, 2005), 70.

28. Mandel, phone interview, April 2, 2010.

29. Howard Rumsey, phone interview by Marc Myers, July 8, 2009.

30. John Levy, phone interview by Marc Myers, January 2, 2010.

31. Rick Moss, "Not Quite Paradise: The Development of the African American Community in Los Angeles through 1950," *California History* 75, no. 3 (Fall 1996): 229.

32. Ibid., 232.

33. Tad Hershorn, *Norman Granz: The Man Who Used Jazz for Justice* (Berkeley: University of California Press, 2011), 397.

34. Ibid., 234.

35. Abraham L. Davis and Barbara Luck Graham, *The Supreme Court, Race, and Civil Rights* (Thousand Oaks, Calif.: Sage Press, 1995), 68.

36. Becky M. Nicolaides, *My Blue Heaven: Life and Politics in the Working-Class Suburbs of Los Angeles, 1920–1965* (Chicago: University of Chicago Press, 2002), 211–12.

37. Bryant et al., *Central Avenue Sounds*, 385.

38. Ibid., 386.

39. Buddy Collette, phone interview by Marc Myers, February 15, 2010.

40. Bryant et al., *Central Avenue Sounds*, 391.

41. Ibid., 396.

42. Ibid., 398.

43. Ibid., 404.

44. Mina Yang, "A Thin Blue Line Down Central Avenue: The LAPD and the Demise of a Musical Hub," *Black Music Research Journal* 22, no. 2 (Autumn 2002): 220

45. Mina Yang, *California Polyphony: Ethnic Voices, Musical Crossroads* (Champaign: University of Illinois Press, 2008), 68.

46. Hampton Hawes, *Raise Up Off Me: A Portrait of Hampton Hawes* (New York: Da Capo, 1979), 29–30.

47. David Bryant, quoted in Yang, "Thin Blue Line," 226.

48. Art Farmer, quoted in ibid., 227.

49. Ibid., 218.

50. Levy, phone interview, January 2, 2010.

51. Ibid.

52. Collette, phone interview, February 15, 2010. Further quotations of Collette in this paragraph and the next are from the same interview.

53. Mandel, phone interview, April 2, 2010.

54. Rumsey, phone interview, July 8, 2009.

55. Pell, phone interview, April 27, 2010.

56. Rumsey, phone interview.

57. Mandel, phone interview.

58. Collette, phone interview, February 15, 2010.

59. Chico Hamilton, phone interview by Marc Myers, May 26, 2008.

60. Herb Geller, phone interview by Marc Myers, March 21, 2010.

61. Pell, phone interview, April 27, 2010.

62. Creed Taylor, phone interview by Marc Myers, April 26, 2008.

63. Pell, phone interview. Quotations of Pell in the paragraphs that follow are from the same interview.

64. Lennie Niehaus, phone interview by Marc Myers, March 31, 2010. Further quotations of Niehaus in this paragraph and the paragraphs that follow are from the same interview.

65. Sonny Rollins, quoted in Marc Myers, liner notes, *Sonny Rollins: Way Out West*, Concord Records, CD re-issue, 2010.

6. BMI, R&B, AND HARD BOP

1. Howard Reich and William Gaines, *Jelly's Blues: The Life, Music, and Redemption of Jelly Roll Morton* (Cambridge, Mass.: Da Capo Press, 2003), 90.

2. Ibid., 144.

3. Ibid., 182.

4. Ibid., 183.

5. Ibid., 215.

6. David Sanjek, *BMI and Black Music History* (New York: Broadcast Music Inc., 2002), 4.

7. "Editorial: MOA [Music Operators of America] and Depreciation," *Billboard*, July 24, 1954, 63.

8. William A. Richter, *Radio: A Complete Guide to the Industry* (New York: Peter Lang, 2006), 55.

9. Gene Seymour, "Hard Bop," *The Oxford Companion to Jazz*, ed. Bill Kirchner (New York: Oxford University Press, 2000), 373.

10. Lyman Ray Patterson, *Copyright, in Historical Perspective* (Nashville, Tenn.: Vanderbilt University Press, 1968), 143.

11. Mary Brandt Jensen, *Does Your Project Have a Copyright Problem?* (Jefferson, N.C.: McFarland, 1996), 47.

12. Elizabeth C. Axford, *Song Sheets to Software* (Lanham, Md.: Scarecrow Press), 30.

13. Ibid.

14. William Benjamin Hale, *A Treatise on the Law of Copyright and Literary Property* (New York: New York Law Book, 1917), 1,035.

15. William F. Patry, *Copyright Law and Practice Vol. II* (Washington, D.C.: Bureau of National Affairs, 1994), 887.

16. Richard A. Peterson, "Why 1955? Explaining the Advent of Rock Music," *Popular Music* 9, no. 1 (January 1990): 101.

17. *The Rise of BMI: 1940–2008*, Broadcast Music Inc., corporate history, author's copy, 3.

18. "Juke Box Disc Purchases Up to 50,000,000 a Year," *Billboard*, January 19, 1952, 1.

19. Ibid., 73.

20. "BMI Drive for Cleffer Pacts Net 3 More," *Billboard*, January 19, 1952, 16.

21. "14 Publishing Houses Grab 697G From 37 Million Discs," *Billboard*, June 28, 1952, 19.

22. "2-Speed Disk Trend Grows; Dealers' Confab Looks Big," *Billboard*, August 2, 1952, 1.

23. "BMI Issues 'Meet the Artist' Biog Tome," *Billboard*, January 19, 1952, 17.

24. "TV 'Sketch Book' Hot: Outlets Go for BMI Ideas, Want More," *Billboard*, February 16, 1952, 20.

25. "ASCAP Radio Cash on Par with 1951," *Billboard*, September 13, 1952, 19.

26. "New Boom in Bids for AM Stations Under Way," *Billboard*, August 9, 1952, 6.

27. "$27\frac{1}{2}$ Million Cars Have Radios Now," *Billboard*, August 9, 1952, 4.

28. "Survey Shows Radio Outpulls Newspapers by 46 to 29 Ratio," *Billboard*, August 9, 1952, 4.

29. "Alley's Tin Pan Clatter As New 'Buck BMI' Pot Boils," *Billboard*, October 25, 1952, 54.

30. Ibid., 1.

31. "BMI Income Reaches New Record with $5,607,841," *Billboard*, November 1, 1952, 1.

32. "Past Year One of Evolutionary Growth for Music Industry," *Billboard*, December 27, 1952, 13.

33. Ibid., 16.

34. "1952 Witnessed Developments at Many Levels," *Billboard*, December 27, 1952, 13.

35. "1952 Marks Banner Record Retail Year," *Billboard*, June 20, 1953, 1.

36. "All-Industry Levels High for Dec./Jan: Hits Are Spread Wide; No Slump After Christmas," *Billboard*, February 7, 1953, 1.

37. "Study Underlines Radio's Solid Grip in the Face of TV," *Billboard*, August 1, 1953, 1.

38. "Production Statistics Point to Strong Radio Comeback," *Billboard*, September 5, 1953, 1.

39. "Auto Radios Booming Trade for Set Building Industry," *Billboard*, September 19, 1953, 3.

40. "How Liberty Does It: Chain Sells $1,000,000 in Disks Per Year," *Billboard*, November 28, 1953, 17.

41. "Prolific Cleffers: '53 Big Year for Music Copyrights," *Billboard*, December 26, 1953, 15.

42. "Radio's Expansion: Despite TV, Stations Approach 2,550 Record," *Billboard*, January 13, 1953, 1.

43. "Jazz Best since '30s: Disks, Road, Clubs Enjoy Crazy Year," *Billboard*, January 24, 1953, 1.

44. Ibid.

45. "Business is Pressing: Major Labels Find Profit in Making Disks for Indies," *Billboard*, March 13, 1953, 17.

46. "Bumper Crop of New Labels Poses Questions for Industry," *Billboard*, May 2, 1953, 14.

47. Ibid.

48. "Key to Profits: Care in Programming Box," *Billboard: Jukebox 65th Anniversary Section*, May 23, 1953, p. 60.

49. "Columbia Launches Disk Club Experiment in Ohio," *Billboard*, December 26, 1953, 18.

50. Ibid.

51. "Phono Dealers Grow: High-Price Sets Also Move Faster," *Billboard*, March 20, 1954, 19.

52. "The R&B Deejay: A Growing Factor," Annual Music-Record Programming Guide, *Billboard*, February 28, 1953, 57.

53. See the epigraph to Gene Seymour, "Hard Bop," in The *Oxford Companion to Jazz*, 373.

54. Benny Golson, phone interview by Marc Myers, April 27, 2008.

55. Big Jay McNeely, phone interview by Marc Myers, July 29, 2009.

56. Ibid.

57. Blue Notes Records Discography Project, JazzDisco.org./blue-note-records.

58. Denny Mellé, e-mail interview by Marc Myers, August 9, 2010.

59. Rudy Van Gelder, e-mail interview by Marc Myers, March 27, 2010.

60. Richard Cook, *Blue Note Records: The Biography* (Boston: Justin, Charles, 2004), 59.

61. Marc Myers, CD liner notes, *The Fabulous Miss D: The Keynote, Decca, and Mercury Singles, 1943–1953* (Universal Music, 2010), 10. "'In the singles era, Dinah knew she had to get her big personality through those tiny jukebox and radio speakers if she was going to leave an impression,' said drummer Jimmy Cobb, who recorded with Washington during those years."

62. Lou Donaldson, phone interview by Marc Myers, May 2, 2010.

63. Ibid.

64. Blue Note Jazz Discography, JazzDisco.org.

65. David H. Rosenthal, *Hard Bop: Jazz and Black Music, 1955–1965* (New York: Oxford University Press, 1992), 39.

66. Donaldson, phone interview.

67. Gary Giddins and Scott DeVeaux, *Jazz*, (New York: Norton, 2009), 356.

68. McNeely, phone interview, July 29, 2009.

69. Van Gelder, e-mail interview, March 27, 2010. Quotations of Van Gelder in the paragraphs that follow are from the same interview.

70. "12-Inch Platters Now Account for Half of LP Disk Output," *Billboard,* October 9, 1954, 11; "Coast Jazz Indies Drop Prices on LPs," *Billboard,* July 9, 1955, 14.

71. Van Gelder, e-mail interview.

72. Golson, phone interview, April 27, 2008. The quotation of Golson in the paragraph that follows is from the same interview.

73. Horace Silver, *Let's Get to the Nitty Gritty: The Autobiography of Horace Silver,* (Berkeley: University of California Press, 2006), 40, 155.

74. Robin D. G. Kelley, *Thelonious Monk: The Life and Times of an American Original* (New York: Free Press, 2009), 94.

75. Donaldson, phone interview, May 2, 2010.

76. Kelley, *Thelonious Monk,* 194.

77. Sonny Rollins, phone interview by Marc Myers, September 16, 2010.

78. Golson, phone interview, April 27, 2008.

79. Ibid.

7. BIAS, AFRICA, AND SPIRITUAL JAZZ

1. Sonny Rollins, in-person interview with Marc Myers, August 8, 2010.

2. Jennifer Guglielmo and Salvatore Salerno, *Are Italians White? How Race Is Made in America* (New York: Routledge, 2003), 161–76.

3. Michael C. Johanek and John L. Puckett, *Leonard Covello and the Making of Benjamin Franklin High School: Education As If Citizenship Mattered* (Philadelphia: Temple University Press, 2007), 109.

4. Ibid., 203.

5. Rollins, in-person interview, August 8, 2010.

6. Guglielmo and Salerno, *Are Italians White?* 161–76.

7. Ibid.

8. Ibid.

9. Rollins, in-person interview, August 8, 2010.

10. Dan Morgenstern, phone interview by Marc Myers, September 30, 2010.

11. Colin Grant, *Negro with a Hat: The Rise and Fall of Marcus Garvey* (New York: Oxford University Press, 2008), 73.

12. Ibid., 152.

13. Brenda Haugen, *Marcus Garvey: Black Nationalist Crusader and Entrepreneur* (Bloomington, Minn.: Compass Point, 2008), 44.

14. Colin Grant, *Negro with a Hat,* 90.

15. Tony Martin, *Race First: The Ideological and Organizational Struggles of Marcus Garvey and the Universal Negro Improvement Association* (Dover, Mass.: Majority Press, 1986), 91.

16. Edmund David Cronon, *Black Moses: The Story of Marcus Garvey and the Universal Negro Improvement Association* (Madison: University of Wisconsin Press, 1969), 49.

17. Rupert Lewis, *Marcus Garvey, Anti-Colonial Champion* (Trenton, N.J.: Africa World Press, 1988), 80–81.

18. *The Philosophy and Opinions of Marcus Garvey*, ed. Amy Jacques Garvey (Dover, Mass.: Majority Press, 1986), 23.

19. Rollins, in-person interview, August 8, 2010.

20. Nat Hentoff, phone interview by Marc Myers, September 2, 2010.

21. Herbert Berg, *Elijah Muhammad and Islam* (New York: New York University Press, 2009), 21.

22. Peter B. Clarke, ed., *Encyclopedia of New Religious Movements* (New York: Routledge, 2006), 20.

23. Edward E. Curtis, *Encyclopedia of Muslim-American History*, vol. 1 (New York: Facts on File, 2010), 32.

24. Ingrid Tolia Monson, *Freedom Sounds: Civil Rights Call Out to Jazz and Africa* (New York: Oxford University Press, 2007), 147.

25. Yusef Lateef with Herb Boyd, *The Gentle Giant: Autobiography of Yusef Lateef*, (Irvington, N.J.: Morton Books, 2006), 56–57.

26. Yusef Lateef, phone interview by Marc Myers, July 26, 2010.

27. C. Eric Lincoln and Lawrence H. Mamiya, *The Black Church in the African American Experience*, Duke University Press, 1990, pp. 2–3.

28. Ibid., 211.

29. Ibid., 348.

30. Ibid., 365.

31. Hentoff, phone interview, September 2, 2010.

32. Horace Silver, *Let's Get to the Nitty Gritty: The Autobiography of Horace Silver* (Berkeley: University of California Press, 2006), 4.

33. Tim Brooks, *Lost Sounds: Blacks and the Birth of the Recording Industry, 1980–1919* (Champaign: University of Illinois Press, 2004), 298.

34. Bill Moody, *The Jazz Exiles* (Reno: University of Nevada Press, 1993), 4.

35. Sonny Rollins, phone interview by Marc Myers, September 16, 2010. Further quotations of Rollins in the paragraphs that follow are from the same interview.

36. Lateef, phone interview, July 26, 2010. Quotations of Lateef in the paragraphs that follow are from the same interview.

37. Penny M. Von Eschen, *Satchmo Blows Up the World* (Cambridge, Mass.: Harvard University Press, 2004), 59.

38. Terry Teachout, *Pops: A Life of Louis Armstrong* (New York: Houghton Mifflin Harcourt, 2009), 330–31.

39. Rollins, phone interview, September 16, 2010.

40. Ibid.

41. Hentoff, phone interview, September 2, 2010.

42. Creed Taylor, phone interview by Marc Myers, October 15, 2010. Quotations of Taylor in the paragraphs that follow are from the same interview.

43. Randy Weston and Willard Jenkins, *African Rhythms: The Autobiography of Randy Weston* (Durham, N.C.: Duke University Press, 2010), 82.

44. Randy Weston, phone interview by Marc Myers, August 9, 2010.

45. Bill Moody and Stanley Dance, *The Jazz Exiles: American Musicians Abroad* (Reno: University of Nevada Press, 1993), 37.

8. INVASION AND JAZZ-POP

1. Carol Sloane, phone interview by Marc Myers, June 7, 2008. Quotations of Sloane in the paragraphs that follow are from this interview.

2. "Births in the United States: 1930 to 2007," *Statistical Abstract of the United States*, About.com.

3. Kerry Segrave, *Payola in the Music Industry: A History, 1880–1991* (Jefferson, N.C.: McFarland, 1994), 98.

4. Ibid., 99.

5. Ibid., 100.

6. Ibid., 156.

7. Ibid., 157.

8. "Payola Not Dead; Now 'Underground,' " *Billboard*, August 19, 1960, 1.

9. Nigel Parker, *Music Business: Infrastructure, Practice and Law* (London: Sweet and Maxwell, 2004), 78.

10. Michael T. Bertrand, *Race, Rock, and Elvis* (Champaign: University of Illinois Press, 2000), 84–85.

11. Ben Fong-Torres, *The Hits Just Keep On Coming: The History of Top 40 Radio* (San Francisco: Backbeat Books, 2001), 128.

12. Hal Blaine, in-person interview by Marc Myers, March 16, 2011.

13. Iain Anderson, *This Is Our Music: Free Jazz, the Sixties, and American Culture* (Philadelphia: University of Pennsylvania Press, 2007), 83.

14. John Broven, *Record Makers and Breakers: Voices of the Independent Rock 'n' Roll Pioneers* (Champaign: University of Illinois Press, 2009), 22.

15. Russell Sanjek and David Sanjek, *American Popular Music Business in the 20th Century* (New York, Oxford University Press, 1991), 88.

16. Philip Furia, *Skylark: The Life and Times of Johnny Mercer* (New York: St. Martin's Press, 2004), 166.

17. "Capitol Sale Would Stiffen Disk Battle," *Billboard*, January 22, 1955, 1.

18. Ibid.

19. "EMI Paid $8 Million," *Billboard*, March 19, 1955, 22.

20. "Cap's Wallichs Placed on EMI Director Board," *Billboard*, May 21, 1955, 39.

21. "Cap Exec Shift Has Wallichs Chairman, Livingston Prexy, *Billboard*, October 20, 1962, 6.

22. Craig Cross, *The Beatles: Day-by-Day, Song-by-Song, Record-by-Record* (London: iUniverse, 2005), 82.

23. Ibid. 82.

24. Bob Spitz, *The Beatles: The Biography* (New York: Little, Brown, 2005), 389.

25. Ibid., 440.

26. Ibid., 430.

27. Ibid., 441.

28. Stuart Shea and Robert Rodriguez, *Fab Four FAQ: Everything Left to Know about the Beatles . . . and More!* (New York: Hal Leonard, 2007), 35.

29. Martin Lewis, "Tweet the Beatles: How Walter Cronkite Sent The Beatles Viral . . . in 1963!" *Huffington Post*, July 18, 2009.

30. Ibid.

31. Ibid.

32. Spitz, *The Beatles*, 444.

33. *The New York Times Guide to Essential Knowledge* (New York: St. Martin's Press, 2007), 823.

34. Joel Whitburn, *Billboard Hot 100 Charts: The Sixties* (Menomonee Falls, Wis.: Record Research, 1990).

35. David Kamp, "The Oral History: The British Invasion," *Vanity Fair*, November 2002, 261.

36. Ibid., 265.

37. Jack Tracy, phone interview by Marc Myers, March 27, 2010. Quotations of Tracy in the paragraphs that follow are from the same interview.

38. Dick LaPalm, phone interview by Marc Myers, October 16, 2010.

39. Ibid.

40. Harvey Kubernik, "Berry Gordy: In His Own Write," *Mojo*, February 1995.

41. Bill Miller, "Motown Magician," *The History of Rock*, no. 24 (1982), 470–73.

42. Kubernik, "Berry Gordy: In His Own Write."

43. Miller, "Motown Magician," 470–73.

44. Mick Brown, "Berry Gordy: The Man in the Middle," *Sunday Times* (London), 1984.

45. Ibid.

46. Ibid.

47. Ibid.

48. Ibid.

49. Liner notes, *Motown: The Complete No. 1s*, 10-CD box set (Universal, 2008).

50. Michael Lydon, "Smokey Robinson," *Rolling Stone* (September, 28, 1968), 20.

51. Ibid.

52. Serene Dominic, *Burt Bacharach: Song by Song* (New York: Schirmer, 2003), 332.

53. Burt Bacharach, in-person interview by Marc Myers, October 17, 2011.

54. Marc Myers, "Bacharach Looks Back—and Forward to a New Musical," *Wall Street Journal*, November 22, 2011.

55. Bill DeMain, "What's It All About, Bacharach?" *Switch*, June 1997.

56. Bacharach, in-person interview.

57. "Burt Bacharach: The Music Man, 1970," *Newsweek*, June 22, 1970, 50–54.

58. Dionne Warwick, phone interview by Marc Myers, September 30, 2010.

59. Tom Lord, *The Jazz Discography*, online database, LordDisco.com.

60. Sonny Rollins, phone interview by Marc Myers, February 12, 2008.

61. Dominic, *Burt Bacharach: Song by Song*, 161.

62. Warwick, phone interview.

63. Cilla Black, *What's It All About?* (London: Ebury Press, 2003), 138.

64. Myers, "Bacharach Looks Back." Quotations of Bacharach in the paragraphs that follow are from the same article.

65. Dominic, *Burt Bacharach: Song by Song*, 162.

66. "Chappell Will Handle Liberty Overseas Publishing Interests," *Billboard*, May 14, 1966, 30.

67. Joel Whitburn, *Billboard's Top Pop Singles, 1955–1996,* (Menomonee Falls, Wis.: Record Research, 1997).

68. Eric Nisenson, *Open Sky: Sonny Rollins and His World of Improvisation* (Cambridge, Mass.: Da Capo Press, 2000), 181.

69. Phil Ramone, phone interview by Marc Myers, July 23, 2008.

70. John Levy, phone interview by Marc Myers, March 11, 2011.

71. Creed Taylor, phone interview by Marc Myers, March 23, 2011. Quotations of Taylor in the paragraphs that follow are from the same interview.

9. ALIENATION AND THE AVANT-GARDE

1. Joseph Jarman, phone interview by Marc Myers, December 3, 2010. Quotations of Jarman in the paragraphs that follow are from the same interview.

2. Alex Haley, "The Playboy Interview: Miles Davis," in *The Playboy Interview*, ed. G. Barry Golson (New York: Playboy Press, 1981), 5.

3. Ibid.

4. Nat Hentoff, *The Jazz Life* (Cambridge, Mass.: Da Capo Press, 1978), 102–3.

5. Robert K. McMichael, " 'We Insist—Freedom Now!': Black Moral Authority, Jazz and the Changeable Shape of Whiteness," *American Music*, Winter 1998, 385.

6. Eric Nisenson, *Open Sky: Sonny Rollins and His World of Improvisation* (Cambridge, Mass.: Da Capo Press, 2000), 172.

7. Ornette Coleman, "I Was a B-flat Man," interview, 1969, by Arthur Taylor, in Taylor, *Notes and Tones: Musician-to-Musician Interviews* (New York: Perigee Books, 1977), 40.

8. Howard Mandel, phone interview by Marc Myers, November 11, 2010.

9. James R. Ralph Jr., *Northern Protest: Martin Luther King, Jr., Chicago, and the Civil Rights Movement* (Cambridge, Mass.: Harvard University Press, 1993), 13.

10. George E. Lewis, *A Power Stronger Than Itself: The AACM and American Experimental Music* (University of Chicago Press, 2009), 85–86.

11. Ralph Jr., *Northern Protest*, 13.

12. Ibid.

13. Ibid., 14.

14. Ibid., 16.

15. Ibid., 15–21.

16. Molefi Kete Asante, *Malcolm X as Cultural Hero and Other Afrocentric Essays* (Trenton, N.J.: Africa World Press, 1993), 29.

17. Ralph, *Northern Protest*, 1.

18. Ibid., 2.

19. Lewis, *A Power Stronger Than Itself*, 93.

20. Ibid., 97.

21. Ibid.

22. Jarman, phone interview, December 3, 2010.

23. Lewis, *A Power Stronger Than Itself*, 101–2.

24. Ibid., 112.

25. Ibid.

26. Ibid., 112–14.

27. Ibid., 116.

28. Mandel, phone interview, November 11, 2010.

29. Larry Kart, phone interview by Marc Myers, November 10, 2010. The quotation of Kart in the paragraph that follows is from the same interview.

30. Mandel, phone interview. Further quotations of Mandel in this paragraph and the one that follows are from the same interview.

31. Lewis, *A Power Stronger Than Itself*, 118.

32. Jarman, phone interview, December 3, 2010. Quotations of Jarman in the paragraphs that follow are from the same interview.

33. John Litweiler, phone interview by Marc Myers, November 14, 2010.

34. Kart, phone interview, November 20, 2010.

10. LIGHTS, VOLUME, AND FUSION

1. Bill Hanley, phone interview by Marc Myers, December 21, 2010. Quotations of Hanley in the paragraphs that follow are from the same interview.

2. Associated Press, *The World in 1966: History as We Lived It* (New York: Western Printing, 1967).

3. Ibid., 92.

4. Ibid., 91–93.

5. Ibid.

6. "LSD Manufacture," U.S. Department of Justice, Drug Enforcement Administration.

7. Grace Slick, phone interview by Marc Myers, April 22, 2011.

8. Hal Blaine, in-person interview by Marc Myers, October 30, 2011.

9. Harvey Kubernik, *Canyon of Dreams: The Magic and the Music of Laurel Canyon* (New York: Sterling, 2009), 68.

10. Julie Coryell and Laura Friedman, *Jazz-Rock Fusion: The People, the Music* (New York: Delacorte Press, 1978), 112–13.

11. Gary Burton, phone interview by Marc Myers, January 7, 2011. Quotations of Burton in the paragraphs that follow are from the same interview.

12. Chick Corea, phone interview by Marc Myers, October 24, 2011.

13. Miles Davis, quoted in Coryell and Friedman, *Jazz-Rock Fusion*, 40.

14. John McLaughlin, e-mail interview by Marc Myers, November 17, 2011. Quotations of McLaughlin in the paragraphs that follow are from the same interview.

15. Herbie Hancock, liner notes, CD reissue of *Head Hunters* (Columbia), 1996.

16. Michael C. Keith, *Talking Radio: An Oral History of American Radio in the Television Age* (Armonk, N.Y.: M.E. Sharpe, 2000), 136.

17. Steve Waksman, "Grand Funk Live! Staging Rock in the Age of the Arena," in *Listen Again: A Momentary History of Pop Music*, ed. Eric Weisbard (Durham, N.C.: Duke University Press, 2007), 158–59.

18. Edward "Chip" Monck, phone interview by Marc Myers, December 19, 2010. Quotations of Monck that follow in this paragraph and the next are from the same interview.

19. Hanley, phone interview, December 21, 2010.

20. Miles Davis with Quincy Troupe, *Miles: The Autobiography* (New York: Simon and Schuster, 1989), 297–98.

21. Ron Carter, phone interview by Marc Myers, April 13, 2008.

22. Corea, phone interview, October 24, 2011.

23. Randy Brecker, phone interview by Marc Myers, January 11, 2011. Quotations of Brecker in the paragraphs that follow are from the same interview.

24. Corea, phone interview. Quotations of Corea in the paragraphs that follow are from the same interview.

25. Monck, phone interview, December 19, 2010. Quotations of Monck in the paragraph that follows are from the same interview.

11. JAZZ HANGS ON

1. Art D'Lugoff, phone interview by Marc Myers, May 9, 2008.

2. Gary Burton, phone interview by Marc Myers, January 7, 2011.

3. Jack Azizo, in-person interview by Marc Myers, January 4, 2012.

Index

LP records: development of, 8, 71–73,
103, 165; fabrication of, 86, 89, 90,
129; as favorable format for jazz,
7, 70–71, 90, 92, 128, 135, 136,
175; 10-inch, 7, 70–73, 75, 77–78,
83–88, 90, 129–30, 133–36, 175,
182, 235n2; 12-inch, 7, 75–80, 85,
88–92, 136, 175
LSD, 207–8
Lubahn, Doug, 221
Lunceford, Jimmie, 43

Macero, Teo, 59
Machito and His Afro Cubans, 151,
158
Madison Square Garden, New York,
217
Magnetophon tape recorder, 82
Mahavishu Orchestra, 212, 216, 222
Malcolm X, 193, 194–95, 201
Mancini, Henry, 64
Mandel, Howard, 191, 197, 199
Mandel, Johnny, 96–97, 103–4, 111,
113
Manhattan School of Music, 58, 60,
61, 68
Mann, Barry, 163
Manne, Shelly, 96, 112, 114, 116, 117
Manor Records, 31, 35, 38
Marmarosa, Dodo, 13
Martin, Dean, 167
Martin, George, 179, 184
Martyn, Quedellis, 53
Marvelettes, the, 174
Masterworks label, 88
Mathias, Frank, 54, 55
Mathis, Johnny, 176
Mayfield, Curtis, 225
McCall, Steve, 187, 194, 195
McCartney, Paul, 181, 184
McFarland, Gary, 181
McGuinn, Roger, 209
McKinley, Ray, 67
McKusick, Hal, 30, 53
McLaughlin, John, 4, 212, 214–15,
216, 220, 222, 223
McLean, Jackie, 158

McLemore, William, 56
McNeely, Big Jay, 128, 131, 132, 135
McRae, Teddy, 137
McShann, Jay, 17
Mellé, Gil, 73, 132
Melotone Music, 138
Mercer, Johnny, 165–66
Mercury Records, 80, 168, 170
Meredith, James, 189
Merritt, Jymie, 131
"Message from Kenya," 134
Metronome magazine, 12, 34, 35, 38,
39, 40, 41, 42, 58, 59, 60, 64, 115
Metropolitan Opera Orchestra, 59
Metzner, Ralph, 207
Miami Pop Festival, 203
Middle Eastern music, 154
Miles in the Sky, 213
Milhaud, Darius, 58, 60, 62–63, 66,
177
military, U.S., musicians in, 49,
51–56
Miller, Glenn, 52, 59, 135
Millinder, Lucky, 16, 17
Mills College, Oakland, California,
62–63
Milstein, Nathan, 77
Mingus, Charles, 69, 150, 156, 185,
187, 189
Minton's Playhouse, New York, 15
Miracles, the, 175
Mitchell, Blue, 131
modernism: and classical music, 58;
and cool jazz, 67; and visual art, 32
Modern Jazz Quartet, 63
Monck, Edward "Chip," 217–18, 224
Monk, Thelonious, 44, 73, 120, 137
Monroe, Clark, 15
Monterey Pop Festival, 9, 218
Montgomery, Wes, 104, 182–83, 184
"The Mooche," 151
"Mood Indigo," 5
Moody, Bill, 160
Moore, Phil, 109
Moreira, Airto, 223
Morgan, Frank, 110
Morgan, Lee, 183

Text: 10/13 Aldus
Display: Aldus
Compositor: Toppan Best-set Premedia Limited
Indexer: Andrew Joron
Pritner and Binder: Maple-Vail Book Manufacturing Group